Business Communications
—Theory and Technique

商务沟通
——理 论 与 技 巧

曹荣光　胡宏斌　编著

云南大学出版社

总　序

　　云南大学经济学院对外贸易系的国际经济与贸易专业是改革开放以后全国最早的 13 个外贸重点专业之一，是云南省省级重点学科，最近又被列为云南省人才培养模式改革试点专业、省院省校合作重点学科。

　　自从加入世界贸易组织（WTO）以来，我国加快了对外开放的步伐，社会主义市场经济体制在对外开放中不断完善，内地同香港特别行政区更加紧密地开展贸易和投资合作，上海合作组织各国之间的合作进一步发展，特别是中国——东盟自由贸易区建设已经启动，将在 2010～2015 年建成。中国正在稳步地、全方位、多层次、宽领域地扩大对外开放，逐步融入全球化的世界经济。随着新的国际国内经济形势的发展及我国对外开放的扩大，对对外经贸及国际商务管理人才的需求也随之增加。为适应这种日益增大的需求，培养新型的国际经贸及商务管理人才，云南大学经济学院对外贸易系组织编写了一系列丛书。这一系列丛书内容涉及国际贸易理论与政策、国际贸易实务、国际商务管理、国际金融学、国际商法、国际企业管理、商务沟通等，可应用于国际经济与贸易、国际商务等涉外经济类专业的本专科教学，也可应用于从事国际经贸与商务管理的在职人员培训，以及作为高校双语教学的辅助教材。

　　《商务沟通——理论与技巧》的编写者是云南大学长期从事对外经贸及商务管理专业教学工作的教师。本书是他们多年教学实践的总结。

　　在本系列丛书的编写过程中，我们参考了国内外同类教材的体例和内容，同时力求编出自己的特色，但由于受到客观条件及编写水平的限制，难免存在各种问题，我们诚挚地希望同行和读者提出批评意见，共同促进有中国特色的对外经贸及国际商务管理的专业教学工作。

2006 年 2 月于昆明

内容简介

在世界经济全球化和一体化的进程中，商务沟通的重要作用日益显现。书面的商务沟通通常分为对外沟通与对内沟通两部分，内容涉及不同类型的商务应用文写作。本书在编写时汲取了国外最新出版的英文原版商务沟通书籍的精华，并借鉴了国内相关出版物成功的经验。为让学习者学到规范的商务英语，本书选用的书信范例大部分选自英文原著，并根据编撰需要和中国国情进行了适当改写。本书全部用英文编写而成，有助于学习者在学习过程中进一步提高运用英语的能力。

本书重点论述对外沟通商务文体的撰写原理与技巧，内容涉及国际贸易、国际金融、合资、独资企业及其他商务机构进行书面沟通时经常撰写的各类商务书信。

全书分为 15 章，其中第 1 ~ 2 章介绍了英文书信的格式、特点和写作技巧；第 3 ~ 11 章为对外商务书面沟通经常撰写的商务应用文，主要分为以下几类：Enquiries and Replies（询价函与复函）、Sales Letters（推销信）、Order and Confirmation Letters（订货与确认信函）、Payment and Collection Letters（付款与收款信函）、Complaints and Adjustments（索赔与理赔）、Modes of Transportation and Shipping（运输与海运）、Credit（信用相关信函）、Banking（银行业务）、Agents and Agencies（代理商与代理机构）；第 12 章为 Public Relation Letters（公共关系信函），包括 Invitations（邀请函）、Letters of Appreciation（感谢信）、Letters of Sympathy（慰问信）及其他日常对外沟通常用的信函；第 13 章主要阐述 Employment Related Letters（个人求职、求学相关信函）的撰写方法，包括 Letters of Application（求职/求学信）、Resume（简历）、Personal Statements（个人自述）、Letters of Recommendation（推荐信）等；第 14、15 章以备忘录和商务报告的写作为例介绍了对内沟通商务书信的格式、行文特点及技巧。

本文的编写顺序为课文正文、词汇和练习三大部分。正文部分着重介绍相关书信的撰写原则及行文特点，并通过大量的例句和书信范例阐述了相应的写作技巧；每一章所附的词汇旨在方便读者阅读正文，并供其学习撰写相关信函时参考；各章练习有助于提高学习者的综合运用能力。

本书可供大专院校主修国际商务、国际经济与贸易、金融学、工商管理或其他涉外专业的学生学习商务英语写作时使用，也可供国际商务、外资企业、银行等部门的在职人员及有志到国外留学者学习使用。

通过本书的学习，有助于学习者掌握商务英语信函的基本行文方法、格式、语言和文体特点以及相关专业词汇，从而能按要求或根据所提供的材料撰写商务信函、与商务活动密切相关的公共关系信函及个人信函，从而提高其在工作和学习过程中运用商务英语进行书面沟通的能力。

由于编写者水平有限，编写时间仓促，文中难免出现不足和疏漏之处，敬请读者和专家学者见谅。

编 者

2005 年 12 月

PREFACE

With the globalization and integration of world economy, people all over the world spend more time communicating than doing anything else. In fact, communication is one activity that we human beings clearly do better than the other forms of life on earth. As a result, we human beings have been playing a dominant role in this world for thousands of years. It is undeniable that communication is vital to our success and well-being in civilized society.

The importance of communication in business becomes even more apparent when we consider an organization's communication activities from an overall perspective. As far as business communication is concerned, these activities roughly fall into two broad categories: internal and external. Though both communication are vital to business success, our emphasis is on the external one for we human beings tend to be extroverted.

The purpose of this book is to provide you with an understanding of the basic skill required to become an effective communicator and with the practice necessary to become confident in your abilities as a writer. At the same time, the book stresses the importance of effective writing skills to your success in school and at work, regardless of what career you choose.

CONTENTS

Chapter 1　Structure and Layout of Business Letter
（商务书信的结构和格式）··· （1）

Chapter 2　The Fundamentals and Techniques of Business Writing
（撰写商务书信的基本原理和技巧）··· （24）

Chapter 3　Enquiries and Replies
（询价函与复函）··· （52）

Chapter 4　Sales Letters
（推销信）·· （70）

Chapter 5　Order and Confirmation Letters
（订货与确认信函）··· （84）

Chapter 6　Modes of Payment and Collection
（付款与收款信函）··· （98）

Chapter 7　Complaints and Adjustments
（索赔与理赔）·· （115）

Chapter 8　Modes of Transportation and Shipping
（运输与海运）·· （137）

Chapter 9　Credit
（信用相关信函）··· （152）

Chapter10　Banking
（银行业务）·· （176）

Chapter 11　Agents and Agencies
（代理商与代理机构）··· （197）

· 1 ·

Chapter 12　Public Relation Letters
（公共关系信函）······(216)

Chapter 13　Employment Related Letters
（个人求职、求学相关信函）······(240)

Chapter 14　Memos
（备忘录）······(273)

Chapter 15　Business Report Writing
（撰写商务报告）······(288)

References
（参考文献）······(333)

CHAPTER 1

STRUCTURE AND LAYOUT OF BUSINESS LETTER

STRUCTURE OF BUSINESS LETTER

A typical business letter usually consists of the following parts:

Letterhead

The first and most obvious element of a business letter is its letterhead or heading. A letterhead's two functions are to *identify* where the letter comes from, and to *look good*. A letterhead usually contains the organization's name, address, telephone number, fax number as well. Sometimes a trademark or slogan is effectively incorporated. Many large companies add department identification, and companies that do business internationally usually add their cable address. e. g.

A&C (Records) Ltd

4-43 Broadway, Manchester M2 58p

Directors: J. Allen, P. D. Robins M. A. , R. C. Frial

Reg. No. 901107	Telephone: 061 832 4397
VAT No. 821 621 531	Fax: 061 832 4397

References

References are quoted to indicate what the letter refers to (Your Ref.) and the correspondence to refer to when replying (Our Ref.).

References may either appear in figures, e. g. 661/17 in which case 661 may refer to the chronological number of the letter and 17 to the number of the department, or in initials, as in DS/MR (or ds/mr), in which case DS stands for Donald Sampson, the writer, and MR for his secretary, Mary Rogers, e. g.

Your ref: *6 November 2005*
Our ref: *DS/MR*
Date: *8 December 2005*

Dateline

The dateline includes the complete date. You should use the conventional date form, with month, day, and year (e. g. "*November 14, 2005*"). Abbreviated forms such as "12 – 11 – 2005", or "Dec. 8, ' ×04'" are informal and do not leave the best impressions on most people.

There are two styles in which letters are dated: the American style and the British Style. You may see the difference between these two styles in the following examples:

The American style is

    A: month (spelled out in full);
    B: day of the month (in digits, without-th, -nd, etc, followed by a comma);
    C: year (in digits).

    e. g. *March 8, 2005, December 25, 2006*

The day of the month is read as an ordinal (second, twenty-third, etc), but the ordinal suffixes are omitted in writing. Likewise, many Americans insert "the" in reading the dates (May the eighth), but this definite article is never written, except in formal invitations where all numbers are spelled out (April the fifth, two thousand and five).

On the contrary, **the British Style** is ordered as follows:

    A: day of the month (in digits);
    B: month (spelled out in full);
    C: year (in digits).

    e. g. 1 *April 2005, 1 May 2006*

You may have found that there is no comma between the name of the month and the year, which is quite different from the American style.

Inside address

The mailing address, complete with the addressee's title, makes up the inside address or receiver's address. Preferably, type it without abbreviations, except for state or province names and those words commonly abbreviated (e. g. Dr. , Mr. , Mrs. , Ms.)

It is not advisable to write dates in all digits, for example, 1. 5. 2005, because it is ambiguous. As you can see in the above example, this would signify January 5, 2005 in American English, whereas, in British English it would mean 1 May 2005.

> e. g. *Ms. Anna Brown, Chair*
> *Department of Linguistics*
> *Right State University*
> *1415 University Drive*
> *Felicity, OH 45434*

Salutation

You should choose the salutation on the basis of your familiarity with the reader and the formality of the situation. As a general rule, if the writer and reader know each other well, the address may be by first name ("Dear Jane"). An address by last name ("Dear Mr. Bush") is appropriate in most cases. In formal or impersonal situations, the forms "Dear Sir" and "Dear Madam" are in order. Nowadays there is some movement toward eliminating the salutation and the complimentary close (especially in the Simplified Form), but this letter style has not yet gained the support of a major section of business.

In addition, as a result of the women's rights movement, the term "Ms. " is used for all women instead of "Mrs. " And "Miss. ", just as we use "Mr. " for all men. The impersonal plural greetings "Gentlemen" and "Dear Sirs" have a similar status. Clearly, they greet the readers as males when in fact females may be among them. One suggested solution is the salutation "Ladies and Gentlemen" (or "Ladies and /or Gentlemen").

Attention line

Some executives prefer to emphasize the company address rather than the individual offices. Thus, they address the correspondence to the company in the inside address. Then they use an attention line to direct the letter to a specific officer or department. Typical forms of this reference are as follows:

Attention of Mr. LW. Lowe, Sales Manager
For Ms. Barbara Blake, Director
Attention: Mr. Lionel Crane, Office Manager
Attention, Ms. Mary Smith, Managing Director

Subject line

To enable sender and receiver to quickly identify the subject of correspondence, many writers use subject lines in their letters. The subject line tells what the correspondence is about. In addition, it contains any specific identifying material that may be helpful—date of previous correspondence, invoice number, order number, and the like. It is placed on a line below the salutation. Usually it begins at the left margin, although it may be centered or indented (if the paragraphs are indented). Take a look at the following examples:

Subject: Your November 8 inquiry about leather shoes
Reference your October 5 order for Walnut Meat

SUBJECT: Applying for a job position
Illustrated catalogues

Body of the letter

The body contains the actual message of a letter. Generally speaking, the letter should be carefully planned and paragraphed, with the first paragraph referring to any previous correspondence and the last paragraph to future actions or plans.

It is best to keep an initial business letter short. Business people are busy and do not have time to read long letters! In a one-page letter, you will usually only need three or four paragraphs, single spaced. Use a double space in between paragraphs.

Second page heading

When a letter must go beyond one page, you should set up the following pages for quick identification. It is general practice to type or print the following pages on plain paper (not letterhead). Of the various forms used to identify these pages, the following three are the most common:

Mr. Bill Clinton   2   *December 8, 2004*

Mr. Bill Clinton December 8, 2004, page 2

Complimentary close

If the letter begins with Dear Sir, Dear Sirs, Dear Madam or Dear sir or Madam, it will close with Yours faithfully. If the letter begins with a personal name—Dear Mr. James, Dear Mr. Robinson, Dear Ms. Jasmin—it will close with Yours sincerely. Avoid closing with old-fashioned phrases such as *We remain yours faithfully*, *Respectfully yours* etc. The comma after the complimentary close is optional (Yours faithfully, or Yours faithfully).

Note that Americans tend to close even formal letters with Yours truly or Truly yours, which is unusual in the UK in commercial correspondence. But a letter to a friend or acquaintance may end with Yours truly or the casual Best wishes.

The position of the complimentary close—on the left, right or in the center of the page—is a matter of choice. It depends on the style of the letter (blocked letters tend to put the close on the left, indented letters tend to put them in the center) and on your firm's preference.

    e. g.

Sincerely,

Jonathan Wilson

Jonathan Wilson

Signature block

The typed or printed signature conventionally appears on the fourth line below the complimentary close, beginning directly under the first letter in the block form. A short name and title may appear on the same line, separated by a comma. If either is long, the title appears on the following line, blocked under the name. The writer's signature appears in the space between complimentary close and typed signature.

Always type your name after your handwritten signature. Even though you may think your signature is easy to read, letters such as a, e, o, r and v can easily be confused.

It is, to some extent, a matter of choice whether you sign with your initials (s) (D. Jenkins) or your given name (David Jenkins), and whether you include a courtesy title (Mr., Mrs., Miss, Ms.) in your signature or not. But if you give neither your given name nor your title, your correspondent will not be able to identify your sex and may give you the wrong title when he/she replies. It is safer, therefore, to sign with your given name, and safest of all to include your title.

Including titles in signature is, in fact, more common among women than among men, partly because many women like to make it clear either that they are married (Mrs.) or unmarried (Miss) or that their marital status is not relevant (Ms.), and partly because there is still a tendency to believe that important positions in a company can only be held by men. It would do no harm for men to start including their titles in their signatures.

Look at the following examples:

Yours faithfully,
T Shurgold
(Miss) T. Shurgold

Yours sincerely,
J. Howatt
J. Howatt (Mr.)

Per Pro

The term per pro (p. p.) is sometimes used in signatures and means for and on behalf of, as indicated as follows:

Yours faithfully,
p. p. Watson & Jervis Ltd.
R. Nod
Sales Manager

Secretaries sometimes use p. p. when signing letters on behalf of their bosses:

Yours faithfully,
(Mrs) Rosemary Phipps
p. p. J. Mane
Managing Director

When signing on behalf of your company, it is useful to indicate your position in the firm in the signature:

Yours faithfully,
(Ms) T. Lovette
(Ms) T. Lovette
Chief Account

Enclosures

If there are any enclosures, e.g. leaflets, prospectuses etc. , with the letter, these may be mentioned in the body of the letter. But many firms in any case write Enc. or Encl. at the bottom of the letter, and if there are a number of documents, these are listed.

Enc.
Bill of Lading (6 copies)
Insurance certificate (1 copy)
Certificate of origin (1 copy)
Bill of exchange (1 copy)

Copies

c. c. (= carbon copies) is written, usually at the end of the letter, when copies are sent to people other than the named recipient:

c. c. Messrs. Poole & Jackson Ltd. , Solicitors
c. c. Mr. J. Cooper

Addressing envelopes

Envelope addresses are written in a similar way to inside addresses, but, for letters in or going to the UK, British Telecom recommends that the postcode is written on a line by itself at the end of both the town and the country are written in capital letters.

It is general practice to have the return address printed in the upper left corner of the envelope. Name and address of the receiver should be typed about half way down the envelope, leaving enough space for the postmark or stamps. Post notations such as Certified or Confidential should be placed in the bottom left-hand corner.

```
┌─────────────────────────────────────────────────────────────────┐
│  Mr. G. Penter                                                    │
│  49 Memorial Road                                   ( Stamp)      │
│  ORPINGTON                                          Registered    │
│  Kent                                                             │
│  BR6 9UA                                                          │
│                                                                   │
│                      Messrs W. Brown & Co.                        │
│                        600 Grand Street                           │
│                        LONDON                                     │
│                        UNITED KINGDOM                             │
│                        WIN 9UZ                                    │
│  Confidential                                                     │
│                                                                   │
└─────────────────────────────────────────────────────────────────┘
```

LAYOUT OF BUSINESS LETTER

When we apply communication theory to business letter situations, it becomes evident that the letter's appearance is a part of the message. Readers judge the writer by what they see as they look at the typed page. Thus, for the very best communication result, you should make certain that your letter looks good—that it gives a good impression of you. For your guidance in this effort, the following review of letter form is presented.

The ideal letter layout is one that has the same shape as the space in which it is typed. It fits the space much like a picture in a frame (see Figure 1), that is, a rectangle bordering the typing has the same shape and it is proportionate to the space under the page letterhead. This layout is marked at the top by the dateline, on the left by the line beginnings, on the right by the average line length, and at the bottom by the last line of the typed signature. Because it looks better to the eye, the layout is best placed slightly high on the page. Slide margins should be equal and no less than an inch.

Most offices use fixed margins for all routine letters. Typically they use lines of about six inches and vary the heights of the letters by using more or less space, as needed, between date and inside address. The arrangements in Figure 2 and Figure 3 typify this practice.

Figure 1

Modified Block, Blocked Paragraphs, Margins
Adjusted to Form Ideal Layout

(*LETTERHEAD*)

December 13 , 2004

↑

3 TO 8 LINES

↓

– – – – – – – – – –

Ms. Loretta R. . Gunnison , President
Port City Investments , Inc.
3117 Avenue E
Seattle , WA 20103

Dear Ms. Gunnison :

Sincerely ,
THE SWANSON COMPANY
3 LINES
C. l. Breen President

Figure 2

Block Style, Fixed Margins Using Subject Line

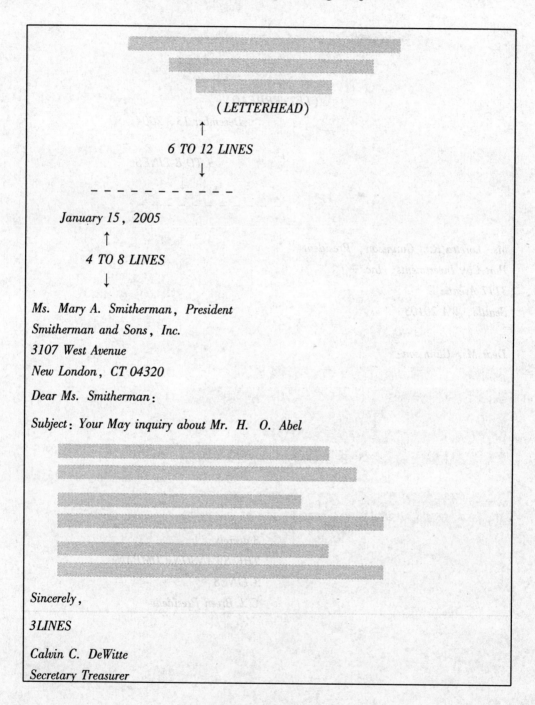

(*LETTERHEAD*)

↑

6 TO 12 LINES

↓

– – – – – – – – – – –

January 15, 2005

↑

4 TO 8 LINES

↓

Ms. Mary A. Smitherman, President
Smitherman and Sons, Inc.
3107 West Avenue
New London, CT 04320
Dear Ms. Smitherman:
Subject: Your May inquiry about Mr. H. O. Abel

Sincerely,
3 LINES
Calvin C. DeWitte
Secretary Treasurer

Figure 3

Modified Block , Indented Paragraphs , Fixed Margins

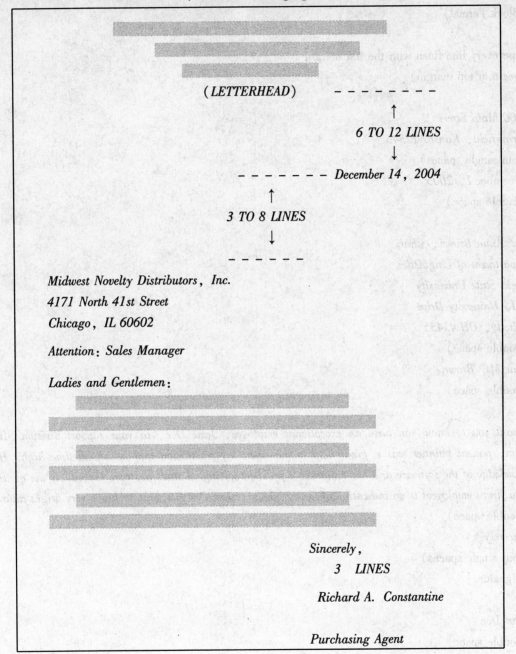

(*LETTERHEAD*) – – – – – – –

↑

6 TO 12 LINES

↓

– – – – – – – *December 14 , 2004*

↑

3 TO 8 LINES

↓

– – – – – –

Midwest Novelty Distributors , Inc.

4171 North 41st Street

Chicago , IL 60602

Attention: Sales Manager

Ladies and Gentlemen:

Sincerely ,

3 LINES

Richard A. Constantine

Purchasing Agent

Sample letters

Example 1
(Block Format)

Type every line flush with the left margin
(begin at top margin)

1600 Main Street
Springfield, Kansas 12345
(four single spaces)
December 1, 2005
(double space)

Ms. Anna Brown, Chair
Department of Linguistics
Right State University
1415 University Drive
Felicity, OH 45435
(double space)
Dear Ms. Brown:
(double space)

I want you to know you have an exceptional employee, Jane Doe, in your support division. Her calm, patient manner was a great help to me when my frustration was at an all-time high. Her knowledge of the software and her remarkable problem-solving abilities are rare indeed. If the quality of a firm's employees is an indication of future success, then Doe Corporation has a very bright future.
(double space)
Sincerely,
(four single spaces)
[Signature]

John Doe
(double space)
Enclosure

Example 2
(Indented Forma)

Indent your return address, the closing, your typed name, and the optional enclosure to the approximate center of the page (position 4. 25 " to 4. 5 ").

(begin at top margin)

600 Main Street
Springfield , Kansas 12345

(four single spaces)

December 1 , 2005
(double space)

Ms. Anna Brown , Chair
Department of Linguistics
Right State University
1415 University Drive

Felicity , OH 45435
(double space)
Dear Ms. Brown :
(double space)

I am writing to thank you for the training seminar you arranged , and to especially thank you for sending Mr. Doe to be our primary instructor. He did his homework well , and was more aware of our needs than any of our previous instructors. We appreciate the time he took to study samples of our work in advance so his comments were immediately applicable. We would welcome his instruction again. Please convey our thanks to Mr. Doe.
(double space)
Sincerely ,
(four single spaces)
[Signature]

John Doe
(double space)
Enclosure

Example 3
(Indented Format)

Indent your return address, the closing, your typed name, and the optional enclosure to the approximate center of the page (position 4. 25 " to 4. 5").
Additionally, indent each paragraph approximately five spaces.

(begin at top margin)

1600 Main Street
Springfield, Kansas 12345

(four single spaces)

December 1, 2003
(double space)

Ms. Anna Brown, Chair
Department of Linguistics
Right State University
1415 University Drive
Felicity, OH 45435
(double space)
Dear Ms. Brown:
(double space)

As manager of our computer department, I commend your employee, John Doe, for the prompt and courteous service he gave us last week. He determined our cable needs and produced a fair written estimate very quickly. Once he started the work, he stayed on location until he had installed all additional computers. You can be certain that we shall ask for him personally to serve our future needs.

(double space)
Sincerely,
(four single spaces)
[Signature]

John Doe
(double space)
Enclosure

USEFUL WORDS & EXPRESSIONS

letterhead/heading/the return address	信头
inside address/receiver's address/ recipient's address	封内地址/收信人地址
registered number	注册/登记号码
VAT number	增值税号码
salutation	称呼语
courtesy title	礼貌的头衔
complimentary close	结束礼貌语/结尾礼貌语
blocked style	齐头式/平头式
indented style	缩行式
attention line / for the attention of	转交
reference	有关的信件或发信人
subject title/subject line/caption	标题
p. p. /per pro. (procuration) /by authority of	经授权
Enc. /Encl. (enclosure)	附录
c. c. (carbon copy)	抄送
b. c. c. (blind carbon copy)	信件的复写副本
PLC/plc (public limited company)	股票上市公司
(USA) Inc. (incorporated)	股份有限公司
& Co. (and company)	公司
Sole Trader	专营商
Joint Stock Company	股份公司
Board of Directors	董事会
Chairman, (USA) President	董事长
Managing Director, (USA) Chief Executive	总经理
Chief Executive Officer (CEO)	执行总裁，首席执行官

Finance Director	财务经理，财务处长
Chief Accountant	总会计师，会计处长/主任
Esq. （Esquire）	先生，绅士
Accounting Assistant	会计助理
Accounting Clerk	记账员
Accounting Manager	会计部经理
Accounting Staff	会计部职员
Accounting Supervisor	会计主管
Administration Manager	行政经理
Administration Staff	行政人员
Administrative Assistant	行政助理
Administrative Clerk	行政办事员
Advertising Staff	广告工作人员
Airlines Sales Representative	航空公司订座员
Airlines Staff	航空公司职员
Application Engineer	应用工程师
Assistant Manager	副经理
Bond Analyst	证券分析员
Bond Trader	证券交易员
Business Controller	业务主任
Business Manager	业务经理
Buyer	采购员
Cashier	出纳员
Chemical Engineer	化学工程师
Civil Engineer	土木工程师
Clerk/Receptionist	职员/接待员
Clerk Typist & Secretary	文书打字员兼秘书
Computer Data Input Operator	计算机资料输入员

Computer Engineer	计算机工程师
Computer Processing Operator	计算机处理操作员
Computer System Manager	计算机系统部经理
Copywriter	广告文字撰稿人
Deputy General Manager	副总经理
Economic Research Assistant	经济研究助理
Electrical Engineer	电气工程师
Engineering Technician	工程技术员
English Instructor/Teacher	英语教师
Export Sales Manager	外销部经理
Export Sales Staff	外销部职员
Financial Controller	财务主任
Financial Reporter	财务报告人
F. X. (Foreign Exchange) Clerk	外汇部职员
F. X. Settlement Clerk	外汇部核算员
Fund Manager	财务经理
General Auditor	审计长
General Manager/President	总经理
General Manager Assistant	总经理助理
General Manager's Secretary	总经理秘书
Hardware Engineer	(计算机)硬件工程师
Import Liaison Staff	进口联络员
Import Manager	进口部经理
Insurance Actuary	保险公司理赔员
International Sales Staff	国际销售员
Interpreter	口语翻译
Legal Adviser	法律顾问
Line Supervisor	生产线主管
Maintenance Engineer	维修工程师

Management Consultant	管理顾问
Manager for Public Relations	公关部经理
Manufacturing Engineer	制造工程师
Manufacturing Worker	生产员工
Market Analyst	市场分析员
Market Development Manager	市场开发部经理
Marketing Manager	市场销售部经理
Marketing Staff	市场销售员
Marketing Assistant	销售助理
Marketing Executive	销售主管
Marketing Representative	销售代表
Marketing Representative Manager	市场调研部经理
Mechanical Engineer	机械工程师
Mining Engineer	采矿工程师
Music Teacher	音乐教师
Naval Architect	造船工程师
Office Assistant	办公室助理
Office Clerk	职员
Operational Manager	业务经理
Package Designer	包装设计师
Passenger Reservation Staff	乘客票位预订员
Personnel Clerk	人事部职员
Personnel Manager	人事部经理
Plant/Factory Manager	厂长
Postal Clerk	邮政人员
Private Secretary	私人秘书
Product Manager	生产部经理
Production Engineer	产品工程师
Professional Staff	专业人员

Programmer	电脑程序设计师
Project Staff	（项目）策划人员
Promotional Manager	推销部经理
Proof-reader	校对员
Purchasing Agent	采购（进货）员
Quality Control Engineer	质量管理工程师
Real Estate Staff	房地产职员
Recruitment Coordinator	招聘协调人
Regional Manger	地区经理
Research & Development Engineer	研究开发工程师
Sales and Planning Staff	销售计划员
Sales Assistant	销售助理
Sales Clerk	店员/售货员
Sales Coordinator	销售协调人
Sales Engineer	销售工程师
Sales Executive	销售主管
Sales Manager	销售部经理
Salesperson	销售员
Seller Representative	销售代表
Sales Supervisor	销售监管
School Registrar	学校注册主任
Secretarial Assistant	秘书助理
Securities Custody Clerk	保安人员
Security Officer	安全人员
Senior Accountant	高级会计
Senior Consultant/Adviser	高级顾问
Senior Employee	高级雇员
Senior Secretary	高级秘书
Service Manager	服务部经理

Simultaneous Interpreter	同声传译员
Software Engineer	(计算机)软件工程师
Supervisor	监管员
Systems Adviser	系统顾问
Systems Engineer	系统工程师
Systems Operator	系统操作员
Technical Editor	技术编辑
Technical Translator	技术翻译
Technical Worker	技术工人
Telecommunication Executive	电信(业务)管理人员
Telephonist/Operator	电话接线员，话务员
Tourist Guide	导游
Trade Finance Executive	贸易财务主管
Trainee Manager	培训部经理
Translation Checker	翻译核对员
Translator	翻译员
Trust Banking Executive	银行高级职员
Word Processing Operator	文字处理操作员
Chief Accountant	总会计师
Chief Architect	总建筑师
Chief Designer	总设计师
Chief Editor；Editor-in-Chief	总编辑
Chief Engineer；Engineer-in-Chief	总工程师
Chief of General Affairs	总务主任
Chief of the General Staff	总参谋长
Commander-in-Chief	总司令
General Accountant	总会计师
General Agent	总代理商
General Consul	总领事

General Designer	总设计师
General Dispatch Officer	总调度员
General Manager	总经理
General Secretary; Secretary-General	总书记；总干事
General Store Supervisor	总务管理员
Auditor-General	总稽查
Consul-General	总领事
Director-General	总干事
Chairman; President	总裁
Controller	总监；总管
Dean of General Affairs	总务长
Governor	总督
Head Clerk	总管
President	总统
Prime Minister; Premier	总理
Head Office	总公司
Branch Office	分公司
Business Office	营业部
Personnel Department	人事部
Human Resources Department	人力资源部
General Affairs Department	总务部
General Accounting Department	财务部
Sales Department	销售部
Sales Promotion Department	促销部
International Department	国际部
Export Department	出口部
Import Department	进口部
Public Relations Department	公共关系部
Advertising Department	广告部

Planning Department	企划部
Product Development Department	产品开发部
Research and Development Department（R&D）	研发部
Secretarial Pool	秘书室

EXERCISES

I. Plan the layout according to the following particulars：

 Sender：China National Import & Export Corporation ，Yunnan Branch，Kunming China

 Receiver：H & G Co. Ltd, Sherman Oak，California 91403，U. S. A.

 Date：Twenty second of March，1998.

 Our Reference No：351/10578

II. Address an envelope based on the following addresses：

 Sender：Johan Adams & Co. ，361 Cross Street，New York，N. Y. ，U. S. A.

 Receiver：Paul Simon & Co. ，Fernhall Drive，Redbridge London E. C. I，England

III. Plan the layout according to the following particulars and order the letter in the best way：

 Sender：W. Brown & Co. ，600 Grand Street LONDON UNITED KINGDOMWIN 9UZ

 Recipient：Ms. Loretta R. Gunnison，Managing Director，Port City Investments，Inc. 3117
    Avenue E Seattle，WA 20103

 Caption：Applying for being buying an agent Date：The tenth of May，2005

 Enclosure：Two copies of draft contracts

My company already acts for several firms in Europe and America and we specialize in buying domestic appliances（家用电器用品）and other household goods（家用物品）for these markets. We have contacts with all leading brand manufacturers so we are able to obtain specially reduced export prices for their products and we can offer excellent terms for freight and insurance.

I am replying to your advertisement in the trade magazine ' House care' in which you said you were looking for a buying agent in the UK to represent your group of stores in West Africa.

I have enclosed our usual draft contact for you to consider，and if you are interested，I would be pleased to hear from you.

Our usual commission is 5 per cent on c. i. f. invoiced values（票面价值），and we make purchases in our principals'（客户）names, sending them accounts for settlement.

We will keep you well informed of new products that come on to the market, sending you any information or literature（推销资料、产品说明书）that we think will be helpful.

CHAPTER 2

THE FUNDAMENTALS AND TECHNIQUES OF BUSINESS WRITING

Business English is not a special language, it is English used in English context. As a result, great importance should be attached to the following aspects while compiling a business letter.

OBJECTIVES OF THE BUSINESS LETTER

Our study of business letters appropriately begins with an analysis of letter objective. By *objectives* we mean what the writer wants to achieve by writing the letter. As we shall see, the objectives of a letter determine the techniques we should use in writing it.

The primary goal

The primary goal is the immediate business reason for writing—collects money, exchange information. This goal is the one that moves us to write the letter in the first place. In each instance there is a definite need to communicate, and fulfillment of that need becomes the letter's primary objective.

The public relation goal

The primary objective is not the only goal. There is at least one more objective in the typical business letter situation, one that may be equally important in some cases—the public relations objective.

The public relations goal involves making or keeping a friend for the business. People form images about companies from many sources. As a result, organizations work hard to keep their images favorable—to keep or make good impressions in people's minds. Correspondence is a major part of the organization's public relation effort.

TECHNIQUES OF WRITING BUSINESS LETER

Techniques are of great significance to writers as far as business writing is concerned. While writing business letters, great importance should be attached to the following techniques.

The seven Cs of business letter writing

Effective letter writing boils down to knowing why you are writing a letter, understanding your reader's needs and then clearly writing what you need to say. Every letter should be clear, human, helpful and as friendly as the topic allows. The best letters have a conversational tone and read as if you were talking to your reader. In brief then, discover the Seven Cs of letter writing. You should be

- Clear
- Concise
- Correct
- Courteous
- Conversational
- Convincing
- Complete

When you write a letter, you are trying to convince someone to act or react in a positive way. Your reader will respond quickly only if your meaning is crystal clear.

Put yourself in the reader's shoes and write in a friendly and helpful tone. Don't represent your company as one that cannot make a mistake and must always be in the right. Try not to reply in the normal bland and defensive way of organizations—write a sincere and helpful letter.

Show you are interested in the reader's circumstances. If he or she has mentioned something personal in the letter, refer to it in your reply. This builds a bridge between you and the reader. Read the original letter carefully and see if there is something you can put in your letter to show your interest.

Putting your reader first

For all writers the most important people are their readers. If you keep your readers in mind when you write, it will help you use the right tone, appropriate language and include the right amount of detail.

What do readers want from writing? They want relevant information, presented in a clear, easy-to-understand style. They don't want muddled thinking, background information they already know, business-speak and jargon or waffle(无聊话,动听而无意义的话). Above all,they want to get the gist of your message in one reading—they don't want to dig for the meaning through long sentences and a boring style. So if you always keep your readers in mind, you will have to adapt your style and content to meet their needs.

Getting a clear picture of your readers before you start to write helps to focus your writing to get your message across. The better picture you have of your readers, the better you can direct your writing.

Ask questions to get a clear picture of your readers.
- Who are my readers?
- What do they already know about the subject?
- What do they need to know?
- Will they understand technical terms?
- What information do they want?
- What do I want them to do?
- What interests or motivates them?
- What prejudices do they have?
- What worries or reassures them?
- What will persuade them to my view?
- What other arguments do I need to present?
- How are they likely to react to what I say?
- If you imagine yourself in your reader's position, you're more likely to write a good letter.

Getting the right tone to your business letter

When you write a business letter, it's important to use a tone that is friendly but efficient. Readers want to know there's someone at the other end of the letter who is taking notice and showing interest in their concerns. Try to sound—and be—helpful and friendly.

To do this, write as you would speak and talk on paper. This doesn't mean you should use slang, bad grammar or poor English, but try to aim for a conversational style and let the reader hear your voice.

Imagine that your reader is sitting opposite you at your desk or is on the telephone. You'd be unlikely to say "please be advised" or "I wish to inform you"; instead you'd be more informal and say, "I'd like to explain" or "Let me explain" or use other everyday expressions.

Here are some ways to change your writing style to a conversational style.

1. Use contractions

Using contractions such *as it's, doesn't, I'm, you're, we're, they're, isn't, here's, that's, we'll* gives a personal and human feel to your writing.

If there are no contractions in your writing, put some in. You don't have to use contractions at every opportunity. Sometimes writing "do not" comes more naturally than "don't". When you speak, you probably use a combination of these styles—try to reflect this in your writing.

2. Use personal references

Use words such as *I, we, you, your, my,* and *our* in your writing. Don't be afraid to identify yourself—it makes writing much more readable. This is a useful trick to make writing look and sound more like face-to-face talk.

Using *I, we and you* also helps you to avoid using passive verbs. It makes your style more direct and clear.

So instead of writing: *Our address records have been amended ...*
Write: *We've changed your address in our records ...*

Instead of writing: *The company policy is ...*
Write: *Our policy is ...*

Using active verbs with personal references is a quick and dramatic way to make your writing readable and more direct.

3. Use direct questions

Direct questions are an essential part of the spoken language. Using them gives your writing much more impact and is a common technique in marketing and advertising material. Marketing people use this technique to put information across clearly and to give their writing impact.

In much business writing, we hide questions in our writing by using words such as whether to introduce them. Look for these in your writing and change them into direct questions. For example:

Original: *We would appreciate your advising us whether you want to continue this account or transfer it.*
Redraft: *Do you want to continue your account or transfer it?*

Original: *Please inform us whether payment against these receipts will be in order.*
Redraft: *Can we pay against these receipts?*

Apart from making your style more conversational, direct questions liven up your writing—it's as though you change the pitch in your voice. There's nothing like a direct question to get some reaction from your reader and to give your writing impact.

Writing your business plan in plain English

Good writing is effortless reading that makes you want to read more. It is clear and concise, uses short sentences and simple words. It keeps to the facts and is easy to read and to understand.

Plain English is clear English. It is simple and direct but not simplistic or patronizing. Using plain English doesn't mean everyone's writing must sound the same. There is no one "right" way to express an idea. There's plenty of room for your own style—but it will only blossom once you have got rid of the poor writing habits that are typical of most business writing. Here are some of the key techniques to help you write in plain English:

1. Use active verbs rather than passive verbs
Using active verbs rather than passive verbs is the key to good writing. Why? Because passive verbs are longwinded, ambiguous, impersonal and dull. Active verbs make your writing simpler, less formal, clearer and more precise. Here are some examples:

Passive: *It was agreed by the committee...*
Active: *The committee agreed...*

Passive: *At the last meeting a report was made by the Secretary...*
Active: *At the last meeting the Secretary reported...*

Passive: *This form should be signed and should be returned to me.*
Active: *You should sign the form and return it to me.*

In switching your style from passive verbs to active verbs throughout your writing, you face several problems. You must accurately spot them. Often writers miss passive verbs or try to change verbs that are already active. You need to measure your use of passive verbs. One or two passive verbs a page will not ruin your style, nine or ten will. You need to know how to turn passive verbs to active verbs.

2. Keep your sentence average length low

Sentence length is crucial to good writing. Almost everything written by good writers has an average sentence length of between 15 and 20 words. This doesn't mean writing every sentence the same length. Good writers naturally vary the length and rhythm of their sentences—longer sentences balanced with shorter ones—but they keep their average sentence length well below 20 words. Compare these examples:

Long sentence:

I refer to my letter of 13th June and am writing to advise you that if we do not receive your completed application form within the next fourteen days, I shall have no alternative but to arrange property insurance on the bank's block policy.

(One Sentence—45 words)

Shorter sentences:

I have not yet received your reply to my letter of 13th June. If we do not receive your completed application form within fourteen days, I shall have to arrange property insurance on the bank's block policy.

(Two sentences—13 words and 24 words)

3. Use simple words rather than complex ones

Many writers have difficulty keeping their message simple and clear. Instead of using everyday words they use complex or unfamiliar words. Simple, everyday words will help you get your message across. Too often we use words such as *additional*, *indicate*, *initiate* and *proliferate* for *extra*, *show*, *start and spread*.

Complex words

As we noted in the preceding section, if you purchased additional printer options, such as a second printer tray, it is a requirement you verify its correct installation.

Simple words

As we noted in the previous section, if you bought extra printer equipment, such as a second printer tray, you must check you install it correctly.

4. Edit wordy phrases

Padding is the enemy of good writing. Unnecessary words and phrases clutter up sentences and obscure meaning. By comparison, economy of words is the mark of good writing. You have to learn to make every word count in technical documents. You must edit ruthlessly, cutting any extra word. Set yourself a target of cutting 10 to 20 percent of the words in your document.

Look for wordy phrases such as these in your writing and replace them with a single word or cut them out completely:

Wordy	Concise
at a later date	later
at the present time	now
for the purpose of	for
have no alternative but	must
in addition to	besides, as well as, also
in order to	to
in relation to	about, in, with, towards, to
on a regular basis	regularly

5. Avoid jargon and technical terms

It's up to you to judge how much you need to explain your industry jargon and specialist terms by putting yourself in your readers' shoes. Don't overestimate your readers' understanding of terms because they may have a hazy idea of the true definition.

It doesn't insult the intelligence of your readers to explain terms clearly. Imagine a customer was sitting with you when you mentioned a technical term and asked "What's that?" You would explain in everyday language. Do the same when you write.

6. Avoid abbreviations

The most common and irritating form of jargon is overuse of abbreviations. Here are some abbreviations. How many do you know?

Acronym	Meaning
CRA	Camera-Ready Artwork
DPI	Dots Per Inch
DTP	Desktop Publishing
PMS	Pantone Matching System
SC	Spot Color
UGD	User Guide Documentation

How many did you get right? Two out of six? Probably DPI for dots per inch and DTP for desktop publishing as these are industry terms. Many people would not recognize these two. As for CRA, camera-ready artwork would be better. SC for spot color is an unnecessary shortened form and UGD for User Guide Documentation is jargon for a manual.

Avoid abstract words and phrases

One habit you should avoid, common to many writers, is overusing abstract words. Here's a list of the most common ones to avoid in your writing.

Abstract words to avoid in technical writing

activities	devices	inputs	sectors
amenities	elements	operations	structures
amenity	facilities	outputs	systems
aspects	factors	processes	variables
concepts	functions	resources	

Avoiding overused business letter phrases

Many business letters contain hackneyed phrases that detract from a clear, natural style. You need to look for them in your writing and use fresh, clear expression instead. Look at this list and see if you recognize any from your letters:

- according to our records
- after careful consideration
- any further action
- as you are aware
- at your earliest convenience
- detailed information
- enclosed for your information
- for your convenience
- further to
- in receipt of

- on receipt of
- please do not hesitate to
- please find enclosed
- please forward
- trust this is satisfactory
- under separate cover
- upon receipt of
- urgent attention
- we acknowledge receipt
- we regret to advise

Look at these examples from typical business letters and you'll see how removing the business clichés changes the tone of the sentence. The originals have a formal and impersonal tone; the redrafts sound more personal and genuine.

Original

We trust this is satisfactory, but should you have any further questions please do not hesitate to contact us.

Redraft

We hope you are happy with this arrangement but if you have any questions, please contact us.

Original

Further to your recent communication. Please find enclosed the requested quotation. . .

Redraft

Thank you for contacting us. I enclose the quotation you asked for. . .

Hackneyed business phrases ruin a clear natural style; so avoid using them and choose your own words instead.

Use of "rubber stamps"

Rubber stamps are expressions used from habit every time a certain situation occurs. They give routine rather than customized treatment. Expressions from the old language of business are rubber stamps. So are some more recent ones. You can avoid rubber stamps by writing in your conversational vocabulary.

The difference between stilted and conversational writing styles are perhaps best described in the following examples.

Dull and Stiff	Friendly and Conversational
This is to advise that we deem it a great pleasure to approve subject of your request as per letter of the 12th August.	*Yes, you certainly may use the equipment you asked about in your August 12 letter.*
Pursuant to this matter, I wish to state that the aforementioned provisions are unmistakably clear.	*These contract provisions are quite clear on this point.*
Thanking you in advance. . .	*I'll sincerely appreciate. . .*
Herewith enclosed please find. . .	*Enclosed is. . .*
I deem it advisable. . .	*I suggest. . .*
I herewith hand you. . .	*Here is. . .*
Kindly advise at an early date. . .	*Please let me know soon. . .*
The undersigned wishes to advise that the aforementioned contract is at hand.	*I have the contract.*
Please be advised that you should sign the form before the 1st. . .	*You should sign the form before the 1st.*
I hope this meets with your approval.	*I hope you approve.*

The you-viewpoint

Because we are self-centered, we tend to see each situation from our own points of view. In letter writing situations, this attitude may lead us to a writer-oriented, we-viewpoint approach—one that places emphasis on ourselves and our interests rather than on our readers and their interests. Such approaches obviously do not elicit the most responses in our readers, for they too are self-centered. The result is not conductive to building goodwill, nor does it help get your readers to do things you want them to do. You can achieve more positive effects by writing in the reader's point of view.

The you-viewpoint or you-attitude involves seeing situations from your readers' standpoint and choosing words and strategies that will bring about a favorable response in their minds.

You-viewpoint writing emphasizes the reader's interests. It is an attitude that focuses on the reader's point of view. The following contrasting examples provide additional proof of the different effects changes in viewpoint produce.

We-Viewpoint	You-Viewpoint
We are happy to have your order for Kopper products, which we are sending today by Railway Express.	*Your selection of Kopper products should reach you by Saturday, as they were shipped by Railway Express today.*
We sell the Forever cutlery set for the low price of $ 4 each and suggest a retail price $ 6. 50.	*You can reap a nice $ 2. 5 profit on each Forever set you sell at $ 6. 50, for your cost is only $ 4.*
We have been quite tolerant of your past-due account and must now demand payment.	*If you are to continue to enjoy the benefits of credit buying, you have no choice but to clear your account now.*
We have received your report of May 1.	*Thank you for your report of May 1.*
We have shipped the two dozen Crown desk sets you ordered.	*Your two dozen Crown desk sets should reach you with this letter.*

Effects of words

Whether your letter achieves its goal often depends to a large extent on the words you use to carry your message. As you know, there are many ways of saying anything, and each way conveys a meaning different from the others. Much of the difference, of course, lies in the words' meaning. Words that stir up positive meanings in the reader's mind usually are best for achieving your letter objectives. This is not to say that negative words have no place in business writing. They do. They are strong, and they give emphasis. There are times when you will want to use them. But most of the time your need will be for positive words, for such words are more likely to produce the effects you seek. If you are seeking some action, for example, they are the words most likely to persuade. They tend to put the reader in the right frame of mind, and they place emphasis on the more pleasant aspects of your objectives. In addition, positive words create the goodwill atmosphere we seek in most letters.

On the other hand, negative words produce the opposite effect. The negative meanings they create in the mind may stir up your reader's resistance to your objective. Also, they are likely to be highly destructive of goodwill. Thus, in reaching your letter writing goals, you will need to carefully study the degrees of negativeness and positiveness your words convey. You will need to select those words that will do the most for you in each case.

Examples of word choice

To illustrate your positive-to-negative word choices in handling letters, take the case of a corporate executive who must write a local civic groups to deny its requests to use the company's meeting facilities. To soften the refusal, the executive can let the group use a conference room, which may be somewhat small for its purpose. Of the many ways to word the response, the executive could come up with this totally negative ones:

*We **regret** to inform you that we **cannot** permit you to use our clubhouse for your meeting, as the Ladies Book Club asked for it first. We can, however, let you use our conference room; but it seats **only** 60.*

Had the writer sought a more positive way to cover the same situation, this tactful response might have resulted:

Because the Ladies book club has reserved the clubhouse for Saturday, the best we can do is offer you our conference room, which seats 60.

Not a single negative word appears in this version. Both approaches achieve the letter's primary objective of denying a request, but the effects on the reader would differ sharply. There is no question as to which techniques does the better job of building and holding goodwill for the company.

As the following negative-filled version illustrates, the effect on the reader is destructive of goodwill:

*We received your claim in which you **contend** that we were responsible for damage to three cases of Madame Dupree's lotion. We assure you that we sincerely **regret** the **problems** this has caused you. Even though we feel in all sincerity that your receiving clerks may have been negligent, we shall assume the **blame** and replace the **damaged** merchandise.*

Obviously, the words "in which you contend" clearly imply some doubt of the claim's legitimacy. Even the sincerely intended expression of regret serves only to recall to the reader's mind the ugly picture of the event that has caused all the trouble. Negatives such as **blame** and **damage** serve only to strengthen this recollection. Certainly, such an approach is not conductive to goodwill.

In the following version of the message, the writer uses only positive aspects of the situation—what can be done to settle the problem. The writer does it without a single negative word. There is no reference to correcting the situation or to suspicions concerning the claim's legitimacy. The goodwill effect of this approach is likely to maintain good business relations with the reader:

Three cases of Madame Dupree's lotion are on their way to you by Rocket Freight and should be on your sales floor by Saturday.

For additional illustration, compare the differing results obtained from the following positive-negative versions of letter messages. Boldface types mark the negative words.

Negative	Positive
*You **failed** to give us the fabric specifications of the chair you ordered.*	*So that you may have the one chair you want, will you please check your choice of fabric on enclosed card?*
*Smoking is **not** permitted anywhere except in the lobby.*	*Smoking is permitted in the lobby only.*
*We **cannot** deliver until Friday.*	*We can deliver the goods on Friday.*
*You were **wrong** in your conclusion for paragraph 3 of our agreement clearly states...*	*You will agree after reading paragraph 3 of our agreement that...*
*We **regret** to inform you that we must deny your request for credit.*	*For the time being we can serve you only on a cash basis.*

*Your May 7 **complaint** about our Pronto mini-dryer is **not** supported by the evidence.*	*Review of the situation described in your May 7 letter explains what happened when you used the Pronto mini-dryer.*

Avoiding anger

There may be times when anger is justified and letting off steam may benefit us emotionally. But anger helps us achieve a goal of a letter only when the goal is to anger the reader. The effect of angry words is obvious. Angry words destroy goodwill. They make the reader angry. And with both writer and reader angry, there is little likelihood that the two can get together on whatever the letter is about.

To illustrate the effect of anger, take an insurance company correspondent who must inform a policyholder that the latter has made a mistake in interpreting the policy and is not covered on the case in question. Feeling that any fool should be able to read the policy, the correspondent uses these angry words:

If you had read Section IV of your policy, you would know that you are not covered on accidents that occur on water.

In a sense, we might say that this statement "tells it like it is". The information is true. But because it shows anger, it lacks tact. A more tactful writer would refer to the point of misunderstanding in a positive and impersonal manner:

As a review of Section IV of your policy indicates, you are covered on accidents that occur on the grounds of your residence only.

Most statements made in anger do not concern information needed in the letter. They are comments that let the writer blow off steam. They may take many forms—sarcasm, insults, or exclamations. You can see from the following examples that it is better to omit them from your letters:

No doubt you expect us to hold your hand.

I cannot understand your negligence.

This is the third time you have permitted your account to be delinquent.

We will not tolerate this condition.

Your careless attitude has caused us a loss in sales.

We have had it!

We have no intention of permitting this condition to continue.

Avoid overdoing goodwill

To write sincerely, you should keep in mind two major checkpoints. First, you must avoid overdoing any of your goodwill techniques. Perhaps through insincerity in what you are doing, or perhaps as a result of an overzealous effort, you can easily overuse these techniques. As the following example shows, the you-viewpoint effort can exceed the bounds of reason:

So that you may be able to buy Kantrell equipment at an extremely low price and sell at a tremendous profit, we now offer you the complete line at a 50 percent price reduction.

Likewise, this example from a form letter from a company president to a new charge customer has a touch of unbelievability:

I was delighted today to see your name listed among Mogan's new charge customers.

Or how about this one, taken from an adjustment letter of a large department store?

We are extremely pleased to be able to help you and want you to know that your satisfaction means more than anything to us.

Avoid exaggeration

As a second checkpoint for sincerity, you will need to watch out for exaggerated statements. Most exaggerations are easy to see through; thus, they can give a tone of insincerity to your letter. Exaggerations, of course, are overstatements of facts. Although a form of exaggerations is conventional in sales writing, even here there are bounds of propriety. The following examples clearly overstep these limits:

Already thousands of new customers are beating paths to the doors of Martin dealers.

Never has there been, nor will there ever be, a fan as smooth running and whispering—quiet as the

North Wind.

Everywhere people meet, they are talking about the amazing whiteness Supreme gives their clothes.

Most exaggerated comments likely involve the use of superlatives. We all use them, and only rarely do they fit the reality about which we communicate. Words such as **greatest**, **most amazing**, **finest**, **healthiest**, and **strongest** are seldom appropriate and often disbelieved. Other strong words may have similar effects-for example, **extraordinary**, **stupendous**, **delicious**, **ecstatic**, **sensational**, **terrific**, **revolutionary**, **colossal**, and **perfection.** Such words cause us to question; rarely do really believe them.

Tie-in sentences

By structuring your strategy such that one idea sets up the next, you can skillfully relate the ideas; that is, you can design sentences to tie in two successive ideas. Notice in the following example how a job applicant tied in the first two sentences of the letter:

As a result of increasing demand for precision instruments in the Billsburg boom area, will you soon need another experienced and trained salespersons to call on your technical accounts there?

With seven successfully years of selling Morris instruments and a degree in civil engineering, I believe I have the qualifications to do this job.

Contrast the smooth connecting sentence above with the abrupt shift this second sentence would create:

I am 32 years of age, married, and am interested in exploring the possibilities of employment with you.

As another case, compare the following contrasting examples of sentences following the first sentence of a letter refusing an adjustment on a trenching machine. As you can see, the strategy of the initial sentence is to set up the introduction of additional information that will clear the company of responsibility:

Good Tie-in	**Abrupt Shift**
In this same spirit of friendly objectivity, we are confident that you will want to consider some additional information we have assembled.	*We have found some additional information you will want to consider.*

Repetition of key words

By repeating key words from one sentence to the next, you can make smooth connections of successive ideas. The following successive sentences from a letter refusing a request to conduct a lecture series for an advertising clinic illustrate this transitional technique:

*Because your advertising clinic is so well planned, I am confident that it can provide a really **valuable** service to practitioners in the community. To be truly valuable, I know you will agree, the program must be given the **time** a thorough preparation requires. As my **time** for the coming weeks is heavily committed, you will need to find someone who is in a better position to do justice to your program.*

EFFECTIVE WRITING OF BUSINESS LETTER

Writing a strong opening to your business letter

Your first job in writing any letter is to gain your reader's attention. It's an important principle of effective writing to put the most important information first. Your opening paragraph is both the headline and the lead for the message that follows in the rest of the letter.

Don't weigh down the front of your letter with boring repetition of information that your reader already knows. Many letters fail to start well because they follow the standard paragraph of every business letter. Here are some typical examples of openings in business letters:

Thank you for your letter of 8th March 1998, which has been passed to me for my attention.

I refer to previous correspondence in respect of the above and note that to date we have not received your cheque for the outstanding arrears.

I write with reference to our telephone conversation yesterday regarding the above matter.

Starting with a reference to the incoming letter is weak and wastes your reader's time. Most readers skip it, looking to the second and third paragraphs to get the answer to their questions. If you step right into your subject in the first paragraph, you'll show your reader you do not intend to waste valuable time. So get rid of any opening reference to the reader's letter and answer the most important question or give the most relevant information in your first sentence.

Make your first paragraph do something other than just referring to known information—so plunge straight into your message and don't waste your reader's time. For example, you could

- answer a question
- ask a question
- explain an action taken
- express pleasure or regret
- give information

As the opening paragraph sets the tone for your letter, try to avoid using tired phrases that are wordy, give little information and create a formal and impersonal tone. Using the classic business-speak opening of Further to... almost guarantees the rest of the letter will be a typical, long-winded, standard piece of business writing.

These opening phrases are so popular because we don't have to think of what to write. Watch out for standard phrases in opening paragraphs. Examples are:

Further to my recent
I am writing
I refer to my letter dated
I refer to previous correspondence
I write in reference to
In respect of the above
Recent correspondence
Regarding
With reference to
With regards to

So be sure your opening paragraph sets the right tone for your letter. Be direct and use your words positively so your reader has a good impression from the beginning of your letter. Decide what is the most important information—and put it in your first paragraph. Don't be afraid to start your letter strongly.

Writing a strong close to your business letter

If the average business letter starts poorly, then it invariably finishes poorly. Your closing paragraph should bring your letter to a polite, businesslike close. Typical final paragraphs in business letters invite the reader to write again or use overused and meaningless phrases that detract from the impact of the letter. Take a look at these examples of good closing sentences for business letters:

I would again apologize for the delay in replying and I trust that this has clarified the points you have raised, however, if you wish to discuss any points I have not clarified, or need any further information, you may wish to telephone or contact me accordingly.

I look forward to hearing from you and in the meantime, should you have any queries, please do not hesitate to contact me.

I regret that I cannot be of more assistance in this matter, and should you have any further queries, please do not hesitate to contact me.

Your last paragraph should do something. In a longer letter it can summarise the key points or repeat the key message. If some action is needed, explain what you want the reader to do or what you will do. Use positive words such as *when* not *if*.

Make sure you avoid using weak phrases and overused business phrases in your closing paragraph.

Thanking you for your. . .
Hoping for a prompt reply. . .
Thanking you in advance for your assistance. . .
Trusting this answers your questions. . .
Please do not hesitate to contact me.
I trust this clarifies the situation.

End your letter positively and politely. Don't leave your reader in mid-air, but use the final paragraph to explain or repeat what you want your reader to do.

BUSINESS LETTER WRITING CHECKLIST

When you write a business letter, use this checklist to remind you of the key principles of effective letter writing.

- Keep it short.
- Cut needless words and needless information.
- Cut stale phrases and redundant statements.
- Cut the first paragraph if it refers to previous correspondence.
- Cut the last paragraph if it asks for future correspondence.
- Keep it simple.
- Use familiar words, short sentences and short paragraphs.
- Keep your subject matter as simple as possible.
- Keep related information together.
- Use a conversational style.
- Keep it strong.

Answer the reader's question in the first paragraph.

- Give your answer and then explain why.
- Use concrete words and examples.
- Keep to the subject.
- Keep it sincere.
- Answer promptly.
- Be human and as friendly as possible.
- Write as if you were talking to your reader.

AN EFFECTIVE APPROACH OF WRITING BUSINESS LETTER

The following approach has proved effective in writing business letter.

A business letter can be drafted according to the following stages:

Stage 1   Identify the task
Lay your answer out as a letter.

Stage 2   Layout
Normal layout is:

your company address:	top right hand corner （右上角）
date:	top right hand corner below sender's address （右上角，在发信人地址之下 3~6 行）

name/address of recipient（收信人名称/地址）	beneath date on left hand side（在左上角，日期之下）
correct salutation：	"Dear..."
complimentary close：	Yours sincerely（Dear Sir/Madam/Sirs）
signature：	your signature
name：	printed name
position：	your position

Stage 3　Identify relevant information

Decide exactly why you are writing, what information you need to give or what information you need to receive. You are often asked to make up any necessary information. This may include your position, name of company and address, as well as other details.

Stage 4　Group/Order relevant information

Group the information in the best way and then order it so that one point follows on to the next.

Stage 5　Write the letter

Language in letters is usually polite. Useful starting phrases are "Thank you for your letter of 28 January 2005", or "I am writing to you because ..." A useful finishing phrase is " I look forward to hearing from you. "

Example of layout

24 High Street
Newcastle
NE46 4AB

29 October 2005

Mr. J Smith
28 Broom Street
Hexham
NE71 2SV
Dear Mr. Smith

....

Yours sincerely
Ena Brown

Ena Brown
Sales Manager

Stage 6　Check your work

Checklist: Letter

The following is a list of points to check when you write a letter.

- Have you completed the task?
- Is your layout correct?
- Do you have all the correct information?
- Is it ordered in the best way?
- Is the language appropriate for a letter?
- Have you checked spelling, grammar and punctuation?

Example 1

Situation: You are the Marketing Manager of a computer company, and a local college has written to your department asking if you would consider sponsoring their week-long drama festival to be held in the summer.

Task: Write a letter to the Principal of the college explaining that while you sympathize with (赞同) their aims and needs, your company has a fixed budget (固定预算) for sponsorship (赞助) and no new ventures can be considered until next year.

Note: Lay your answer out as a letter. Make up any necessary details.

Stage 1　Identify the task

Lay out your answer as a letter.

Stage 2　Layout

- your company address—Funtime Computers Ltd, 28 Blackwell Street, Newcastle, NE12 4AB
- the date—28th June 1991
- the name and address of the person to whom you are writing—The Principal, Newcastle College of Technology, 35 High Street, Newcastle, NE 14 3 LJ
- the correct salutation—Dear Sir/Madam
- complimentary close—Yours faithfully
- a signature—your signature
- name—your printed name
- position—Marketing Manager

Stage 3   Identify relevant information

- interested to hear about drama festival
- sympathize with aims
- unable to help
- fixed budget for sponsorship
- no new ventures until next year
- good luck with sponsorship
- hope all goes well
- try again next year

Stage 4   Group/Order relevant information

- Thank for letter
- Interested to hear about drama festival
- Sympathize with aims and needs
- Unfortunately unable to help
- Fixed budget for sponsorship
- No new ventures until next year
- Hope it all goes well
- Perhaps try again next year
- Good luck

Stage 5   Write the letter

Funtime Computers Ltd
28 Blackwell Street
Newcastle
NE12 4AB

28th June 1991

The Principal
Newcastle College of Technology
35 High Street
Newcastle
NE14 3LJ

Dear Sir/Madam:

Thank you for your letter of 24th June.

I was very interested to hear about the drama festival you are holding in the summer and sympathize with your aims and needs.

Unfortunately I am unable to help you as our company has a fixed budget for sponsorship and at present no new venture will be considered until next year.

I hope your festival is successful and can only suggest that perhaps you contact us again next year.

In the meantime, good luck!

Yours faithfully.

(your signature)
(printed name)
Marketing Manager

Stage 6   Check your work

Checklist: Letter

- Have you completed the task?
- Is your layout correct?
- Do you have all the correct information?
- Is it ordered in the best way?
- Is the language appropriate for a letter?
- Have you checked spelling, grammar and punctuation?

Example 2

Situation: You are working temporally in your local tourist office and your boss has asked you to find a writer to produce a short guide to your town/city.

Task: A colleague, Archie Leach, has recommended a friend of his, Michael Rees, the famous author of the "London Book". Write to Mr. Rees, at 21 Meadowcourt Road, London, SE3 9EU, asking if he would be interested in the project. Specify what want and the details of payment.

Note: Lay your answer out as a letter and make up any necessary details.

Stage 1   Identify the task

Lay your answer out as a letter and make up any necessary details.

Stage 2　Layout

- your company address—Tourist Office, 19 Eldon Gardens, Perth, Ph13 4NL
- the date—28 April 2005
- the name and address of the person to whom you are writing—Mr. M. Rees, 21 Meadow-court Road, London, SE3 9EU
- the correct salutation—Dear Mr. Rees
- complimentary close—Yours sincerely
- a signature—your signature
- name—your printed name
- position—no position

Stage 3　Identify relevant information

- want a writer to produce guide
- Archie Leach gave his name
- already written " The London Guide"
- Is he interested in the project?
- guide would include:
  - —places to visit
  - —places to eat
  - —places of historical interest
  - —places of outstanding beauty
- payment
  - —expenses during research period
  - —sum in advance
  - —percentage of every book sold

Stage 4　Group/Order relevant information

- Need someone to write a short guide.
- Got his name through Archie Leach, a colleague.
- Know of his book " The London Book".
- Required guide would give information on:
  - —places to visit
  - —places of historical interest
  - —places of outstanding beauty
  - —places to eat
- Payment would be
  - —a sum in advance
  - —expenses during research

—percentage of every book sold
- If he's interested, meet to discuss details.

Stage 5　Write the letter

Tourist Office
19 Eldon Gardens
Perth
PH13 4NL

28 April 2005

Mr. M. Rees
21 Meadowcourt Road
London
SE3 9 EU

Dear Mr. Rees:
The Tourist Office in Perth is looking for someone to produce a guide to the town and local area. I was given your address by a work colleague, Archie Leach. I am familiar with the "The London Guide" which you have written and am hoping to find a writer to produce a similar work about Perth.

Ideally the guide would include information about places to visit, places of historical interest, places of outstanding beauty and also good places to eat.

The payment package would provide a sum in advance, cover all expenses during the research period and the author would receive 10% percentage of every book sold.

If you are interested, I would suggest we arrange a date to discuss details.

I look forward to hearing from you.
Yours sincerely

(your signature)

(printed name)

USEFUL WORDS & EXPRESSIONS

abbreviations	缩写，缩写词
ambiguous	暧昧的，不明确的
commercialese	商业用语；商业中滥用的词句
stereotyped phrase	陈腐的词句
order and sequence	次序，顺序，序列
idiom	成语，方言，土语，习惯用语
colloquial language	通俗语，白话
tie-in	相配物；搭配销售的商品；关联、关系

EXERCISE

I. Rewrite and improve the following sentences according to the principles you've learned in this chapter.

1. We believe these goods are what you want.

2. It is impossible to meet your demands.

3. I wish to acknowledge receipt of your letter of October 18.

4. You failed to give us the texture specifications of the shirts you ordered.

5. Smoking is not permitted anywhere except in the lobby.

6. We cannot deliver the goods until Friday.

7. No doubt you expect us to hold our hand(手下留情).

8. We cannot understand your negligence.

9. This is the third time you have permitted your account to be delinquent(拖欠债务的).

10. We will not tolerate this condition.

11. Your careless attitude has caused us a loss in sales.

12. The undersigned is not in a position to effect payment for the time being.

13. You must correct your mistake as soon as possible.

14. We cannot dispatch the goods because you didn't establish the L/C.

15. We look forward to your valued order at your earliest convenience.

II. Rewrite and improve the following letter based on the seven Cs.

Because Mr. Jones is out of the office for the next two weeks, I am acknowledging receipt of your estimated letter dated May 20, 2005. It will be brought to his attention immediately upon his return.

If the undersigned may be of any assistance during Mr. Jones' absence, please do not hesitate to call.

III. Complete Stage 4 and Stage 5 of the following letter according to the given stages

Situation: You are Geoff Pullar, Director of Personnel at Aegis Insurance Company. Next month the Managing Director, Dr Glen Turner, of your Australian branch is to visit the headquarters of your company for two days.

Task: Send a letter to him at Lake View Tower, 264 High Street, Allambie, NSW2100, Australia, confirming the dates of his visit. Indicate who will meet him at the airport, where he will stay and a brief outline of his two-day program.

Note: Lay out your answer as a letter. Make up any necessary details.

Stage 1 Identify the task

Lay your answer out as a letter.

Stage 2 Layout

- your company address—Aegis Insurance Company, 24 High Street, Newcastle, NE46 4AA, England
- the date—25th April 2003
- the name and address of the person to whom you are writing—Dr Glen Turner, Aegis Insurance Company, Lake View Tower, 264 High Street, Allambie, NSW2100, Australia.
- the correct salutation—Dear Dr. Turner
- complimentary close—Yours sincerely
- a signature—your signature
- name—Geoff Pullar
- position—Director of Personnel

Stage 3 Identify relevant information

- visit HQ for 2 days
- confirm dates and arrival times (Monday 28th April, 6.30pm)
- Tim Taylor, Sales Manager-will meet at airport (he will have a sign)
- stay at Maritime Hotel, 21 Front View, Newcastle
- visit includes:
  —meeting with Marketing Manager, Tom Brown—Marketing Strategies
  —sales report on Uk by Tim Taylor
  —trip to Bamburgh Castle
- take him back to airport

Now complete the following stages.

Stage 4   Group/Order relevant information

Stage 5   Write the letter

IV. Complete the Stage 2 – Stage 5 of the following letter.

Situation: As the Office Manager of a large fruit-packing company, you have been asked to investigate the cost of a day's summer outing for both the office and the factory workers.

Task: Write a letter to a local coach company asking for a quotation for the hire of coaches for a day's excursion of your choice. Specify the number of people, the time of departure and return, and the destination.

Note: Lay out your answer as a letter. Make up any necessary details.

Stage 1   Identify the task

Lay your answer out as a letter.

Now complete the following stages.

Stage 2   Layout

your company address— ··

the date— ···

the name and address of person to whom you are writing— ·····················

the correct salutation— ···

complimentary close— ···

a signature/name/position—···

Stage 3   Identify relevant information

  ···

Stage 4   Group/Order relevant information

  ···

Stage 5   Write the letter

  ···

Chapter 3

Enquiries and Replies

Enquiries

An enquiry is made to seek a supply of products, service or information.

Methods of enquiry

An enquiry can be made by telephone, telegram (cable) or facsimile (fax), or postcard. If you use a postcard, it is not necessary to begin with a salutation (Dear Sir etc.) nor end with a complimentary close (Yours faithfully etc.). Your address, the date and reference is sufficient.

If you need to give more information about yourself or ask the supplier for more information, you will need to write a letter. The contents of this will depend on three things: how well you know your supplier; whether your supplier is at home or abroad; and the type of goods you are enquiring about—there is a difference between asking IBM about the cost of installing a complex computer and asking a publisher how much a book would cost.

Writing letters of enquiry

Opening

Tell your supplier what sort of firm you are.

We are a co-operative wholesale society based in New York.

Our company is a subsidiary of Universal Business Machines and we specialize in PC computers.

We are one of the main producers of industrial chemicals in Canada, and we are interested in establishing direct business relations with you in this line.

How did you hear about the firm you are writing to? It might be useful to point out that you know a firm's associates, or that they were recommended to you by a consulate or Trade Association.

We were given your name by the Hoteliers' Association in Paris.

You were recommended to us by Mr. John King, of Lasworn & Davis, Merchant Bankers.

We were advised by Spelt Marco Gennovisa of Milan that you were interested in supplying . . .

The Spanish consulate in London told us that you were looking for an agent in England to represent you.

It is possible to use other references

We were impressed by the selection of gardening tools that were displayed on your stand at this year's Gardening Exhibition held in Hamburg.

Our associates in the packaging industry speak highly of your Zeta packing machines and we would like to have more information about them. Could you send us. . .

Asking for catalogues, price-lists, prospectuses

It is not necessary to give a lot of information about yourself when asking for catalogues, brochures, booklets, etc. This can be done by postcard, but remember to supply your address, phone number and fax number if you have one. It would also be helpful if you could briefly point out any particular items you are interested in.

Could you please send your current catalogue and price-list for exhibition stands? We are particularly interested in "furniture display" stands.

Would you let us have your summer brochure for holidays to Greece and the Greek Islands, and supply details of any low fares and tariff for the month of September?

I would appreciate your sending me an up-to-date price list for your building materials.

I will be attending your College next autumn and I would like a prospectus giving me information a-bout fees and special courses in computing.

Asking for details

When asking for goods or services you must be specific and state exactly what you want. If replying to an advertisement you should mention the journal or newspaper, the date, and quote any box number or department number given, e. g. Box no. 3451; dept. 4/12 B. and if referring to, or ordering from a catalogue, brochure, leaflet, or prospectus, always quote the reference, e. g. Cat. No. A149; Holiday no. J/M3; Item No. 351; Course BL 362.

I am replying to your advertisement in the June edition of "Tailor and Cutter". I would like to know more about the "steam pressers" which you offered at cost price.

I will be attending the auction to be held in turner house on 16th February this year, and am particularly interested in the job lot listed as Item No. 351.

Could you please give me more information about course BL362 which appears in the language learning section of your summer prospectus?

I would appreciate more details about the "University Communications System" which you are advertising on Grampian Television.

Asking for samples, patterns, demonstrations

You might want to see what a material or item looks like before placing an order. Most suppliers are willing to provide samples or patterns so that you can make a selection.

When replying, could you please enclose a pattern card?

We would also appreciate it if you could send some samples of the material so that we can examine the texture and quality.

Before selling toys we prefer to test them for safety. Could you therefore send us at least two examples of these children's cars in the "Sprite" range?

I would like to discuss the problem of maintenance before deciding which model to install in my factory. I would be grateful if you could arrange for one of your representatives to call on me within the next two weeks.

Suggesting terms, methods of payment, discounts

Firms sometimes state prices and conditions in their advertisements or literature and may not like prospective customers making additional demands. However, even if conditions are quoted, it is possible to mention that you usually expect certain connections. Although it is true that once a supplier has quoted a price and stated terms, he may be unwilling to change them. By suggesting your terms, you would be indicating that certain conditions maybe persuade you to place an order.

As a rule our suppliers allow us to settle by monthly statement and we can offer the usual references if necessary.

We usually deal on a 30% trade discount basis with an additional quantity discount for orders over 1,000units.

We would like to point out that we mainly settle our accounts on a documents against acceptance basis with payment by 30-day bill of exchange.

We would appreciate it if you could let us know if you allow cash or trade discounts.

We intend to place a substantial order and would therefore like to know what quantity discounts you allow.

Closing

Usually a simple "thank you" is sufficient to close an enquiry. However, you could mention that a prompt reply would be appreciated, or as the examples show, that certain terms or guarantees would be necessary.

Finally, we would like to point out that delivery before Christmas is essential and hope that you can offer us that guarantee.

We would be grateful for an early reply.

If the concessions we have asked for could be met, we would certainly place a substantial order.

Prompt delivery would be necessary as we have a fast turnover in this trade. We would therefore need your assurance that you could meet all delivery dates.

You can also indicate further business, or other lines you would be interested in if you think they could be supplied. If a supplier thinks that you may become a regular customer, rather than someone who has placed the odd order, he would be more inclined to quote competitive terms and offer concessions.

If the product is satisfactory, we will place further orders with you in the future.

If the price quoted are competitive, and the quality up to standard, we will order on a regular basis.

Provided you can offer favorable quotations, and guarantee delivery within four weeks from receipt of order, *we will place regular orders with you*.

Checklist For Requests and Inquiries

- Have you identified yourself and explained the reason(s) for the inquiry or request?
- Are your questions clear and specific?
- Have you listed the questions to help your reader to organize the answers?
- Have you closed your letter courteously?

SPECIMEN LETTERS

Short enquiries

Example 1
(Request for a catalogue and price-list)

Dear Sir,

Please would you send me your Spring catalogue and price-list quoting c. i. f. prices, Bombay? Thank you.

Yours faithfully,

Example 2
(Request for a prospectus)
Dear Sir,

I would like some information about your Proficiency courses in English beginning this July.

Please send me a prospectus, details of your fees, and information about accommodation in London for the period July – December. If possible I would like to stay with an English family. Thank you.

Yours faithfully,

Example 3
(Request for general information)

Dear Sir,

Could you please send me details of your tubeless tires which are being advertised in garages around the country?

I would appreciate a prompt reply quoting trade prices.

Yours faithfully,

Example 4
(Reply to an advertisement)

In this letter the customer is replying to an advertisement for cassettes which he saw in a trade journal. The advertiser gave little information, so the writer will have to ask for details.

Dear Sirs,

We are a large record store in the center of Manchester and would like to know more about the tapes and cassettes you advertised in this month's edition of " Hi Fi News".

Could you tell us if the cassettes are leading brand names, or made by small independent companies, and whether they would be suitable for recording classical music or only dictations and messages? It would also be helpful if you could send us some samples.

Yours faithfully,

REPLY TO LETTERS OF ENQUIRY

Opening

Mention your prospective customer's name. If the customer signs the letter Mr. B. Green, then begin with Dear Mr. Green, not Dear Sir, which would indicate that you have not even bothered to remember the enquirer's name.

Thank the writer for his enquiry. Mention the date of his letter and quote any other references that appear.

Thank you for your enquiry of June 6th 2005 in which you asked about. . .

I would like to thank you for your enquiry of May 10 and am pleased to tell you that we would be able to supply you with the . . .

We were pleased to hear from your letter of 10 December that you were impressed with our selection of. . .

Thank you for your letter, NJ 1691, which we received this morning.

Confirming that you can help

Let the writer know as soon as possible if you have the product or can provide the service he is enquiring about. It is irritating to read a long letter only to find that the firm cannot help.

We have a wide selection of sweaters that will appeal to all ages, and in particular the teenager market which you specified.

Our factory would have no problem in turning out the 6, 000 units you asked for in your enquiry.

We can supply from stock and will have no trouble in meeting your delivery date.

I am pleased to say that we will be able to deliver the transport facilities you require.

We can offer door-to-door delivery services.

"Selling" your product

Encourage or persuade your prospective customer to do business with you. A simple answer that you have the goods in stock is not enough. Your customer might have made ten other enquiries, so remember it is not only in sales letters that you have to persuade. Mention one or two selling points of your product, including perhaps any guarantees you offer.

We think you have made an excellent choice in selecting this line, and once you have seen the samples we are sure you will agree that this is unique both in texture and color.

Once you have seen the Delta 800 in operation we know you will be impressed by its trouble-free performance.

We can assure you that the Omega 2005 is one of the most outstanding machines on the market today, and our confidence in it is supported by our five-year guarantee.

Suggesting alternatives

If you do not have what the enquirer has asked for, but have an alternative, offer it to him. But do not criticize the product he originally asked for.

... The model has now been improved, its steel casing having been replaced by plastic which is lighter, more durable, and stronger.

... and while this engine has all qualities of the model you asked for, the "Powerdrive" has the added advantage of having fewer moving parts, so less can go wrong. It also saves on oil as it...

Of course leather is an excellent material to work with in the upholstering of furniture, but escalating costs have persuaded customers to look for something more competitive in price. Fortunately Tareton Plastics have produced an amazing substitute, "Letherine", which has the same texture, strength and quality of leather, but is less than a quarter of the cost. The samples enclosed will convince you...

Referring the customer elsewhere

It is possible, of course, that you may not be able to handle the order or answer the enquiry. Your correspondent may be asking about a product you do not make or a service you do not give. If this is so, tell him and if possible refer him elsewhere.

I regret to say that we no longer produce the type of stapler you refer to, since we find there is no longer sufficient demand for it. I'm sorry we cannot be of help to you.

The book you mention is not published by us, but by Greenhill Education Ltd.. If you would care to write to them, their address is ...

Even if the product is yours, you may still have to refer the enquirer elsewhere.

I confirm that the product you require is one of ours, but since we are able to deal only with wholesalers, not retailers, may I refer you to Bright & Co. Ltd. at ...?

Our agents in Italy are Intal S. p. A, Via Alberto Poerio 79, Rome, and they carry a full stock of our goods.

Catalogues, price-lists, prospectuses, samples

Make sure that you enclose current catalogue and price-lists if you are sending them. And if prices are subject to change, then let your customer know. If you are sending samples, let your customer know they will follow the letter immediately by separate post.

Please find enclosed our current catalogue and price-list quoting c. i. f. prices Kobe. The units you referred to in your letter are featured on pp. 25 – 28 under catalogue numbers Y15 – Y18.

When ordering could you please quote these numbers? The samples you asked for will follow by separate post.

. . . and we have enclosed our price-list, but should point out that the prices are subject to change as the market for raw materials is very unstable at present.

Closing

Always thank the customer for writing to you. If you have not done so in the beginning of the letter, you can do so at the end. You should also encourage further enquiries.

Once again we would like to thank you for writing to us and would welcome any further points you would like us to answer.

Please write to us again if you have any questions, or call us at the above telephone number.

I am sorry we do not have the model you asked for, but I can promise you that the alternatives I have suggested will certainly meet your expectations, and remember we offer a full guarantee for three years.

We hope to hear from you again, soon, and can assure you that your order will be dealt with promptly.

Quotations

In your reply to an enquiry, you may want to go as far as giving your prospective customer a quotation. Below is a guide to the subjects you should cover in your quotation.

When a manufacturer, wholesaler or retailer quotes a price, he may or may not include other costs and charges such as transport, insurance and taxes (e. g. in the UK, Value Added Tax or VAT). Prices which include these extra costs are known as gross prices; those which exclude them are known as net prices.

The net price of this article is £ 10. 00, to which must be added VAT at 8% making a gross price of £ 10. 80.

We can quote you a gross price, inclusive of delivery charge, of £ 37. 50 per 100 items. These goods are exempt from VAT.

A firm's quotation is not necessarily legally binding, i. e. they do not always have to sell you the goods at the price they quoted in their reply to an enquiry. However, when prices tend to fluctuate, the supplier will add a provision to their quotation stating that their prices are subject to change. If the company makes a firm offer, it means they will hold the goods for a certain time until you order, e. g. firm 14 days. Again, this is not legally binding, but suppliers generally keep to their offer to protect their reputation.

The prices quoted above are provisional, since we may be compelled by increased costs of raw materials to increase our prices to customers. I will inform you immediately if this happens.

We can offer you a price of £ 6. 29 per item, firm 21 days; after which the price will be subject to an increase of 5%.

Whenever possible you should quote prices in your customer's currency, allowing for exchange fluctuations.

The price of this model of CD-player is 2800 Belgian francs at today's rate of exchange.

We can quote you a price of 150,000 Italian lire per 100 units, though I regret that, because of fluctuating exchange rates, we can only hold this price for four weeks from today's date.

TRANSPORT AND INSURANCE COST

In commerce there are a number of abbreviations that explain which price is being quoted to the customer. The list below is in rough order of the greatest number of extra costs to be carried by the buyer.

- **Ex-works** (ex-factory, ex-mill, ex-warehouse)
  The buyer will have to pay all the costs once the goods have left the factory, mill, or warehouse. If you are quoted any of these prices you will have to pay for insurance and transport yourself.
- **f. o. r.** (free on rail)
  The price quoted covers the cost to the nearest railway station.
- **f. a. s** (free alongside ship)
  There are no extra charges up to taking the goods to the side of the ship. In some ports small boats (barges, lighters) are used to take the goods to the ship and a f. a. s. quotation means that there

will be no charge for this, but there will be charges for loading the goods on to the ship.

- **f. o. b.** (free on board)

Loading on to the ship is included in the price quoted.

- **c. & f.** (cost and freight)

In this case the price includes cost and shipping to the destination named, e. g. £ 300. 00 **c. & f.** Hong Kong. But note that insurance is not included.

- **c. i. f.** (cost, insurance and freight)

As the term indicates, the price includes all costs up to the named destination, e. g. £ 500. 00 **c. i. f.** Bombay. Note that some of the above abbreviations may also be written without full stops and /or in capital letters (e. g. CIF, F. O. R.). This book uses these abbreviations as above, but you may come across variations elsewhere.

- **ex-ship**

The importing port is named, and the price includes delivery to this port, e. g. ex-ship Manila.

- **franco quay**

The price includes all costs up to the importer's dockside, e. g. franco quay New York.

Two other terms which should be noted but are usually used only in the U. K. are:

- **carriage paid** (c. p. or C/p)

Charges will be paid by **the sender**, e. g.

We are replacing the damaged goods and will send replacements carriage paid.

- **carriage forward** (c. f. or C/f)

The transport charges are paid by the receiver, e. g. *We will send the replacement glasses, but as you were responsible for the breakages, we will send them carriage forward.*

- **Discounts**

Manufacturers and wholesalers sometimes allow discounts to be deducted from the net or gross price. They may allow a trade discount to sellers in similar trades; or a quantity discount for orders over a certain amount; or a cash discount if payment is made within a certain time, e. g. seven days.

We allow a 3% discount for payment within one month.

The net price of this model is £ 7. 50, less 10% discount for quantities up to 100 and 15% discount for quantities over 100.

We do not normally give discounts to private customers but because of your long association with our company we will allow you 20% off the retail price.

Methods of payment

When quoting terms, you may require, or at least suggest, any of several methods of payment (letter of credit, bill of exchange, etc.) .

If you would kindly send us your personal cheque for the amount quoted, we will then send the article by registered mail.

Payment for initial orders should be made by sight draft, payable at Den Norske Creditbank, Kirkegaten 21, Oslo1, cash against documents.

Quoting delivery

If the enquiry specifies a delivery date, confirm that it can be met, or if not, suggest an alternative date. Do not make a promise that you cannot keep; it will give you a bad reputation, and if a delivery time is a condition of ordering, the customer could sue you if you break the contract, or he could reject the goods.

... and we are pleased to say that we can deliver by December 1st for the Christmas rush.

As there are regular sailings from Liverpool to New York, we are sure that the consignment will reach you well within the time you specified.

We have the materials in stock and will ship them immediately we receive your order.

As there is a heavy demand this time of year for heaters, you will have to allow at least six weeks for delivery.

We could not deliver within two weeks of receipt of order, as we would need time to prepare the materials. However, if you could let us have a month, we could guarantee delivery within that period.

Fixed terms and negotiable terms

It is possible to quote terms in two ways: by stating your price and discounts without leaving room for negotiation, or by implying that the customer could write again and discuss them. In the two examples below, the companies make firm quotes, indicating that methods of payment and discounts are fixed.

All list-prices are quoted f. o. b. Hong Kong and are subject to a 25% trade discount with payment by letter of credit.

The prices quoted are ex-works, but we can arrange freight and insurance if required, and unless otherwise stated, payment is to be made by 30-day bill of exchange, documents against acceptance.

In the next two examples, the use of the adverbs normally and usually soften the tone of the statements to indicate that although the firm prefers certain – terms, these can at least be discussed. In the final example the supplier even asks "if this arrangement is satisfactory".

We usually offer an 18% trade discount on f. o. b. prices, and would prefer payment by irrevocable letter of credit.

Normally we allow a 23% trade discount off net prices with payment on a documents against payment basis. Please let us know if this arrangement is satisfactory.

SPECIMEN LETTERS (SHORT REPLIES)

Reply to Example 1
(Catalogue and price-list)

Dear Mr. Raval,

Thank you for your enquiry of 31 January, and we are enclosing our Spring catalogue and current price-list quoting c. i. f. prices Bombay.

We would like to draw your attention to the trade and quantity discounts we are offering in our Special Purchases section pp. 19 – 26 which may be of particular interest to you.

Please contact us if we can be of any further help to you.

Yours sincerely,

Reply to Example 2
(College prospectus)

Dear Miss Iwanammi,

Please find enclosed our prospectus covering courses from July to December. Details of fees and accommodation in London for that period are covered in the booklet "Living in London" which accompanies the prospectus.

At present we still have places available for students taking the Proficiency course beginning in July, but would ask you to book as soon as possible so that we can reserve a place for you in the class and arrange accommodation with an English family.

We are sure you will enjoy your stay here and look forward to seeing you.

Yours sincerely,

Reply to Example 3
(General information)

Dear Mr. Wymer,

Thank you very much for your enquiry, and you will find enclosed a catalogue giving detailed information about our tubeless tires and including the impressive results we have achieved in rigorous factory and track tests. Please note the items on safety and fuel economy which have proved the main selling points of this product.

With regard to trade discounts, we are allowing 25% off list prices to bona fide retailer and wholesalers, with quantity discounts for orders over £ 3000. 00.

We will be pleased to supply any further information you require.

Yours sincerely,

Reply to Example 4

Dear Mr. Allen,

Thank you for your enquiry of 20 December in which you asked about the tapes we advertised in this month's edition of "Hi Fi News".

The cassettes are ferrous based and high quality chromium dioxide which as you know means they would be suitable for any type of recording. They are "Kolby" products which is a brand names you will certainly recognize, and the reason their prices are so competitive is that they are part of a bankrupt stock that was offered to us.

Because of their low price and the small profit margin we are working on, we will not be offering any trade discounts on this consignment. But we sell a wide range of cassettes and have enclosed a price-list giving you details of trade, quantity, and cash discounts on our other products.

We have sent, by separate post, samples of the advertised cassettes and other brands we stock, and would urge you to place an order as soon as possible as there has been a huge response to our advertisement. Thank you for your interest.

Yours sincerely,
B. Lyndon
B. Lyndon
Southern Importers Ltd.

Encl. price-list

CHECKLIST FOR RESPONSES TO REQUEST AND INQUIRIES

- Have you answered all questions clearly and accurately?
- Have you emphasized the positive features of your product or service?
- Does the closing paragraph enhance the chances of future business or better working relations?
- Have you offered to give your reader further help?

USEFUL WORDS & EXPRESSIONS

to make an inquiry/enquiry about a product, to enquire/inquire about a product	就某种商品进行询（盘）价
a supplier	供应者，补充者，厂商，供给者
a wholesaler/distributor	批发商
a retailer	零售商
wholesale price	批发价
retail price	零售价
a bulk buy	大量购买
a bulk buyer	大量购买者
a principal	委托人
a customer	消费者
a consumer	消费者

a client	顾客，客户，委托人
an end-user	终端用户
an associate	合作人，同事
a representative	代表
a subsidiary company	子公司
a co – operative society	合作社
an illustrated catalogue	合作社
a brochure	小册子
a booklet	小册子
prospectus	内容说明书，样张
a price-list	价格（目）表
a leaflet	传单
a circular letter	通知、通函
to offer concession	作出让步
to quote a price	报价
to suggest/state terms	提出条件/条款
cash discount	现金折扣
trade discount	商业折扣，同行折扣，批发折扣
quantity discount	数量折扣，大量购买折扣
monthly/quarterly statement	月/季度报表
annual financial statement	年度财务报表
documents against acceptance	承兑交单
acceptance bill	承兑汇票
bill of exchange	汇票
to place an order	下订单
goods on approval	供试用的货物
goods on sale or return	无法销售可退货
to hold/carry（a）stock of a product	储存货物
to ask for trade reference	要求商行备(咨)询

to provide/supply trade reference	提供商行备(咨)询
a stockist	有库存的批发商或零售商
net price	净价，实价
gross price	总价,毛价(未打折扣前的价格)
to quote a firm price	报约定价格
to hold a price for 21 days（firm 21 days）	报价在 21 天内有效
goods exempt from VAT	免税商品
negotiable terms	可谈判的条款
sight draft	即期汇票，见票即付票据
cash against documents	凭票据付款
documents against payment	付款交单
ex-works/ex-factory	工厂交货价
franco quay	目的港码头交货价
carriage paid	运费已由收件人缴付
carriage forward	运费未付，运费由收件人支付

EXERCISES

I. Begin a letter to a foreign company by first identifying yourself，and then stating that you want the latest illustrated catalogue as well as current price list on their cars. Conclude the letter with a request.

II. Write a brief but courteous letter sending the catalogue and price list requested by receiver in a previous letter. End your letter with a request for specific enquiry.

III. Write to IBM, Incorporated, asking for detailed information about the kind of business machines available at the moment and the terms and conditions for prompt delivery.

IV. Write a reply to the following inquiry.

Gentlemen:

We are one of the leading importers of textiles in this country and are interested to buy large quantities of your Bed-sheets(床单) and Printed（印花的）Shirting(衬衫衣料). We'd like you to send us as soon as possible your current price list, together with some samples and an illustrated(有插图的) catalogue.

We shall be pleased to have you inform us of your best terms and conditions, and also your references (资信证明人). Ours are the Pittsburg National Bank, Pittsburgh.

We look forward to hearing from your soon.

CHAPTER 4

SALES LETTERS

The sales letter is a form of advertising. It aims to sell particular kinds of goods or services to select-ed types of customers. There are mainly three types of sales letters: direct mail letters, retail letters and sales promotion letters. Direct mail letters are sent to sell your product or service to a target buy-er; retail letters aim to provide necessary information about a sale or a special offer; while sales pro-motion letters are to urge the reader to enquire about what you have to supply.

The sales letter sells a product or service. The application letter sells a person's ability to work.

THE PRINCIPLES OF SALES WRITING

- Attract the reader's attraction.
- Stimulate the reader's interest in the product.
- Stress the benefits of the offer to the reader.
- Convince the reader to act immediately.

VALUE OF SALES WRITING

Knowing selling techniques will help you in writing other types of letters
Even though you probably will not have to write sales letters in business, you will benefit from the experience of writing them as a student. You will profit even if your efforts appear amateurish. Espe-cially you will benefit from the experience of using the techniques of selling that all sales letters em-ploy. This experience will help you in writing other types of letters for, in a sense, every letter you write is a sales letter. In every letter case, you are selling something—an idea, a line of reasoning, your company, yourself. To do this selling in each of these letter situations, you use general selling techniques.

It will help you in everyday living, because much of what you will do involves selling
Even in your daily life you will find good use for the selling techniques. From time to time, all of us are called on to sell something. If we are engaged in selling goods and services, our sales efforts will, of course, be frequent. In other business areas, our selling efforts may consist only of selling

intangibles such as an idea, our own competency, and our firms' goodwill. In all such cases, you can make good use of the selling techniques. Thus, sales writing and the techniques used actually are more valuable to you than you might at first think.

Need for Preliminary Knowledge

Begin work on a sales letter by studying the product or service to be sold

Before you can begin writing, you must know something about your product or service and your readers. You simply cannot sell most goods and services unless you know something about them. To sell, you have to tell your prospects what they need to know. You must tell how the product is made, how it works, what it will do, what it will not do, and the like. Thus, as an initial step in sales writing, you should study your product or service.

Study your prospects. Research can help you learn about them. If research is not possible, use your best logic

You will need to know something about the people who will read your message. You will especially need to know their needs for your product or service. In the progressive business organization, a marketing research department or agency gathers this information. If you have no such source of information, you will need to gather the data yourself. The nature of the product or service should give you some guidance. For example, people with technical backgrounds would be likely to buy industrial equipment. Expensive French perfumes and cosmetics would be most attractive to people in high-income brackets. Burial insurance would appeal to older members of lower economic strata.

Determination of Appeal

Decide on which appeals to use

By appeals, we mean the strategies you use to present a product or service favourably to the readers. You could, for example, introduce a product in terms of its beauty. You could present its taste qualities. You could stress the fun the product will give or how it will make one more attractive to members of the opposite sex. You could attempt to sell your readers through appeals to profits, savings, durability, and the like.

Appeals may be emotional (to the feeling) or rational (to the reason)

Generally speaking, we can divide appeals into two broad groups. In one group are the emotional approaches to persuasion—those that affect how we feel. Included here are all the appeals to our senses—tasting, smelling, feeling, hearing, and seeing. These appeals also include all strategies designed to arouse us through love, anger, pride, fear, and enjoyment. Rational appeals are appeals to reason—to the thinking mind. Included in this group are persuasion efforts based on saving or making money, doing a job better or more efficiently, and getting better use from a product.

Select the appeals that fit the product or service and the prospect
Any specific case offers many possible appeals. You must consider all those that fit your product or service and your prospect. Those you select should be based on an analysis of these factors. Some products or services for example, are well suited to emotional selling. Perfume, travel, stylish merchandise, candy, and exotic food lend themselves to emotional reasons for buying. On the other hand, products such as automobile tires, tools, and industrial equipment are best sold through rational appeals. Automobile tires, for example, are not bought because they are beautiful. People buy them for very rational reasons—because they are durable, grip the road, and promote safety.

Prospects' uses of the product often determine the best appeal to use
How the buyer will use the product may be a major determinant of the best sales strategy to use. Cosmetics sold to ultimate users might well be sold through emotional appeals. The same product sold to retailers (who are interested primarily in reselling the product) would require rational appeals. Such readers would be interested in the emotional qualities of the product only to the extent that these characteristics will influence customers to buy. Retailers'main concerns about the product involve questions such as these: Will it sell? What is the likely turnover? How much money will it make?

An Approach to the Subject

Writing sales letters involves imagination
Writing sales letters is as creative as writing short stories, plays, and novels. In addition to imagination, it probably involves applied psychology and skillful use of words. There are as many different ways to handle sales letters as there are ideas in the brain. The only sure way to judge each is by the sales the letter brings in.

Sales letter plans vary in practice, but the following plan is used most often
Because sales letters can vary so much, it is hard to describe their order. Even so, most follow a traditional pattern. In addition, most use conventional techniques. This pattern and these techniques are the subjects of the following paragraphs. As you study them, however, keep in mind that in actual practice only your imagination will limit the possibilities open to you.

SOME MECHANICAL DIFFERENCES

Sales letters differ in makeup somewhat from ordinary letters. For example, they may use impersonal headlines for inside addresses and attention-gaining devices:

IT'S GREAT FOR PENNICILLIN,
BUT YOU CAN DO WITHOUT IT
ON YOUR ROOF....

We're referring to roof fungus, which, like penicillin, is a moldlike growth. However, the similarity ends there. Unlike penicillin, roof fungus serves...

Sales letters may use a variety of mechanical techniques to gain attention. Pictures, lines, diagram, and cartoons are common; so is the use of varying colors of ink. Devices such as coins, stamps, sandpaper, rubber bands, pencils, and paper clips may be affixed to the letter to gain interest and help put over the appeal. As you can see, the imaginative possibilities in sales writing are boundless.

THE ATTENTION-GETTING OPENING

The main requirement of the opening is that it gain attention

Opening words must meet one fundamental requirement: They must gain attention. If they don't, your letter will fail. The reason for this requirement should be apparent from your own experience. Sales letters are sent without invitation. They are not likely to be favourably received, and in fact, may even be unwanted. Thus, unless the opening words do something to overcome the barriers and gain the reader's attention, the letter will end up in the wastebasket.

The opening should also set up the strategy

Your plan for gaining attention is part of your creative effort. But whatever you do, it should assist in presenting the sales message; that is, it must help set up your strategy. It should not be just attention for attention's sake. Attention is really easy to get if nothing else is needed.

One of the most effective attention-gaining opening is a statement or question that introduces a need the product will satisfy. For example, a rational-appeal letter to a retailer would clearly tap the reader's strong needs with these words:

Here is a proven best seller—and with a 12 percent greater markup!

Another rational-appeal beginning is this first sentence of a letter seeking to place metered personal computers in hotel lobbies:

Can you use an employee who not only works free of charge but also pays you for the privilege of serving your clientele 24 hours a day?

Yet another rational-appeal beginning is this opening device from a letter selling a trade publication to business executives:

How to move more products,
Win more customers,
And make more money
... for less than $ 1 a week

PRESENTATION OF THE SALES MATERIAL

After your attention-gaining opening has set up your sales strategy, you develop this strategy.

Emotional appeals usually involve creating an emotional need

The plan of your sales talk will vary with your imagination. But it is likely to follow certain general patterns determined by your choice of appeal. If you select an emotional appeal, for example, your opening probably has established an emotional atmosphere that you will continue to develop. Thus, you will sell your product in terms of its effects on your reader's senses. You will describe your product's appearance, texture, aroma, and taste so vividly that your reader will mentally see it, feel it—and want it. In general, you will seek to create an emotional need for your product.

Rational appeals stress fact and logic

If your appeal is rational, your sales description is likely to be based on factual material. In such a case, you should describe your product in terms of what it can do for your reader rather than how it appeals to the senses. You should write matter-of-factly about such qualities as durability, savings, profits, and ease of operation.

Sales writing is not ordinary writing. Still, it is ethical

Generally speaking, sales writing is highly conversational, fast moving, and aggressive. It even uses techniques that are incorrect or inappropriate for other forms of business writing-incomplete sentences, one-sentence paragraphs, folksy language, and such. It uses mechanical emphatic devices (underscore, capitalization, exclamation marks, color) to a high degree. Often its paragraphing appears choppy. Apparently, direct-mail professionals feel that whatever helps to sell is appropriate.

However, you are morally bound to present a true message. In sales letters, it is easy to deviate from this standard. You can easily get carried away with the persuasive techniques and to overdo the effort—to exaggerate, to deceive. Thus, you must take special care to persuade truthfully and honorably. Your goal should be simply to arouse a legitimate need and to satisfy this need.

STRESS ON THE YOU-VIEWPOINT

In no area of business communication is you-viewpoint writing more important than in sales writing. In sales writing, you would do well to present the sales points in terms of reader interest. More specifically, you should make good use of the pronoun *you* and the implied *you* throughout the letter.

The techniques of you-viewpoint writing are best described through illustration. The following examples further show the value of the technique:

Matter-of-Fact Statements	**You-Viewpoint Statements**
We make Aristocrat hosiery three colors.	*You may choose from three lovely shades.*
The Regal has a touch as light as a feather.	*You'll like its feather-light touch.*
Lime-Fizz tastes fresh and exciting.	*You'll like the fresh, exciting taste of Lime-Fizz.*
Baker's Dozen is packaged in a rectangular box that has a bright, bull's-eye design.	*Baker's Dozen's new rectangular package fits compactly on your Shelf, and its bright, bull's-eye design is sure to catch the eyes of your customers.*

COMPLETENESS OF THE SALE

The information you present and how you present it are matters for your best judgment. But you must make sure that you present enough information to complete the sale. You should answer all your reader's questions and overcome any likely objections. You must work to include all such basic information in your letter. And you should present this information in a clear, convincing way.

In your effort to include all necessary information, you may choose any of a variety of supplementary sales material — booklets, leaflets, brochures, and the like. You should coordinate the letter with accompanying supplementary sales materials.

As a general rule, you should use the letter to carry your basic sales message. This means that in your letter you should not shift a major part of your sales effort to an enclosure. Instead, you should use the enclosures mainly to supplement the sales letter— to supply the descriptive, pictorial, and other information that is too detailed for inclusion in the letter.

WRITING OF SALES LETTER

The first step in writing a sales letter is to get a list of addresses of prospective buyers. The second step is to send each of the buyers on your list a sales letter. The sales letter that you send represents your company. If it looks good, you look good. If it looks bad, you look bad. If there are mistakes in the letter, the quality of your product is questioned. Effective sales letters generally have four paragraphs and are arranged in the following manner.

Paragraph one: attracting attention

The first sentence must get the reader's attention. Asking a question in which the answer is guaranteed to be "yes" is a good way to start. "Would you like to improve your life?" The opening paragraph, in fact the first sentence, should excite curiosity or attract the attention in some way that will make the reader continue to read the letter.

The most difficult paragraph to write in a sales letter is the first one. You have just a few seconds to get the reader's attention.

Would you like to see your factory's production increase by 15% or more?

Wouldn't you prefer to have your wedding pictures taken by the leader in the field?

Another way to start a sales letter is to write a sentence that will surprise or shock the reader.

In 2004 we helped over 250 small businesses like yours to increase their productivity.

Since 2000 we have grown from a small printing company to one of the largest publishing houses in the city.

If you are contacting the customer for the first time or if your company is unknown, you might start with a general introduction of yourself.

Example 1
Alfred's Textile Marketing Co. Ltd. is a leading Russian manufacturer and exporter of socks and hosiery. The range of our product line, good quality, and competitive prices have made us one of the fastest growing companies of its kind in Russia.

Example 2
Floppy Textile Buying Agency, established in 1987, is one of the fastest growing agents in India. We currently represent a number of major European importers, such as Fe Fe LaMew Mail Order of France and others.

Example 3
The ABC Trading Company was founded in 1996 to serve the construction industry in New York state. Since then we have expanded our market year by year to where we now have customers in 12 countries around the world.

Paragraph two: building interest and desire

The second paragraph must convince the reader of the value of the product. When you have succeeded in getting the reader's attention, you must hold that attention. The best way to hold it is to build interest by describing your product so that the reader can virtually experience it. Use colorful, descriptive words.

In paragraph two you must show the reader that he/she either
 – needs your product (a car)
 – could use your product (an easier inventory system)
 – should not be without your product (insurance)
OR – would benefit from your product (a new line of clothes he/she could sell)

Sentence by sentence you lead the reader through your sales pitch. If he closes his eyes he can see that new car, going home earlier because of his new inventory system, the comfort of having insurance, and increased sells because of the new line of clothes.

Example 1

Located in Moscow, we produce a wide variety of socks and hosiery items in a cotton-woolen-nylon blend for men, women, and children. These socks are of good quality, are popular with customers, and sell well. Our total production averages 10 million pairs per year, 70% for export and 30% for the domestic market.

Example 2

We are happy to announce that we are now offering this same service to American import companies like yours. From our office in New Deli, the heart of low cost and good quality ready-to-wear garments, we can supply your company with whatever kind of apparel you would like.

Paragraph three: convincing the reader

If you have done your work well to this point, the reader is already interested and is partially convinced. You must convince readers that it is to their advantage to buy your product or use your service.

If the reader has read your letter to this point then he/she is interested in your product. Paragraph three convinces him/her to buy it. It is here that you show what buying your product would mean to the reader.

Example 1

The wide range of Indian export companies that we work with insure you of getting just the items that you are looking for. Whether it be baby wear, children's wear, ladies and men's outer and underwear, leather wear, socks, belts, bags, shoes, or household items such as bed linen, towels, bathrobes, or table clothes we can make sure that you get the quantity you need at the best possible price. And our staff of quality controllers insure that the garments are well made.

Examples 2

The machine that we sell is called the Safehouse. It turns the lights on at your house at night when you 're coming home. And you can reverse the process when you leave, turning off the lights when you have locked the door, gone down the steps, and left the yard. Amazingly, the Safehouse weighs only 150 grams and fits easily in your pocket or purse.

Paragraph four: directing favorable action

You have now reached the point where if your letter was successful, you must move the reader to act. The fourth paragraph must tell the reader what to do to get the product. Tell the reader exactly what you want him/her to do and make it easy to do. The desired action is to go to your web site to get more information and, hopefully contact you for specifics or to place an order. Even the most highly motivated and excited customer will not act if the action you are requesting is too difficult.

Example 1

Our company is expanding its market to include the United States and we would like very much to do business with your company. Enclosed is our price list (brochure) describing our wide range of products. I would welcome the opportunity to introduce you to our line socks and hosiery. For more information or to place an order, please visit our web site at www. nicesocks. com. .

Example 2

If you would like to take advantage of the services that Floppy Textile Buying Agency has to offer your company, please log on to our web site at www. floppytextile. com or contact us by fax at (56/324) 785 48 96. Thank you. We look forward to hearing from you.

Example 3

To order, please go to our web site at www. swimsuit. com, or fill out the enclosed order form and send it by fax or post to our office in Washington. Before you know it, you will be wearing this beautiful men's business swim suit—and feeling like royalty.

A typical well written letter for an agent

Star Textile Exports, established in 1989, is one of the fastest growing agents in Turkey. We currently represent a number of major European importers, such as Blue Cloud Mail Order of France and others.

We are happy to announce that we are now offering this same service to American import companies like yours. From our office in Istanbul, the heart of low cost and good quality ready-to-wear garments, we can supply your company with whatever kind of apparel you would like.

The wide range of Turkish export companies that we work with insure you of getting just the items that you are looking for. Whether it be baby wear, children's wear, ladies and men's outer and underwear, leather wear, socks, belts, bags, shoes, or household items such as bed linen, towels, bathrobes, or table clothes we can make sure that you get the quantity you need at the best possible price. And our staff of quality controllers insure that the garments are well made.

If you would like to take advantage of the services that Star Textile Buying Agency has to offer your company, please go to our web site at www. startextile. com, or contact us by fax at (90/212) 123 45 67.

Thank you. We look forward to hearing from you.

A very simple sales letter

Dear Sirs,

We are a Polish company that specializes in making men's shirts and would like to tell you about our line of products.

Our products are special because they are made of good quality cloth. In the 15 years that we have been selling our products we have made a good name for ourselves in countries around the world.

Enclosed is a price list and brochure. If you would like to place an order or receive more information, please log onto our web site at www. polishshirts. com, or contact us by telephone.

Sincerely yours

A simple proposal letter

Dear Mr. Customer:

Thank you for your interest in our company. Enclosed is the proposal that you requested.

The Model XR 17 is designed to help those companies who want to sell the latest model on the market, at the best possible price. This low-cost machine is made in Germany—the land of good quality machines.

This model sells well because:

the price is competitive;
the technology is state-of-the-art;
there is a great demand for such a machine.

We hope that you will soon join the growing list of companies that are selling our model XR 17. If you would like more information, please visit our web site at www. modelxr17. com or contact us directly.

Sincerely yours

Two more complicated sales letters

Example 1

Dear Friend:

Here's an honest-to-goodness attempt to make everything between us as CLEAR as CRYSTAL—

Frankly, I'm thoroughly confused because out of the thousands of readers whose subscription expired with yours several months ago you're one of the very small handful who have not renewed yet. Whatever it is that's holding up your renewal, I wish you'd let me know about it because you're a good customer and we miss you.

I'm sure you haven't lost your hearty interest in the latest news on cars and car repairs, inventions, home workshop projects and ideas, aviation, mechanics, and the hundreds of other exciting things POPULAR SCIENCE brings to your doorstep every months. I'm sure you'll find the lively new features and money-saving home repair articles lined up for coming issues of POPULAR SCIENCE even more inviting than ever!

Chances are you've been intending to renew all along, but just keep putting it off. To make certain you don't delay another minute, I'm going ALL OUT with a special bargain offer that can't be repeated!

I'm going to SLASH the regular rate of 16. 40 a year DOWN TO ONLY $ 12—SAVING YOU A FULL 27%! That means you'll get 12 crisp, new issues of POPLILAR SCIENCE for only $ 1. 00 a copy. You save even more by renewing for 2 or 3 years!

So get on the band wagon. Join the vast majority who have already renewed their subscriptions. All you have to do is to fill in and return the enclosed postage-free order card TODAY. If it isn't convenient to send your remittance now, don't worry about it because your credit is TOPS with me.

This is CLEARLY a bargain you shouldn't miss!

Sincerely,

Example 2

DON' T READ THIS UNLESS YOU HAVE DECIDED NOT TO CLAIM

YOUR <u>FREE TEXAS SALTWATER BIG</u> 3 BOOK.

Frankly, I'm puzzled.

I just don't understand why every fisherman and boat owner in Texas doesn't run—not walk—to the nearest mailbox and return the enclosed FREE BOOK CERTIFICATE.

Here's a guidebook that will bring you better times and better catches each and every time you head for that beautiful Gulf.

PLUS, you get a money-saving bargain on a subscription to THE TEXA FISHERMAN—the news monthly that Texas outdoorsmen swear by.

Month after month you'll be in on all the latest tips about where the big ones are biting. Each issue sports super-big photographs of fishermen grinning their heads off, holding up the catch for the day.

And Dave Ellison is there each month telling you the latest there is about boating. Plus many other boating articles every month.

Over 34,000 Texas boaters and fishermen are subscribing now. And the yearly renewal rate is just fantastic!

But those 34,000 aren't important this morning. The important person to today is YOU. I want YOU as a new subscriber—because I know you'll find more helpful advice here than in any other publication in the state today.

Do yourself a favor. Send off your FREE BOOK CERTIFICATE now, today, while you're thinking about it. Have more fun and catch more fish!

Bob Gray, Publisher

P. S. Please hurry! We have only a limited supply of this FREE BOOK. Get yours now!

USEFUL WORDS & EXPRESSIONS

| direct mail | 直接邮件 |
| money-back guarantee | 退回货款的担保 |

sales department	销售部门
sales letter	销售函
sales promotion	销售宣传
target buyer	目标购买者
prospective customer	预期的客户
potential customer	潜在的用户/客户
retail letter	零售信件

EXERCISES

I. As the sales manager for a textile company, write a sales letter for the promotion of your product.

II. Write a sales letter for the KONKA 208 TV, Chinese made miniature television set, highlighting the main selling points below:

World's most advanced pocket TV—small enough to go anywhere. Size: 5 × 4 × 1 – 1/2 inches. Weight: 22 oz. 2-inch diagonal screen-colour. Has its own telescope antenna. Sound: bell clear, drift free.
Operate on internal rechargeable batteries. AC current.
Rugged stainless steel case. Most advanced electronic design, reliable and efficient. Company has been in business making electronic products 55 years. An old and trusted name.
Price: $ 38.00 traveler cheques acceptable.

III. Your firm, which handles Chinese Silk, is just entering the Canadian Market. Write a sales letter to the Canadian buyers for promoting the sales of Western Lake Silk.

IV. Your firm has put a new product—Model 288 MP4 on the world market. Write a letter offering to supply this new product to your buyers abroad.

CHAPTER 5

ORDER AND CONFIRMATION LETTERS

PLACING AN ORDER

Orders are usually written on a company's official order form which has a date and a reference number that should be noted in any correspondence which refers to the order. Even if the order is telephoned, it must be confirmed in writing, and an order form should always be accompanied by either a compliments slip or a covering letter. A covering letter is preferable as it allows you the opportunity to make any necessary points and confirm the terms that have been agreed.

The guide below is for an outline of a covering letter.

Opening

Explain there is an order accompanying the letter.

Please find enclosed our Order No. B4521 for 25 "Mudan" transistor receivers.

Thank you for your reply of 14 May regarding the computers we wrote to you about.

Enclosed you will find our official order (No. B561) for instrumental products (仪器产品类).

The enclosed order (No. R154) is for 200 reams of A4 bank paper.

Your letter of 12 January convinced me to place at least a trial order for the building materials you spoke about. Therefore, please find enclosed. . .

Payment

Confirm the terms of payment.

As agreed you will draw on us at 60 days, documents against acceptance, with the documents being sent to our bank at 138 Beijing Road, Bank of China, Yunnan Branch.

We would like to confirm that payment is to be made by irrevocable letter of credit which we have already applied to the bank for.

Once we have received your advice, we will send a banker's draft to...

... and we agree that payments would be made against monthly statements...

Discounts

Confirm the agreed discounts.

We would like to thank you for the 30% trade discount and 10% quantity discount you allowed us.

Finally, we would like to say that the 25% trade discount is quite satisfactory.

Although the rather low trade discount of 15% disappointed us, we will place an order and hope that this allowance can be reviewed at some time in the near future.

... and we will certainly take advantage of the generous cash discounts you offered for prompt settlement.

Delivery

Confirm the delivery dates.

It is essential that the goods are delivered before the beginning of August in time for the Mid-autumn Festival rush.

Delivery before January is a firm condition of this order, and we reserve the right to refuse goods delivered after that time.

Please confirm that you can complete the work before the end of April, as the opening of the supermarket is planned for the beginning of May.

Methods of delivery

Many firms use forwarding agents who are specialists in packing and handling the documentation for shipping goods. Nevertheless you should still advise the firm as to how you want the goods packed and sent to ensure prompt and safe delivery, so that if the consignment does arrive late, or in a damaged state, your letter is evidence of the instructions you gave.

... and please remember that only air freight will ensure prompt delivery.

Please send the goods by inter-city express as we need them urgently.

We advise delivery by road to avoid constant handling of this fragile consignment.

Could you please ship by scheduled freighter to avoid any unnecessary delays?

Packing

Advise your supplier how you want the goods packed.

*Each piece of crockery is to be individually wrapped in thick paper, packed in straw, and shipped in wooden crates marked " * " and numbered 1 to 6.*

The carpets should be wrapped in thick grease-proof paper which is reinforced at both ends to avoid wear by friction.

The machines must be well greased with all movable parts secured before being loaded into crates, which must be marked.

Closing

We hope that this will be the first of many orders we will be placing with you.

We will submit further orders, if this one is completed to our satisfaction.

If the goods sell as well as we hope, we shall send further orders in the near future.

I look forward to receiving your advice/shipment/acknowledge/confirmation.

ACKNOWLEDGING AN ORDER

As soon as an order is received by a supplier, it should be acknowledged.

Thank you for your order No. 338B which we received today. We are now dealing with it and you may expect delivery within the next three weeks.

Your order, No. 6712/1 is now being processed and should be ready for dispatch by next week.

We are pleased to say that we have already made up your order, No. 9901/1/5 for 50 canteens of "Silverline" cutlery, and are now making arrangements for shipment to Lagos.

ADVICE OF DISPATCH

When the supplier has made up the order and arranged shipment, the customer is informed of this in an advice. This may be done on a special form or in a letter.

Your order, No. . D/154/T, has now been placed on board the SS Mitus Maru sailing from Kobe on 16 May and arriving Tibury, London, on 11 June. The shipping documents have already been sent to your bank in London for collection.

We are pleased to advise you that the watches you ordered—No. 88151/24—were put on flight BA 165 leaving Zurich 11.009 August arriving Manchester 13.00. Please find enclosed air waybill DC 15161/3 and copies of invoice A 113/3.

Please be advised that your order, No. Y1/151/C, has now been put on the Glasgow-London express and can be collected at Euston station. Enclosed is consignment note No. 1167153 which should be presented on collection. You should contact us immediately if any problems arise. Thank you for your order, and we hope we can be of service in the future.

Placing an order

Sample 1

(covering letter)

Dear Mr. Causio,

Please find enclosed our order, No. DR 4316, for men's and boys' sweaters in assorted sizes, colours and designs.

We have decided to accept the 15% trade discount you offered and terms of payment viz. documents against payment, but would like these terms reviewed in the near future.

Would you please send the shipping documents and your sight draft to Northminster Bank (City Branch), Deal Street, Birmingham?

If you do not have some of the listed items in stock, please do not send substitutes in their place.

We would appreciate delivery within the next six weeks, and look forward to your acknowledgement.

Yours sincerely,

Lionel Crane

Lionel Crane

Chief buyer

Enc. order form No. DR4316

Sample 2

(covering letter)

Mr. Bill Norton
Sales Manager
Glaston Potteries Ltd.
Clayfield

Burnley BB10 1 RQ

Dear Mr. Norton,

Please find enclosed an order (R1432) from our principals, Mackenzie Bros. Ltd. , 1 – 5 Whale Drive, Dawson, Ontario, Canada.

They have asked us to instruct you that the 60 sets of crockery ordered should be packed in six crates, ten sets per crate, with each piece individually wrapped, and the crates marked clearly with their name, the words "fragile", "crockery", and numbered 1 – 6.

They have agreed to pay by letter of credit, which we discussed on the phone last week, and they would like delivery before the end of this month, which should be easily effected as there are regular sailings from Liverpool.

If the colors they have chosen are not in stock, they will accept an alternative provided the designs are those stipulated on the order.

Please send any further correspondence relating to shipment or payment direct to Mackenzie Bros, and let us have a copy of the commercial invoice when it is made up.

Yours sincerely,
L. W. Lowe
L. W. Lowe (Mrs)
Enc. Order R1432

Advice of dispatch

Dear Sirs,

Order R1432

The above order has now been completed and sent to Liverpool Docks where it is awaiting loading onto the SS Manitoba which sails for Dawson Canada on the 20 December and arrives on 30 December.

Once we have the necessary documents we will hand them to Burnley City Bank, your bank's agents here, and they will forward them to the Canadian Union Trust Bank.

We have taken special care to see that the goods have been packed as per your instructions, the six crates being marked with your name, and numbered 1 – 6. Each crate measures 6ft × 4ft × 3ft and weighs 5cwt.

We managed to get all items from stock with the exception of Cat. No. G16 which we only had in red. But we included it in the consignment as it had the Willow pattern you asked for.

If there is any further information you require, please contact us. Thank you very much for your order, and we look forward to hearing from you again soon.

Yours sincerely,

J. Merton

J. Merton (Mr.)

Sales Manager

ORDER FORM

The following is Johnson & Co.'s official order form:

ORDER   No. DR 4316
Johnson & Co. Ltd.

(Head Office), Nesson House, Newell Street, Birmingham B3 3EL

Telephone: 021 236 6571   Fax: 341641

Textile Importers Co. Ltd

21 Sunshine Building High Street

00146 Milan

ITALY   Authorized: *David Copperfield*

Quantity	Item description	Cat. No.	Price cif London
150	V Neck: 50Red/100 Blue	R 432	£ 6.90 each
120	Roll Neck: 80 Black/40 Blue	N154	£ 4.70 each
100	Crew Neck: 70 Green/30 Beige	N154	£ 8.00 each
100	Crew Neck: Plain	R541	£ 6.00 each

Comments: 15% Trade Disc. Pymt. D/P Del. 6 weeks   Date: 14 March 2005

Covering letter with order form

Dear Sirs,

Your Reference LB/AP

We enclose our order No. 345 for four items in your latest catalogue.

We note that you can supply these items from stock and hope you will send them without delay.

Yours sincerely,

Adams & Co. LTD

18 Broadway , Manhattan
New York , NY112536

ORDER

12 November 2005

Order No. <u>348</u>

China National Textiles

IMP&EXP Corporation

Beijing

China

Please supply the following items in accordance with the terms and conditions of Order No. 347.

Qty	Item	Catalogue No.	Price net
43	Quilt, 120 cm, yellow	75	US $ 5. 00 each
30	—do. —120 cm, pink	82	$ 6. 00 each
23	Quilt Cover, blue	150	$ 1. 50 each
20	—do. —pink	162	$ 1. 70 each

FOB China port

For Adams & Co. LTD

Bill Norton

Secretary

When placing an order with a printed order form it is often sufficient merely to attach a compliments

（问候）slip（纸条）like：

Adams & Co. LTD
18 Broadway , Manhattan
New York , NY112536

China National Textiles
IMP&EXP Corporation
Beijing , China

Enclose please find our order No. 348. We would appreciate prompt shipment.

WITH COMPLIMENTS

ACKNOWLEDGEMENT OF ORDERS

The following is a letter of acknowledging an order：

Dear Sirs
We were very pleased to receive your Order No. 345 for men's clothes and children's leather shoes. We accordingly accept the order and shall arrange delivery as soon as possible.

We hope they will reach you in good time and that we may have further orders from you.

Printed Routine Acknowledgments

Example 1

CHINA CHEMICALS CORPORATION

30, _____ Street , Beijing

Tel. _____ Fax _____

Thank you for your order No. _____

We accept your order and will arrange shipment accordingly.

Our letter of acceptance will reach you in a few days.

Example 2

Norton & Smith Inc.

P. O. Box 8789 – 068 – A

Tel. _____ Fax _____

We have received with thanks your order for 50 tons of Minerals .

We are working on your order and will keep you informed in time of the progress.

Example 3

Norton & Smith Inc.
P. O. Box 8789 – 068 – A

Tel. _____ Fax _____

We thank you for your order No. _____ for _____

Because <u>our supply of minerals has been committed to other orders for months in advance</u>, we are unable to accept your order at this time.

Example 4

Norton & Smith Inc.
P. O. Box 8789 – 068 – A

Tel. _____ Fax _____

We accept your order No. _____ for _____ and have arranged shipment for arrival at destination by April 15.

DELAYS IN DELIVERY

If goods are held up either before or after they are sent, you must keep your customer informed. Let him know what has happened, how it happened, and what you are doing to correct the situation.

I was surprised and sorry to hear that your consignment (Order No. B145) had not reached you. On enquiry I found that it had been delayed by a local dispute on the cargo vessel <u>SS Hamburg</u> on which it had been loaded. I am now trying to get the goods transferred to the <u>SS Samoa</u> which should sail for Yokohama before the end of next week. However, I shall keep you informed.

I am writing to tell you that there will be a three week delay in delivery. This is due to a fire at our

Greenford works which destroyed most of the machinery.

Nevertheless, your order has been transferred to our Slough factory and is being processed there. I apologize for the delay which was due to circumstances beyond our control.

We regret to inform you that there will be a hold up in getting your consignment to you. This is due to the cut in supplies from Gara where civil war suddenly broke out last week. We have contacted a possible supplier in Lagos and he will let us know if he can help us. If you wish to cancel your order, you may, but I think you will find most manufacturers are experiencing the same difficulties at present.

REFUSING AN ORDER

There are a number of reasons for a firm refusing an order, and some of the most common are given below. Whatever your reason, you must be polite: the words **reject** and **refuse** have a negative tone to them, and it is better to use **decline** or **turn down** instead.

Out of stock

You may be out of stock of the product ordered, or indeed you may no longer make it. Note that, in either case, you have an opportunity to sell an alternative product, but remember not to criticize the product you can no longer supply.

We are sorry to say that we are completely out of stock of this item and it will be at least six weeks before we get our next delivery, but please contact us then.

We no longer manufacture this product as demand over the past few years has declined.

Thank you for your order for heavy-duty industrial overalls, but unfortunately we have run out of the strengthened denim style you asked for. As you have particularly requested only this material, we will not offer a substitute, but hope we will get delivery of a new consignment within the next two months. We hope you will contact us then.

We received your order for CAN adaptors today, but regret that due to a strike at the CAN factory we are unable to fulfill the order, and we realize that other models will not suit your requirements. Hopefully the dispute will be settled soon so that we will be able to supply you. You can reply on us to keep you informed of the developments.

Bad reputation

The customer may have a bad reputation for settling their accounts or, in the case of a retailer of, say, electrical or mechanical products may have offered a poor after-sales service which could in turn affect your reputation. Even in these cases, it usually serves no purpose to be rude to your correspondent and to refuse his order outright; better is to indicate terms on which you would be prepared to accept his order, or, as in the last three examples, find a diplomatic way of saying 'no'.

We would only be prepared to supply on a cash basis.

We only supply on payment against pro-forma invoice.

USEFUL WORDS & EXPRESSIONS

a trial order	试用的/试验的订货
a provisional order	临时的订货
a firm order	确定订货
to place an order for sth. with	向……定购某物
to confirm an order	确认订货
to refuse/reject/turn down an order	不接受订货
to fill/fulfill/make up/complete/ meet/supply an order	供应订货，执行订货
an order form	订货单
a compliments slip	表示问候/祝贺的纸条
a covering letter	附信
a pro-forma invoice	形式发票；估价发票
a consignment note	（货物的）交托/运送/托付物票据
to draw a bill on a customer	给客户开账单
long-term credit facilities	长期信用透支/信贷组织/融通便利
shipping documents	船（货）运单据
air waybill	空运单

commercial invoice	商务发票，正式签证的贸易发票
goods in stock	现货，存货
goods out of stock	已脱销的货物
to pack goods in crates	板条箱/柳条箱装货
to ship goods	用船运输货物
a forwarding agent	运送经理人,运输行/商,转运公司
air freight	航空运费

EXERCISES

I. Write an order for three of the items listed below, specifying quantity, unit price, total amount and terms of payment, asking for prompt shipment by parcel post.

Item	Ordering No	Unit Price
Ginseng	07—552	$ 50
Maotai	08—332	$ 80
Wu Liang Ye	09—442	$ 60
Dongjiu	10—222	$ 20

Note: Ginseng（Liquors）Maotai（Liquors）Wu Liang Ye（Liquors）
Dongjiu（Liquors）

II. Write a reply to acknowledge the above order, expressing satisfaction at receiving the first order and confirming prompt shipment of the goods.

III. Place the order in Exercise I, using a printed order form and a compliments slip.

IV. Write a letter to your customer, acknowledging receipt of his order, but regret being unable to accept it at the prices as requested. Quote your current prices and ask for your customer's opinion.

CHAPTER 6

MODES of PAYMENT AND COLLETION

After goods have been delivered, the supplier will send an invoice or bill. The buyer can pay in several ways: by cheque, a postal-order, letter of credit, or make a bank transfer. This chapter is intended to discuss modes of payment and problems involved.

INVOICE AND STATEMENTS

Invoices

Invoices are not only requests for payment but also records of transactions which give both the buyer and seller information about what has been bought or sold, the terms of the sale and details of the transaction. The invoice may be accompanied by a short covering letter offering any additional information the customer might need.

Please find enclosed our invoice No. B 1951 for £ 29. 43. The plugs you ordered have already been dispatched to you, carriage forward, and you should receive them within the next few days.

The enclosed invoice (No. D 1167) for £ 56. 00 is for 2 "Layeazee" chairs at £ 40. 00 each less 33 per cent trade discount. We look forward to receiving your remittance and will then send the chairs on carriage forward.

Our invoice No. TR3351/6 for £ 400. 00 net is attached. We look forward to receiving your cheque from which you may deduct 3 per cent cash discount if payment is made within seven days. Your Order No. H615D is at present being processed and will be sent on to you within the next few weeks. Thank you for your order, and we are sure you will be pleased with the units when you receive them.

Pro-forma invoice

A pro-forma invoice is an invoice with the words pro-forma typed or stamped on it, and is used:

- if the customer has to pay for the goods before receiving them, i. e. he pays against the pro-forma.
- if the customer wants to make sure that a quotation will not be changed; the pro-forma will tell him exactly what and how he will be charged.
- if goods are sent on approval, or on sale or return, or on consignment to an agent who will sell them on behalf of the principal.

A covering letter may accompany a pro-forma invoice

The enclosed pro-forma No. 1164 for £ 853.78 is for your order No. C 1534, which is now packed and awaiting dispatch. As soon as we receive your cheque we will send the goods which will reach you within a few days.

We are sending the enclosed pro-forma (No. H9181) for £ 3,160.00 gross, for the consignment of chairs you ordered on approval. We would appreciate your returning the balance of unsold chairs by the end of May as agreed.

Pro-forma invoice, No. PL7715, is for your order, No. 652 1174, in confirmation of our quotation. The total of £ 15, 351.00 includes cost, insurance, and freight.

Statements of account

Rather than requiring immediate payment of invoices, a supplier may grant his customer credit in the form of open account facilities for an agreed period of time, usually a month but sometimes a quarter (three months). At the end of the period a statement of account is sent to the customer, listing all the transactions between the buyer and seller for that period. The statement includes the balance on the account, which is brought forward from the previous period and listed as Account Rendered. Invoices and debit notes are added, while payments and credit notes are deducted.

Statements of account rarely have letters accompanying them unless there is a particular point that the supplier wants to make, e. g. that the account is overdue, or that some special concession is available for prompt payment.

I enclose your statement as at 31 July. May I remind you that your June statement is still outstanding, and ask you to settle as soon as possible?

Please find enclosed your statement of account as at 31 May this year. If the balance of £ 161.00 is cleared within the next seven days, you can deduct a 3 per cent cash discount.

Settlement of Account

Methods of payment: home trade

Here is a list of methods of payment which can be used in the home trade, which refers in this case to trade in the UK.

Postal order

Postal Orders can be bought from the Post Office, usually to pay small amounts, and sent to the supplier direct. They can be crossed or closed, i. e. only to be paid into the supplier's account, or open for cash. Poundage, i. e. the cost of buying the Order itself, is expensive, so they would only be used for small amounts.

Stamps

It is possible to pay someone with postage stamps, but unusual in business.

Giro

This postal check system is run by the Post Office and allows customers to send payments to anyone whether they have a Giro account or not.

C. O. D. (cash on delivery)

The Post Office Offers a service by which they will deliver goods and accept payment on behalf of the supplier.

Check

You must have a current account, or certain types of savings accounts, to pay by check. Checks take three working days to clear through the commercial banks, and can be open, to pay cash, or closed (crossed), to be paid into an account. Unlike in most countries, UK checks are valid up to six months.

Bank transfer

Banks will transfer money by order from one account to another.

Credit transfer

The payer fills out a Bank Giro slip and hands it in to a bank with a check. The bank then transfers the money to the payee.

Bank draft

The payer buys a check from the bank for the amount he wants to pay and sends it to the payee. Banks usually require two of their Director's signatures on drafts, and make a small charge.

Bill of exchange

The seller draws a bill on the buyer. The bill states that the buyer will pay the seller an amount within a stated time, e. g. 30 days. The bill is sent to the buyer either by post, or through a bank, and the buyer signs (accepts) the bill before the goods are sent. If this is done through a bank, the bank will ask the buyer to accept the bill before handing over the shipping documents; this is known as a documents against acceptance (D/A) transaction.

Letter of credit

This method of payment can be used internally, but is more common in overseas transactions.

Methods of payment: foreign trade

Check

It is possible to pay an overseas supplier by check, but it takes a long time before the supplier gets his money. In a German/UK transaction, for example, the supplier could wait up to three weeks for payment.

International Giro

Payment by International Giro, which replaced money Orders, can be made whether the buyer has an account or not, and to a supplier whether he has an account or not. The International Giro form is obtained from any Post Office, filled out, then handed to the Post Office who forwards the order to the Giro centre which will send the amount to a Post Office in the beneficiary's country where the supplier will receive a postal check. He can then either cash it, or pay it into his bank account. Giros are charged at a flat rate.

International money orders

International Money Orders can be bought at most banks in the UK and are paid for in sterling or dollars. The bank fills out the order for the customer, then for a small charge, hands the IMO over, and the buyer sends it to the beneficiary. IMOs can be cashed or credited to the recipient's account.

Bank transfer

Payment can be made by ordering a home bank to transfer money to an overseas account. If telegraphed, the transfer is known as telegraphic transfer (TT), and if mailed, a mail transfer

(MT).

International banker's draft

This is a banker's check which the bank draws on itself and sells to the customer, who then sends it to his supplier as he would an ordinary inland check. So if you have to pay your supplier £ 2,000.00, you purchased the check for that amount, plus charges. Usually the receiver's bank should either have an account with the sender's bank, or an agreement.

Promissory notes

A promissory note is not a method of payment but simply a written promise from a debtor to a creditor that the former will pay the stipulated amount either on demand or after a certain date. In effect a promissory note is an IOU (I owe you).

Bill of exchange

The procedure is the same as for the home trade, but shipping documents usually accompany bills when the bank acts as an intermediary in overseas transactions.

Documentary credit

This term is used to distinguish the normal letter of credit, used in business, from the circular letter of credit, formerly used by foreign travelers and now largely replaced by Eurochecks, traveler's checks, and cash check credits. Documentary credits have to be applied for from the buyer's bank, by filling out a form giving details of the type of credit (i. e. revocable or irrevocable), the beneficiary (the person receiving the money), the amount, how long the credit will be available for (i. e. valid until. . .), the documents involved (bill of lading, insurance, invoice, etc.) and a description of the goods. The money will be credited to the supplier's account as soon as confirmation of shipment is made. This is done when the documents are lodged with the customer's bank.

Examples

Dear Mr. Blake,

Thank you for being so prompt in sending the documents for our last order, No. 14463. We have accepted the sight draft, and the bank should be sending you an advice shortly.

We have been dealing with you on a cash against documents basis for over a year and would like to change to payment by 40-day bill of exchange, documents against acceptance.

When we first contacted you last February you told us that you would be prepared to reconsider terms of payment once we had established a trading association. We think that sufficient time has elapsed for us to be allowed the terms we have asked for. If you need references, we will be glad to supply them.

As we will be sending another order within the month, could you please confirm that you agree to these news of payment?

Yours sincerely,

R. Copperfield

R. Copperfield

Chief Buyer

In the following letter, Johnson Bros. will accept either replacement for the broken crockery or a credit note. Garrison Potteries will claim on their insurance company for the breakages, although they might not get compensation as they have been negligent in their packing.

JOHNSON BROS. LTD.

1 – 8 Whale Drive. Dawson, Ontario, Canada

Branches: Bangkok, Vancouver, New York, Chicago

Tel: (613) 238 1492   Fax: 315515

J. Kennedy   *15 December 2005*

Sales Manager

Garrison Potteries Ltd.

Birmingham

B10 1RQ

UNITED KINDOM

Dear Mr. Kennedy,

We have instructed our bank to arrange for a letter of credit for £ 6,158. 92 to be paid against your pro-forma invoice No. G 1152/S, and the proceeds will be credited to you as soon as Canadian Trust receive the documents.

We usually ask you to wrap each piece of crockery individually and pack no more than ten sets into a crate to allow for easy and safe handling. This was done with our last consignment and as a consequence there were breakages. Attached you will find a list and we would like either replacements to be included in our next shipment, or your credit note.

Could you please pay more attention to our instructions in the future?

Yours sincerely,
Michael Johnson
Michael Johnson

Enc.

DELAYED PAYMENT

Asking for more time to pay

If you are writing to a supplier to tell him why you have not cleared an account, remember that he is mainly interested in **when** the account will be paid. So, while you must explain **why** you have not paid, you must also tell him **when** and **how** you intend to pay.

Remember to begin the letter with your creditor's name (This should always be done once correspondence has been established, but it is essential in this case: if you owe someone money, you should know their name), to refer to the account and to apologize in clear, objective language (i. e. do not use language like 'Please forgive me not setting my indebtedness to you').

I am sorry that I was not able to clear my August account.

We regret we were unable to send a check to settle our account for the last quarter.

Explain why you cannot clear the account. But do not be over-dramatic.

The dock strike which has been in operation for the past six weeks has made it possible to ship our products, and our customers have not been able to pay us, we have not been able to clear our own suppliers' accounts yet.

A warehouse flood destroyed the majority of the components that were to be fitted into Zenith 900. We are waiting for our insurance company to settle our claim so that we can renew our stock and pay our suppliers.

Tell your supplier when you will pay him; as far as he is concerned, this is the most important piece of information in your letter. You may be able to pay some money on account, i. e. to offer some money towards settlement; this shows a willingness to clear the debt, and the gesture will at least gain your creditor's confidence.

We will try to clear your invoice within the next few weeks. Meanwhile the enclosed check for £ 200.00 is part payment on account.

If you cannot offer a part payment, give as precise a date of payment as you can.

Once the strike has been settled, which should be within the next few days, we will be able to clear the balance.

As soon as the insurance company pays us compensation we will settle the account. We expect this to be within the next two weeks.

REQUEST FOR PAYMENT

First request

You should never immediately assume your customer has no intention of paying his account if the balance is overdue. There may be a number of reasons for this. He may not have received your statement. He may have sent a check which has been lost. He might have just overlooked the account. Therefore a first request is in the form of a polite enquiry.

We are writing concerning the outstanding October account for £ 171.63, a copy of which is enclosed and which should have been cleared last month. Could you please let us know why the balance has not been paid?

As you usually clear your accounts promptly, we wondered why the November account for £ 6,324.61 was not paid last month when it was due. If you are experiencing any difficulties please let us know as we may be able to help you. We look forward to hearing from you. Attached, please find a copy of the account.

We think you may have overlooked invoice no. 5A 1910 for £ 351.95 (see copy) which was due last month. Please could you let us have your check to clear the amount? If, however, you have already sent a remittance, then please disregard this letter.

Second requests

If a customer intends to pay, he usually answers a first request immediately, offering an apology for having overlooked the account, or an explanation. But if he acknowledges your request but still does not pay, or does not answer your letter at all, then you can make a second request. As with first requests, you should include copies of the relevant invoices and statements, and mention your previous letter. This will save time. You should also refer to previous correspondence.

We wrote to you on 7 September concerning our July statement which is still outstanding. Enclosed you will find a copy of the statement and our letter.

This is the second letter I have sent you with regard to your March account which has not been cleared. My first letter dated 21 April, asked why the account had not been paid, and you will see from the enclosed that...

State that you have not received payment if this was promised in the reply, or that no reply has been received.

I would like to know why you have neither replied nor sent a check to clear the outstanding balance.

In your reply to my letter of 18 July you promised that the account would be cleared by the end of June, yet I have not received your remittance.

Insist that you receive payment or an answer within a certain time.

We must now insist that you clear this account within the next seven days, or at least offer an explanation for not paying it.

I would like your remittance by return of post, or failing that, your reasons for not clearing this account.

Third requests (Final Demands)

Review the situation from the time the account should have been paid.

We have written you two letters on 22 August and 18 September, and have sent copies of the outstanding invoices with them, but have not received either a reply or remittance.

I have written to you twice, on 8 June and 5 July, concerning your balance of £ 934. 85 which has been outstanding since May, but as yet, have not received a reply.

Explain you have been patient.

When we arranged terms, we offered you payment against monthly statements, yet it has been three months since you wrote promising the account would be cleared. *We now assume that you have no intention of clearing the balance.*

We had expected this matter to have been settled at least two months ago, but you have shown no indication of co-operating with us.

Let the customer know what you intend to do, but do not threaten legal action unless you intend to take it, as it will make you look weak and indecisive. In the two examples below legal action is not threatened.

We feel that you have been given sufficient time to clear this balance and now insist on payment within the next ten days.

We must now press you to clear this outstanding account. Please send your remittance immediately.

In the next two examples legal action is threatened. Notice the language used to do this. Do not use obscure language (e.g. "We will take other steps" or "We will use other methods to enforce payment"), and do not try to sound like a lawyer (e.g. "Unless payment is forthcoming, we will have to take steps to enforce our claims"). A direct statement will produce better results.

We were disappointed that you did not bother to reply to either of our letters asking you to clear your account, and you have left us no alternative but to take legal action.

We are giving you a further seven days to send your remittance after which the matter will be dealt with by our solicitors.

SPECIMEN LETTERS

Request for more time

D. Carter & Co. Ltd write to their supplier to warn them that payment will be delayed.

Dear Mr. Macdonald,

I am sorry that we were not able to clear your November statement for £ 610.00 and December invoices, No. 7713 for £ 92.00. We had intended to pay the statement as usual, but a large cash shipment to one of our customers in Australian was part of the cargo destroyed in the fire on the MV Titanic when she docked in Bombay in late November.

Our insurance company has promised us compensation within the next few weeks, and once we have received this the account will be paid in full.

We know you will appreciate the situation and hope you can bear with us until the matter is settled.

Yours sincerely,
D. Carter
D. Carter

Agreeing to more

This is a reply to the previous letter. Mr. D. MacDonald accepts the request and asks for payment as soon as possible.

Dear Mr. Carter,

Thank you for your letter of the 15 September regarding our June statement and July invoice No. 7713.

We were sorry to hear about the difficulties you have had, and understand the situation, but would appreciate it if you could clear the account as soon as possible, as we ourselves have suppliers to pay.

We look forward to hearing from you soon.

Yours sincerely,
D. MacDonald
D. MacDonald

Request for an extension

In this letter the customer asks for his bill of exchange to be extended for another 60 days.

Dear Mr. Wilson,

I am sorry to tell you that I will not be able to meet my bill, No. BE7714, due on 6 June.

My government has put an embargo (禁运) on all machine exports to Cuba, and consequently we found ourselves in temporary difficulties as we had three major cash consignments for that country.

However, I am at present discussing sales of these consignments with two large Australian importers, and am certain that they will take the goods.

Could you allow me further 60 days to clear my account, and draw a new bill on me, with interest of, say 6% added for the extension of time?

I would be most grateful if you could help me in this matter.

Yours sincerely,
David Williams
David Williams

First request

Below is an example of a first request.

Dear Mr. Simpson,

I am writing to ask why you have not settled our invoice No. T931 for US $ 7,000, a copy of which is enclosed.

I know that since we began trading you have cleared your accounts regularly on the due dates. That is why I wondered if any problems have arisen which I might be able to help you with. Please let me know if I can be of assistance.

Yours sincerely,

Nancy Rice
Nancy Rice

Reply to first request

You will see from Mr. Simpson's reply to Ms. Nancy Rice's above letter that the invoice had been paid, not by check, which as Mr. Simpson's usual method of payment but by credit transfer. If Ms. Nancy Rice had looked at her bank statement, she would have seen that the money had been credited. On the other hand, if Mr. Simpson wanted to change his method of payment, he should have informed his supplier, as banks may not always advise credit transfers.

Dear Ms. Rice,

I was surprised to receive your letter of the 20th November in which you said you had not received payment for invoice No. T 931.

I instructed my bank, the National City Bank of New York, to credit your account in Chartered Bank, Hong Kong, with the US $ 7,000 some time ago.

As my bank statement showed the money had been debited to my account, I assumed that it had been credited to your account as well. It is possible that your bank has not advised you yet. Could you please check this with Chartered Bank, and if there are any problems let me know, so that I can make enquiries here?

Yours sincerely,
W. Simpson
W. Simpson

Second request

This is an example of a second request for payment, but you will see that, even though this is a second letter, Mr. R. Cliff still uses a careful and friendly tone.

Dear Mr. Pope,

We wrote to you on 10 August and enclosed copy invoices which made up your June statement, the balance of which still remains outstanding.

Having dealt with you for some time, we were disappointed in neither receiving your remittance nor any explanation as to why the balance has not been cleared. Please would you either send us a reply, or check to clear the account within the next seven days? Thank you.

Yours sincerely,
R. Cliff
R. Cliff

Credit Controller

Reply to second request

Here is Mr. Pope's reply to the previous letter.

Dear Mr. Cliff,

First let me apologize for not having cleared your June statement or replying to your letter of 10 August. However, I am surprised that you did not receive our circular letter informing all our suppliers that we were moving from London to Hull in Yorkshire. I have checked our post book, and find that a letter was sent to you on June 30.

As you will see from the copy enclosed, we warned suppliers that during the move there might be some delay in clearing accounts and replying to correspondence as the move would involve replacing more than half our staff with new people who needed time to get used to our accounts and filing systems.

You will be pleased to hear that we have now settled into our new offices and will have a fully trained staff by the end of next month. Meanwhile, I am enclosing a check for £ 3,000.00 on account, and will send a full settlement of your June statement within the next few days.

Could you please note our new address, which is on the heading of this letter, for future reference?

Yours sincerely,
Allen Poe
Allen Poe

Enc. Check No. 427322 for £ 3,000.00

Third request (final demand)

Dear Mr. John Milton,

<u>*Account No. TY99018*</u>

I wrote to you on two occasions, 25 October and 18 November, concerning the above account which now has an outstanding balance of £ 2,350.15 and is made up of the copy invoices enclosed.

I have waited three months for either a reply to explain why the balance has not been cleared, or a remittance, but have received neither.

Although I am reluctant to take legal action to recover the amount, you leave me no alternative. Therefore, unless I receive your remittance within the next ten days, my solicitors will be instructed to start proceedings to recover the debt.

Yours sincerely,
W. Grant
W. Grant

Accountant

Encl. Invoice copies

USEFUL WORDS & EXPRESSIONS

an invoice	发票，发货单
a remittance	汇款，汇寄之款，汇款额
a pro-forma（invoice）	估价单，估价发票
a statement of account	对账单，结单
a credit/debit note	借方通知，收款票，借项清单
a balance	收支差额，结余，余额
a refund	偿还额，退款
open account facility	未清结的账目/往来账户便利设施
account rendered	借贷细账，结欠清单
due date（date of maturity）	到期日，期头，支付日
prompt payment	立即付款
to clear/settle an account	结清账户
overdue account	逾期账款，过期未付账款
to extend credit	延期/展期信用/信贷
to recover a debt/recover debts	索回债款
a postal order	汇票，汇单
a Giro（transaction）	汇划转账（交易）
COD（cash on delivery）	货到付款
a current account	经常账户

a saving account	储蓄存款账户
a bank transfer	银行间的转账
	银行汇款
a telegraphic transfer（TT）	电汇
a mail transfer（MY）	邮汇
a bank draft	银行汇票
a money order	汇票，邮政汇票
a promissory note	本票，期票
documentary credit	跟单信用证
postage and packing（p&p）	邮资和包装费
errors and omissions are excepted（E&OE）	错漏不在此限定

EXERCISES

I. Messrs. Bill Johnson &Co. Ltd., purchased 3,000 tons of fine chemicals for delivery in August. As the goods are ready for shipment, draft a letter to the buyers urging them to establish the covering L/C by fax immediately.

II. Write a letter to satisfy the writer of the following letter.

Dear Mr. Smith,

Perhaps you have overlooked the fact, but your account with us is currently overdue. I have enclosed a statement of your account, which shows a balance due of $ 10,000.

If there is some reason why you have failed to remit your payment, please call us, and let's discuss the problem.

If it would be more convenient, please feel free to write a note at the bottom of this letter and send it to my office in the enclosed envelope.

Thank you for your prompt attention to this matter.

Sincerely yours,

Mary Reagan

Mary Reagan

MD

III.　Translate the following letter into Chinese.

(Request for Payment of Unearned Discounts)

Dear Mr. Carl Sandburg,

If you remember, we wrote to you about our terms on open account and are wondering if perhaps the personnel in your accounts payable department are unaware of these terms. If this is the case, we would appreciate it if you would bring this letter to their attention so that we may clear up any misunderstanding in regards to your account.

The 2% discount we offer our customers is only applicable when the merchandise received is paid for within 10 days of delivery. We have not been receiving your payments more than 10 days after delivery. While you are under no obligation to pay sooner, this does not entitle you to take advantage of the discount.

Presently, the 2% discount is being deducted from the face of the invoice and our charges for your earlier unearned discount, which we have added to your statements, are being disregarded.

The total amount due us at this time for unearned discounts is $ 2,000. We must ask that you remit your check in that amount to us as soon as possible.

We do appreciate your business and hope that this letter will help to clarify any misunderstanding.

CHAPTER 7

COMPLAINTS AND ADJUSTMENTS

In order to get your problem resolved, you should put your complaint in writing. A respectful, yet firm, complaint letter may help you accomplish what you want. Complaint letters can be a very effective way of making your voice heard.

PRINCIPLES OF WRITING EFFECTIVE COMPLAINTS

How to write a complaint letter

- Keep in mind that most errors are unintentional, and realize that most businesses and organizations want to address and clear up complaints quickly in order to have satisfied customers or members.
- Be brief. Keep your letter to one page, and write short paragraphs, rather than long ones.
- Be honest and straightforward, and include sufficient detail to back up your claim and to show that you have thoroughly researched the subject. However, omit irrelevant details. Keep your letter concise and professional.
- Maintain a firm but respectful tone, and avoid aggressive, accusing language.
- Send only photocopies of receipts and other documents, and retain all originals. Keep a copy of the letter for your records.
- In many cases, you can increase the effectiveness of your letter by getting several others to sign it with you. This is particularly the case when trying to influence or change legislation, denouncing material from the media, and so forth.
- If a company has repeatedly given you bad service and refuses to correct the situation and you feel that your only recourse is to pursue legal action, voice your feelings in a tactful but firm way. However, don't threaten legal action unless you are willing to follow through with it.
- If your letter focuses on a single individual, avoid making generalizations about the company or organization.
- If you need to make a complaint to or about people that you will still have contact with on a regular basis, your letter needs to accomplish its purpose without destroying the relationship. Use tact, and be direct, but respectful.

- Include your contact information (name, address, phone number, and e-mail address), if desired, so that the person(s) can reach you to discuss any questions or concerns.
- If a first letter does not bring action, assume a stronger but still respectful tone in the next one. If two or three letters do not resolve the problem, send one to the president or CEO of the company or entity. In each case, be firm but polite.

With a well-written complaint letter you can

- Clearly make your complaint to the person(s) involved.
- State plainly and directly your reason(s) for making the complaint.
- Indicate what the reader can or should do to address your complaint, and specify how long you are willing to wait to have your complaint resolved. (Be reasonable)
- Communicate clearly, but respectfully, that you are dissatisfied with the service you have received.
- Explain why your suggestion or request for retribution (报偿) should be granted (if you made one).
- Make your concerns known to politicians and bureaucrats. (Note: Your letter is more likely to be answered if you discuss specific concerns rather than political issues.)

UNJUSTMENT COMPLAINT

To have to complain is annoying, but to complain without good reason will also annoy your correspondent. If you complain, make sure you get your facts right. And if you have to answer an unjustified complaint, be polite and restrained and remember that we can all make mistakes. Below are two examples of unjustified complaints, with the replies to them. Notice how restrained the replies are.

Example 1
(Complaint)

Dear Sir,

I strongly object to the extra charge of £ 9. 00 which you have added to my statement. When I sent my check for £ 56. 00 last week, I thought it cleared this balance. Now I find...

Example 2

(Reply)

Dear Mr. Smith,

We received your letter today complaining of an extra charge of £ 9. 00 on your May statement. I think if you check the statement you will find that the amount due was £ 66. 00 not £ 56. 00 which accounts for the £ 9. 00 difference. I have enclosed a copy of the statement and...

Example 3

(Complaint)

Dear Sir,

I could not believe it when I read that your prices have now been increased by £ 7. 00 to have to pay £ 13. 00 for an article that was £ 6. 00 only a few months ago. It is outrageous! The government is fighting inflation...

Example 4

(Reply)

Dear Mr. Richardson,

Thank you for your letter of October 10. I checked the item you referred to, which is in fact the Scriva Pen catalogue No. G14 on our price-list. The pen has been increased to £ 7. 00, not by £ 7. 00, and I think you will agree that for a gold-plated(镀金的)pen this is not an unreasonable increase considering that the prices of gold has doubled in the past few months.

WRITING GENERAL COMPLAINT

Opening

Do not delay and do not apologize. Complain as soon as you realize a mistake has been made; delay not only weakens your case, but can complicate the matter as the people you are dealing with might forget the details. And there is no need to open your letter by apologizing for the need to complain ("We regret to inform you...", "I am sorry to have to write to you about...") ; this also weakens your case. Begin simply:

· 117 ·

We would like to inform you that . . .

I am writing to complain about. . .

I am writing with reference to Order No. P32 which we received yesterday.

The language of complaints

Terms like "disgusted", "infuriated", "enraged", "amazed" have no place in business. You can express dissatisfaction by saying:

This is the third time this mistake has occurred and we are far from satisfied with the service you offer.

Unless you can fulfil our orders efficiently in the future we will have to consider other sources of supply.

Please ensure that this sort of problem does not arise again.

Don't be rude or personal. In most cases correspondence between firms takes place between employees in various departments. There is nothing to be gained by being rude to the individual you are writing to; you will merely antagonize someone who may have had nothing to do with the error and, rather than getting the error corrected, you may make your correspondent defensive and awkward to deal with. Therefore, do not use sentences like:

You must correct your mistake as soon as possible.

You made an error on the statement.

You don't understand the terms of discount. We told you to deduct discount from net prices, not c. i. f prices.

Use passive and impersonal structures instead.

The mistake must be corrected as soon as possible.

There appears to be an error on the statement.

There seems to be some misunderstanding regarding terms of discount. Discount is deducted from net prices, not c. i. f. prices.

Do not use words like "fault" ("your fault", "our fault") or "blame" ("you are to blame"); these expressions are not only rude, but childish. Therefore, do not write:

It is not our fault, it is probably the fault of your dispatch department.

But:

The mistake could not have originated here, and must be connected with the dispatch of the goods.

Finally, while writing the complaint remember that your supplier wants to help you and correct the mistake. He is not in business to irritate or confuse his customers but to offer them service.

Explaining the problem

If you think you know how the mistake was made, you may politely point it out to your supplier. Sometimes when a mistake occurs several times, you may be able to work out why it is happening more quickly than the firm you are dealing with.

Could you tell your dispatch department to take special care when addressing my consignment? My name is C. J. Williams, 101 Monmouth street, Swansea. But there is a C. Williams at 110 Monmouth Street who also deals in electrical fittings.

Could you ask your accounts department to check my code carefully in future? My account number is 246 – 642, and they have been sending me statements coded 642 – 246.

I think the reason that wrong sizes have been sent to me is that I am ordering in metric sizes, and you are sending me sizes measured in feet and inches. I would appreciate your looking into this.

Suggesting a solution

If you think you know how the mistake can be corrected, let your supplier know.

If I send you a debit note for £ 18. 00 and deduct it from my next statement that should put the matter right.

The best solution would be for me to return the wrong articles to you, postage and packing forward.

Rather than send a credit note, you could send six replacements which would probably be easier than adjusting our accounts.

RESPONDING TO COMPLAINT LETTERS

Responding to complaint letters can be a very sensitive matter. When handling complaints, it is important to know all of the facts and to respond to the complaint in a timely and tactful manner.

7 Tips for responding to complaint letters

- Use a polite, understanding tone, and keep your letter short and to the point.
- Don't argue. Even if you do not agree with the complaint, and can do nothing about it, a considerate response will often help soothe an irate client.
- Write your response letter as soon as you have received and investigated the complaint, especially if you realize that an adjustment needs to be made or that you have made a mistake. Keep in mind that it takes less effort to satisfy a current customer than to attract a new one.
- If you don't have enough information to respond to the complaint immediately, you should ask the customer for more information or inform the customer that you are collecting more information from another source before responding. This lets the customer know that you take the complaint seriously.
- When the company is not at fault, but you agree to grant the customer's request either partially or fully, inform the customer of his or her error, if any, so it will not happen again. Do this tactfully, without accusation. The letter should show that the company values both fairness and customer goodwill.
- If you are not willing to make an adjustment or correct the perceived error, explain why you cannot grant the request, and at the same time seek to retain the customer's business and favor. The denial will probably disappoint the customer, so be tactful.
- When responding to a complaint letter of discrimination or sexual harassment, your letter must show that you take the complaint very seriously and that you are taking appropriate steps to resolve the situation. This letter must be serious and professional.

Opening

Acknowledge that you have received the complaint, and thank your customer for informing you.

Thank you for your letter of 6 August informing us that. . .

We would like to thank you for informing us of our accounting error in your letter of the 8 June.

We are replying to your letter of 10 March in which you told us that . . .

Getting time to investigate the complaint

Sometimes you cannot deal with a complaint immediately, as the matter needs to be looked into. Do not leave your customer waiting, but tell him straight away what you are doing.

While we cannot give you an explanation at present, we can promise you that we are looking into the matter and will write to you again shortly.

As we are sending out orders promptly, I think these delays may have something to do with the haulage contractors and I am making investigations at the moment.

Would you please return samples of the items you are dissatisfied with, and I will send them to our factory in Scotland for tests.

Explaining the mistake

If the complaint is justified, explain how the mistake occurred but do not blame your staff; you employed them, so you are responsible for their actions.

The mistake was due to a fault in one of our machines, which has now been corrected.

There appears to have been some confusion in our addressing system, but this has been adjusted.

It is unusual for this type of error to arise, but the problem has now been dealt with.

Solving the problem

Having acknowledged your responsibility and explained what went wrong, you must, of course, put matters right as soon as possible and tell your customer that you are doing so.

The reason for the weakness in the units you complained about was due to a faulty manufacturing process in production. This is being corrected at the moment and we are sure you will be completely satisfied with the replacement units we will be sending you in the next few weeks.

The paintwork on the body of the cars became discoloured because of a chemical imbalance in the paint used in spraying the vehicles. We have already contacted our own suppliers and are waiting for their reply. Meanwhile we are taking these models out of production and calling in all those that have been supplied.

The material you complained about has now been withdrawn. Its fault was in the weave of the cloth and this was due to a programming error in the weaving machines themselves. This has been corrected and replacement materials are now being sent on to you.

Rejecting a complaint

If you think the complaint is unjustified, you can be firm but polite in your answer. But even if you deny responsibility, you should always try to give an explanation of the problem.

We have closely compared the articles you returned with our samples and can see no difference between them, and in this case we are not willing to either substitute the articles or offer a credit.

Our engineer has examined the machines you complained about and in his report tells us that the machine has not been maintained properly. If you look at the instruction booklet on maintenance that we sent you, you will see that it is essential to take care of ...

Our factory has now inspected the stereo unit you returned last week, and they inform us that it has been used with the wrong speakers and this had overloaded the circuits. We can repair the machine, but you will have to pay for the repairs as misuse of the unit is not included under our guarantee.

Closing

It is useful when closing your letter to mention that this mistake, error or fault is an exception, and it either rarely or never happens, and of course you should apologize the inconvenience your customer experienced.

In closing we would like to apologize for the inconvenience, and also point out that this type of fault rarely occurs in the Benz 600.

Finally, may we say that this was an exceptional mistake and is unlikely to occur again. Please accept our apologies for the inconvenience.

The replacements of the faulty articles are on their way to you and you should receive them within the week. We are sure that you will be satisfied with them and there will be no repetition of the faults. Thank you for your patience in this matter, and we look forward to hearing from you again.

Specimen Letters

Example 1
(Complaint of wrong delivery)

Dear Mr. Williams,

I received a consignment of 6 dressing tables from you yesterday, my order No. 1668, which were ordered from your summer catalogue, Cat No. GR154. But on unpacking them I found that six heavy teak(柚木)-finished dressing tables had been sent, instead of the light pine-finished ones asked for.

As most of my customers live in small flats earning a moderate income, it is doubtful that I will be able to find a market for larger more expensive products.

I also have firm orders for the goods asked for. Would you send someone with my consignment as soon as possible and at the same time pick up the wrongly delivered goods? Thanks.

Yours sincerely,
Robert Lee
Robert Lee

Example 2
(Reply to complaint of wrong delivery)

Dear Mr. Lee.

Thank you for your letter of 3 February in which you said that you had received a wrong delivery to your order (No. B1668).

I have looked into this and it appears that you have ordered from an out-of-date catalogue. Our current catalogue is Winter 2005 – 5, and this lists the dressing tables you wanted under DR189.

I have instructed one of my drivers to deliver the pine-finish dressing tables tomorrow and pick up the other consignment at the same time. Rather than sending a credit note, I will cancel invoice No. T4451 and include another, No. T4467, with the delivery.

There is also a Winter 2005 – 6 catalogue on its way to you in case you have mislaid the one I origi-

nally sent you.

Yours sincerely,
T. Williams
T. Williams

Enc. Invoice No. T4467

Complaint of damage

This letter deals with damage.

Dear Mr. Jefferson

<u>Our Order No. 14478</u>

I am writing to you to complain about the shipment of sweater we received yesterday against the above order.

The boxes in which the sweaters were packed were damaged, and looked as if they had been broken open in transit(在运输过程中). From your invoice No. 18871 we estimate that thirty garments have been stolen to the value of £ 150.00, and because of the rummaging(碎屑)in the boxes, quite a few other garments were crushed or stained and cannot be sold as new articles in our shops.

As the sale was on c. i. f. basis and the forwarding company your agents, we suggest you contact them with regards to compensation.

You will find a list of the damaged and missing articles attached, and the consignment(寄售商品) will be put to one side until we receive your instructions.

Yours sincerely,

L. Crane

L. Crane
Chief Buyer

Reply to complaint of damage

Because **Sunshine Co. Ltd** sells goods on a c. i. f. basis to their retailers, and in this case there was no special instruction to send the goods in a particular way, **Sunshine** will have to find out what happened and whether they can be compensated. Mr. Jefferson could have asked Mr. Crane to keep those items which were not damaged, and return the garments which could not be sold. However, he wants the shipping company to inspect the whole consignment in case they do not accept that the damage was caused by pilfering(盗窃).

Dear Mr. Crane,

Thank you for informing us about the damage to our consignment (Inv. No. 1887).

From our previous transactions you will realize that this sort of problem is quite unusual, nevertheless we are sorry about the inconvenience it has caused you.

Please would you return the whole consignment to us, postage and packing forward, and we will ask the shipping company to come and inspect the damage so that they can arrange compensation. It is unlikely that our insurance company needs to be troubled with this case.

If you want us to send you another shipment as per your order No. 14478, please let us know. We have the garments in stock and it would be no trouble to send them within the next fortnight.

Yours sincerely,
Thomas Jefferson
Thomas Jefferson

Complaint of bad workmanship

When bad workmanship(技艺,作工) is involved the customer can only complain as the fault arises. But they should still complain immediately. The work was completed, but some months later faults began to appear.

Dear Mr. Simpson,

Superbuys' Wembley High Street

I am writing to you with reference to the above premises(前提) which you refitted last February.

In the past few weeks a number of faults have appeared in the electrical circuits and the flooring which has been particularly dangerous to our customers.

With regard to the electrical faults we have found that spotlights on the far wall have either failed to work, or flicker while they are on, and replacing the bulbs has not corrected the fault.

The Duraflooring which you laid has been showing signs of deterioration with some areas being worn through to the concrete creating a hazard to our customers.

Will you please come and inspect the damage and arrange for repairs within the next weeks? The matter is urgent as we can be sued if any of our customers are injured by falling over the cracks in the flooring. I would also take the opportunity to remind you that you have guaranteed all your fixtures and fittings for one year. I look forward to hearing from you soon .

Yours sincerely,
K. Bellon
K. Bellon

Managing Director

Reply to complaint of bad workmanship

Dear Mr. Bellon,

The manager of your Wembley supermarkets has probably told you by now that I came down to inspect the damage you wrote to me about in your letter of 7 July.

I looked at the faulty electrical wiring and this appears to have been caused by gripping water from the floor above. My foreman, who put the wiring in in February, tells me that the wall was dry at the time he replaced the old wires. However, we will make the repairs and seal off that section.

Duraflooring is one of the most hardwearing materials of this kind on the market and I was surprised to hear that it had worn away within six months, so I made a close inspection. I noticed the floor had been cut into and this seems to have been the result of dragging heavy sharp boxes across it, possibly the ones you use to store some perishable products in. The one year guarantee we offer on our workmanship is against normal wear and tear, and the treatment the floor has been subjected to does not come under this category. I am quite willing to have the surface replaced, but I am afraid we will have to charge you for the materials and work involved. If I may, I would like to suggest that you in-

struct your staff to use trolleys when shifting these containers.

I am sorry about the inconvenience you have experienced and will tell my men to repair the damage as soon as I have your confirmation that they can begin work.

The floor repairs should not come to more than £ 60.00 and the work can be completed in less than a day. Perhaps we can arrange for it to be completed on a Sunday when the supermarket is closed.

Yours sincerely,
H. Simpson
H. Simpson

Director

Complaint of non-delivery

Dear Mr. Brown,

<u>Order No. VC 58391</u>

We are writing to you with reference to the above order and our letter of 22 May in which we asked you when we could expect delivery of the 60 dynamos（发电机）(PT model 55) you were to have supplied on 3 December for an export order.

We have tried to contact you by phone, but could not get anyone in your factory who knew anything about this matter.

It is essential that we deliver this consignment to our Canadian customers on time, as this was an initial order from them and would give us an opening in the American market.

Our deadline is 28 December, and the lorries have been completed except for the dynamos that need to be fitted.

Unless we receive the components within the next five days, the order will be cancelled and placed elsewhere. We should warn you that we are holding you to your delivery contact and if any loss results because of this late delivery we will be taking legal action.

Yours sincerely,
John Major

Reply to complaint of non-delivery

The final example in this section is an illustration of a strong complaint to a supplier. In this case the customer, Overseas Co. Ltd. , makes lorries for export. They placed an order with Coventry components Ltd. , to supply them with 60 dynamos for an export shipment of lorries that were to be sent to Canada. Coventry Components have neither delivered and the order, nor answered Overseas' previous letter urging them to make delivery.

Dear Mr. Brown

Thank you for your letter of 6 November concerning your order (No. VC 58319) which should have been supplied to you on 3 November.

First I apologize for your order not being delivered on the due date and for the problems you have experienced in getting in touch with us about it. But as you may have read in your newspapers we have experienced an industrial dispute which has involved both administrative staff and employees on the shop floor, and as a consequence has held up all production over the past few weeks.

However, I can tell you that the dispute has been settled and we are back to normal production. Nevertheless there is a backlog of orders to catch up on, but we are using associates of ours to help us fulfill all outstanding commitments; your order has been given priority, so we should be able to deliver the dynamos before the end of this week.

May I point out, with respect, that your contract with us did have a standard clause stating that delivery dates would be met unless unforeseen circumstances arose, and we think you will agree that a dispute is an exceptional circumstances. However, we quite understand your problem and will allow you to cancel your contract if it will help you to meet your own commitments with your Canadian customers. But we will not accept any responsibility for any action they may take against you.

Once again let me say how much I regret the inconvenience this delay has caused, and emphasize that it was due to factors we could not have known about when we accepted your delivery dates.

Please phone or cable me letting me know if you wish to complete your order or whether you would prefer to make other arrangements.

I look forward to hearing from you within the next day or so.

Your sincerely,

John Major

John Major

Managing Director

Note how this letter is both apologetic but firm. Though Coventry accept responsibility for the problems Overseas face in delivering their consignment to their Canadian customers, Mr. Major rejects the threat of legal action by drawing Mr. Brown's attention to a clause in their contract stating that the company will not be responsible for "unseen circumstances that arise". However, Mr. Major is flexible enough to realize he must not antagonize his customers, so he allows Mr. Brown the opportunity to cancel the order if he can make other arrangements.

Therefore the two main points this letter makers are — First, do not commit yourself to contracts unless you are absolutely certain they can be fulfilled. Second, always try and be as flexible as possible with customers or associates even if you are in a strong position; it will increase your business reputation.

ACCOUNTING ERRORS AND ADJUSTMENT

As we have seen, many letters of complaint arise out of accounting errors, which can be put right by adjustments. Debit notes and credit notes are used for this purpose.

Debit notes

Debit notes are a second charge for a consignment and become necessary if a customer has been undercharged through a mistake in the calculations on the original invoice. An explanation is included on the debit note:

Undercharge on invoice C293. 10 Units @ £ 2. 62 each = £ 26. 20, NOT £ 16. 20 Invoice No. P. 32, one line omitted viz. 100 C90 cassettes at £ 1. 40 each = £ 140. 00.

VAT should have been calculated at 15%, NOT 8% Difference = £ 1. 86. ?

Debit notes are the result of carelessness and show that you should be careful when making up invoices as once a buyer has settled an account, it is annoying to be told that there is an additional payment. A letter of apology should always accompany a debit note.

We would like to apologize for the mistake on invoice No. C293, which was due to an oversight. Please could you send us the balance of £ 10. 00? Thank you.

I am sorry to trouble you, particularly since you were so prompt in settling the account, but I would be grateful if you would let us have the additional amount of £ 140. 00 as itemized on the enclosed debit note.

I regret that we miscalculated the VAT and must now ask you to forward the difference of £ 1. 86.

Credit notes

Credit notes are sent because of accidental overcharges:

10 copies of 'International Commerce' @£ 3. 50 = £ 36. 00 NOT £ 40. 00.
Invoice L283. Discount should have been 12%, not 8%. Credit = £ 6. 60.

A credit note may also be issued when a deposit is being refunded (e. g. on the cartons or cases which the goods were packed in) or when goods are returned because they were not suitable or had been damaged.

Received 3 returned cases charged on Invoice No. 1436@£ 2. 00 each = £ 6. 00.
Refund for 4 copies of 'International Commerce' @£ 3. 50 each(returned damaged) = £ 14. 00.

As with a debit note, a covering letter explanation and apology should be sent with a credit not in the case of mistakes.

I have pleasure in enclosing a credit note for £ 6. 00. This is due to a miscalculation on our invoice dated 12 August. Please accept our apologies for the mistake.

Please find enclosed our credit note No. C23 for £ 6. 60 which is a refund for the overcharge on invoice No. L283. As you pointed out in your letter, the trade discount should have been 12%, not 10%, of the gross price. We apologize for the inconvenience.

Debit note

This note is necessary because the suppliers, Sunshine Furniture Ltd., have made a mistake in their calculations and have undercharged their customers, Universal Stores Ltd.

DEBIT NOTE		*No. 311*

SUNSHINE FURNITURE Ltd.

High Street, Maidenhead, Berks. SL6 5D2   Telephone 0628 26755
Registered No. 18514391 London
VAT No. 231 618831

Universal Stores Ltd.   *31 September   2005*
Kings Road
Harrogate
North Yorkshire

	Invoice No. L8992. <u>UNDERCHARGE</u>	
2005 5 September	*The extension should have read:* *6 Chairs @ £ 6.00 each = £ 36.00* *NOT* *6 <u>Chairs@ £ 6.00</u> each = £ 30.00* *We apologize for the error and ask if you would please pay* *the difference viz. £ 6.00*	
		£ 6.00

Credit note

Sunshine Furniture Ltd. has made a mistake on another invoice and must now send a credit note. Note that the form for a credit note is the same as that for a debit note, except for the heading.

Credit notes, however, are often printed in red.

DEBIT NOTE   No.   C517

SUNSHINE FURNITURE Ltd.

High Street, Maidenhead, Berks. SL6 5D2   Telephone 0628 26755
Registered No. 18514391 London
VAT No. 236 618831

Universal Stores Ltd.   20 October   2005
Kings Road
Harrogate
North Yorkshire

2005 20October	Invoice No. L8996. _OVERCHARGE_ The invoice should have read: 15% off gross price of £ 400.00 = £ 60.00 NOT 10% off gross price of £ 400.00 = £ 40.00 Refund = £ 20.00. Please accept our apologies.	 £ 20.00

Complaint of accounting errors

Mr. Johnson of Johnson & Son Ltd. (Builders' Suppliers) has received a statement in which several accounting errors have occurred.

Dear Mr. Johnson,

I have received your July statement for £ 1,640.32, but noticed that a number of errors have been made.

1. Invoice Y 1146 for £ 128.00 has been debited twice.

2. No credit has been listed for the wallpaper (Cat. No. WR114) which I returned in July. Your credit note No. CN 118 for £ 9. 50 refers to this.

3. You have charged me for a delivery of paint brushes, Invoice No. Y 1162 for £ 31. 00, but I never ordered or received them. Could you check your delivery book?

I have deducted a total of £ 168. 50 from your statement and will send you a check for £ 1,471. 82 once I have your confirmation of this amount.

Yours sincerely,

Tom Hanks
Tom Hanks

Reply to complaint of accounting errors

Dear Mr. Hanks,

Thank you for your letter of 5 August in which you pointed out that three mistakes totaling £ 168. 50 had been made on your statement.

I apologize for the errors which were due to a fault in our computer which has now been fixed. I have enclosed another statement for July which shows the correct balance of £ 1471. 82.

Yours sincerely,
Michael Johnson
Michael Johnson

Encl. Statement

USEFUL WORDS & EXPRESSIONS

complaint	提出异议；索赔
adjustment	理赔
claim	索赔
breach	违背/反，破坏，破裂，裂口

a mistake	错误，过失
an error	错误，过失，误差
a fault	过错，缺点，故障，毛病
non-delivery	不交货；提货不着
match	相配，相称，比赛，相比，匹配
a principal	总部；委托人
an inconvenience	麻烦，不方便之处
a deadline	最终期限
a guarantee	保证，保证书，担保，抵押品
a dispute	争论，辩论，争吵
a backlog	订货
a commitment	委托事项，许诺，承担义务
a contract	合同，契约
credit	贷方；借记
a miscalculation	误算，估错
an overcharge	超载，过重的负担，过度充电
an undercharge	低的索价，充电不足
a debit/credit note	保值单据，信用证
a debit note	借方通知，收款票，借项清单
a refund	归还，偿还额，退款
deterioration	变坏，退化，堕落
out-of-date	老式的，过时的，落伍的
wear and tear	磨损，折磨
workmanship	手艺，技艺，作工，技巧
compensation	补偿，赔偿
legal action	诉讼
legal person	法人
to lodge/file/submit a claim against sb.	向某人索赔

to investigate a complaint	调查索赔
to look into a matter	调查事因
to deny/accept responsibility	拒绝/同意承担责任
to give an explanation	做解释
to solve a problem	解决问题
to put matters right	使恢复正常，纠正错误
to cancel an order	取消订货单

EXERCISES

I. Write a letter of complaint to the supplier, informing them that half of the artworks delivered on 18 November were broken and that the packing appears to have been at fault. Ask them to replace the broken goods.

II. You have bought 15 tons of minerals, delivery of 10 tons was promised within two weeks. One and a half months have passed and the consignment has not been delivered; nor has any explanation been received. Write a letter about this to the supplier in Brazil.

III. Prepare an adjustment letter to satisfy the writer of the following letter.

To whom it may concern,

On April 1, 2005 I received a book entitled "How To Write A Complaint Letter" by the author Roy W. Poe. I believe I was shipped this book in error as I had ordered the book "How To Write A Love Letter" by the author Allen Poe on March 15, 2005 and to date I have not received the book. I am returning this book and including my postage receipt. Please credit my account the amount of the postage and send me the book I had originally ordered entitled "How To Write A Love Letter" by Allen Poe, product-number 011011.

Yours Truly,

IV. Improve the following letter of complaint according to the techniques we've learned in the previous chapters.

Gentlemen,

We duly received the 20 cases Porcelain Wares（瓷器）you sent us，but we regret to find on examination that those in tow cases of them have been wholly damaged in transit.

As they are absolutely of no use to us，we have to request you to substitute good porcelains for the broken ones as soon as possible.

Yours faithfully,

PEARD & Co.
H. J. Peard
H. J. Peard，President

CHAPTER 8

MODES OF TRANSPORTATION AND SHIPPING

ROAD, RAIL AND AIR

The three main methods of transporting goods, besides shipping which we will deal with in a separate section, are road, rail and air.

Road transport

Road transport tends to be comparatively cheaper and more direct than rail, and in the past years haulage (trucking) has doubled in the world. The reasons for this include the increased capacity for lorries to carry goods, particularly with the introduction of containers (large steel boxes which allow for bulk transportation), faster services, with road improvements (motorways, expressway), and accessibility abroad with ferries (boats crossing the channel) offering rolling-on and rolling-off facilities, i. e. trucks can drive on to a channel ferry, cross, and then drive off without unloading.

Rail transport

Rail transport is faster than road, which is necessary especially when transporting perishable goods, i. e. fish, fruit, meat etc., and can haul bulk commodities (oil, grain, coal) in greater volume than road transporters.

There is a link between road and rail through companies such as freightliners, but transshipment (transferring goods from train to truck) can still be a problem. Special ferries are available to take trains across the Channel to link up with European rail services, and British Rail also has containers facilities. Nevertheless, rail transport tends to be comparatively more expensive than road haulage.

Air transport

Air transport has the advantage of saving time, so goods arrive faster, in a better condition, and can be sold quicker, particularly over long distances. Insurance also tends to be comparatively cheaper as consignments spend less time in transit. However, with regard to bulky, cumbersome e-quipment and bulk commodities, air transport is much more expensive.

Documentation

Road and rail use consignment notes, and air transport, waybills. These documents are receipts, and not documents of titles as a bill of lading might be. This means that ownership of the consign-ment note/waybill does not give ownership to the goods. They are also not negotiable, i. e. they cannot be bought, sold, transferred by the consignor (the person sending the goods) or the con-signee (the person receiving the goods).

Consignment notes and waybills are obtained by the consignor filling out an instruction for dispatch form, and paying the freight charges (the cost of sending the goods). These charges are calculated on size (volume), weight, or value, and sometimes risk, particularly if special precautions have to be taken.

Correspondence in transport is generally between the sellers and freight firms, or sellers and for-warding agents, who send goods on behalf of the seller. The customers are behalf of the seller. The customers are kept informed by advice notes which give details of packing, and when the goods will arrive.

SPECIMEN LETTERS

Request for a quotation for delivery by road

In this letter the furniture manufacturer, Homemakers Ltd. , is writing to a road haulage firm asking them for an estimate to deliver furniture to his customer, Mr. Hughes; he describes the packing, states the value of the consignment and mentions a delivery time.

HOMEMAKERS Ltd.
54 – 59 Riverside , Cardiff CF CF1 1JW

Telephone: (0222) 49721   *Registered No:* C135162
Fax: 3821798

Transport Manager   *10 November 2005*

Cartiers Ltd.
516 – 9 Cathays Park
Cardiff CF 1 9VJ

Dear Sir,

Would you please quote for collecting, from the above address, and delivering the following consignment to R. Hughes & Son Ltd., 21 Mead Road, Swansea?

6 divans and mattresses, 6' × 3'6
7 bookcase assembly kits packed in strong cardboard boxes,
Measuring 12 cubic feet each
3 coffee table assembly kits, packed in cardboard boxes, measuring 9
Cubic feet each
4 armchairs 2'6 × 1'6 × 2'

The divans and armchairs are fully protected against knocks and scratches by polythene and corrugated paper wrapping, and the invoiced value of the consignment is £ 830.00.

I would appreciate a prompt reply, as delivery must be made before the end of next week.

Yours faithfully,

R. Cliff
R. Cliff

Quotation for delivery by road

In the reply to Mr. Cliff's letter, note how the writer refers to the consignment note as a "receipt". He also quotes for "picking up and delivering" the consignment; carriers may quote for delivery, as here, or on a time basis, i. e. how long it will take to load or unload the lorry or van.

Kunming CHARTERS Ltd.

218 Beijing Road, Kunming 650031

Reg. No. : 31883512
VAT No: 96 4218792

Telephone: (0871) 5231358
Fax: (0871) 5231358

12 October 2005

Mr. R. Cliff
Homemakers Ltd.
54 – 59 Riverside
Cardiff CF1 1JW

Dear Mr. Cliff,

In reply to your letter of 5 October, we can quote £ 33. 5 for picking up and delivering your consignment from your address to the consignee's premise. This includes loading and unloading, plus insurance.

If you fill out the Dispatch Note enclosed, and let us know two days before you want the delivery made, our driver will hand you a receipt when he calls to collect the consignment.

Yours sincerely,

H. Wells
H. Wells

Supervisor

Enc.

Advice of delivery

Yamano Express Co. , Ltd. now advises their customer.

YAMANO EXPRESS CO. , Ltd

YOKOHAMA , JAPAN

Telephone: 03 1234 5678   Registered No. C135162

Mr. R. Hamilton   *12 October 2005*
R. Hamilton & Son. Ltd.
21 Mead Road
Swansea
Glamorgan 3ST 1DR

Dear Mr. Hamilton,

We are glad to inform you that we have today shipped by N. Y. K. m/s "Heian Marru", your 20 cases Fancy Goods to Honolulu, Hawaii, as per your instruction of October 6.

The ship is to set sail tomorrow noon. Enclosed please find copies of invoice for same to your immediate attention.

Yours sincerely,
R. Cliff
R. Cliff

Enc. Invoice No. DM2561

Complaint of damage in delivery by rail

In this letter, the goods were sent by rail, at the consignee's request, and were received damaged. S & M (Records) Ltd., the customer, is writing to their supplier, Shanghai Importers, complaining about the consignment.

S & M (Records) Ltd.
54 - 59 Riverside, Manchester M2 5BP

Telephone: 061 832 4397   Registered No: C135162
Fax: 3821798   VAT No. 821 6215 31

Mr. Wang Wei
Shanghai Importers Ltd.
18 Nanjing Road
Shanghai 200028

Dear Mr. Wang

Consignment Note 671342 158

Yesterday we received the above consignment to our order, No. T1953, but found on opening boxes 4, 5 and 6 that the records and tapes in them were damaged.

Most of the L. P. S. were either split or warped, in boxes 4 and 5, and the majority of cassette cases

· 141 ·

in box 6 were smashed, with tape spilling out of the cassettes themselves.

The goods cannot be retailed even at a discount and we would like to know whether you want us to return them, or hold them for inspection.

Yours faithfully,

B. Lyndon

B. Lyndon
S & M (Records) Ltd.

Enc.

Reply to complaint of damage

Shanghai Importers Ltd.
18 Nanjing Road, Shanghai 200028

Telephone: (021) 61028598
Fax: (021) 61028598

Registration No: 56783457
VAT No. 243 761028
Your Ref: JA/MR

Mr. B. Lyndon
S & M (Records) Ltd.
54 – 59 Riverside
Manchester M2 5BP
Great Britain

Dear Mr. Lyndon,

I was sorry to hear about the damage to part of the consignment (No. T1953) that we sent you last week.

I have checked with our dispatch department and they tell me that the goods left here in perfect condition. There should be our checker's mark on the side of each box, which is a blue label with a packer's number and date on it.

As you made the arrangements for delivery, I am afraid we cannot help you. However, I suggest you write to British Rail, and if the goods were being carried at "company's risk" I am sure they will consider compensation.

I have enclosed a copy of their receipt from their goods depot at Southampton station, and you can have any other documents that we can supply to help you with your claim.

Yours sincerely,

Wang Wei
Wang Wei
Shanghai Importers Ltd.

Enc.

Complaint to the carrier

S & M (Records) Ltd. writes to the railway company. On receipt of this letter, the railway company will inspect the goods and decide whether the damage was due to negligence. If it was, the customer will receive compensation.

S & M (Records) Ltd.
54 – 59 Riverside, Manchester M2 5BP

Telephone: 061 832 4397   *Registered No: C135162*
Fax: 3821798   *VAT No. 821 6215 31*

Ref: TA/MR   *20 November 2005*

Claims Dept.
British Rail
Railway House
Liverpool SO2 4RG

Dear Sirs,

Consignment Note 671842 158

The above consignment was delivered to our premises, at the above address, on November 16. It consisted of eight boxes of records and cassettes, three of which were badly damaged.

We have contacted our suppliers, Shanghai Importers Ltd., in Shanghai, China, and they inform us that when the goods were deposited at your depot, they were in perfect condition. Therefore we assume that damage occurred while the consignment was in your care.

The boxes were marked FRAGILE, and KEEP AWAY HEAT, but because of the nature of the damage to the goods (records warped, cassette cases split), the consignment appears to have been roughly handled and left near a heater.

We estimate the loss on invoice value to be £ 672.00, and as the goods were sent "carrier's risk" we are claiming compensation for that amount.

You will find a copy of the consignment note and invoice enclosed, and we will hold the boxes for your inspection.

Yours faithfully,

J. Allen

J. Allen

Request for a quotation for delivery by air

Panton Manufacturing Ltd. writes to an airline to find out how much it will cost to send glassware to their agents in Saudi Arabia.

Panton Manufacturing Ltd.
Panton Works, Houslow, Middlesex, TW6 2 BQ

Tel: 353 0215   Registered No: England 266135
Fax: 353 0215

Cargo Manager   16 October 2005
International Airways P. L. C
Palace Road
London SW1

Dear Sir or Madam,

We would like to send from Heathrow to Riyadh, Saudi Arabia, twelve boxes of assorted glassware, to be delivered within the next fortnight.

Each box weighs 40 kilos, and measures 0.51 cubic metres. Could you please quote charges for shipment and insurance?

Yours faithfully,

N. Jay
N. Jay

Director

Quotation for delivery by air

Here is the airliner's reply to Mr. Jay. We saw before that airlines calculate freight charges on weight or volume; in this case both will have been taken into account.

International Airways P. L. C

Airline House, Palace Road, London SW1

Telephone: *01 638 4129*   Reg. No: *London 281395*
Fax: *3812158*   VAT No: *85 116259 15*

20 October 2005

N. Jay
Panton Manufacturing Ltd.
Panton Works,
Houslow
Middlesex
TW6 2 BQ

Dear Mr. Jay,

Thank you for your enquiry of 16 October.

We will be able to send your consignment to Riyadh within two days of your delivering it to Heathrow. The cost of freight Heathrow/ Riyadh is 3.60 per kilo, plus £ 1.50 air waybill, and £ 14.00 customs clearance and handling charges. But you will have to arrange your own insurance.

There are three flights a week from London to Saudi Arabia, Monday, Wednesday, and Saturday.

Please fill in the enclosed Dispatch Form and return it to us with the consign ment and commercial invoices, one of which should be included in the parcel for customs inspection.

Yours sincerely,

H. Weldon
H. Weldon
Cargo Manager
Enc.

<h1 style="text-align:center">SHIPPING</h1>

Types of vessels

There are a variety of vessels available for exporters to use when shipping goods.

Passenger liners are ships that follow scheduled routes and concentrate on passenger services, but also carry cargo.

Passenger cargo vessels, on the other hand, concentrate on cargoes, offer more facilities for loading and unloading, but carry few passengers.

Tramps, so called because they travel anywhere in the world on unscheduled routes, picking up cargo and delivering it.

Tankers are usually oil carriers, and are like bulk carriers which transport bulk consignments such as grain, wheat, and ores.

Containers vessels offer facilities to move containers from one country to another, and have special lifting gear and storage space for the huge steel boxes they transport.

Roll-on roll-off terries are vessels which allow cars and trucks to drive on at one port and off at another without having to load and unload their freight.

Forwarding agents

Forwarding agents are used by exporters to arrange both import and export shipments. In the case of the former, their services include collecting the consignment, arranging shipment, and if required, packing and handling all documentation, including making out the bill of lading, obtaining insurance, sending commercial invoices and paying the shipping company for their clients. They also inform the importer's forwarding agent that the shipment is on its way by sending an advice note, and he in turn, will inform his client, send the goods on to him, or arrange for them to be stored until collected. Many forwarding agents in importing countries also act as clearing agents, ensuring that the goods are cleared through the customs.

Chartering ships

It is general practice to hire the vessels through shipbrokers. Once a broker is contacted he will find a ship owner who is prepared to hire his vessel on either a "voyage charter" or "time charter" basis.

Voyage charter charges, i. e. taking freight from port A to port B, are calculated on the tonnage value of the cargo. For example, if an exporter ships 500 tons of coal at £ 1.20 per ton, he will pay £ 600.00 for the charter.

Time charter charges are calculated on the tonnage of the ship (i. e. the weight of the ship) plus running costs of the vessel, excluding wages. So the larger the ship, the more the charter pays, regardless of whether he ships 500 tons or 500 tons.

There are also mixed charters combining both time and voyage charters. The contract signed by both parties is known as charter party.

Enquiry for a voyage charter

Dear Sirs,

We would like to charter a vessel for one voyage from Hong Kong, to New York, USA, to take a consignment of 7,000 tons of minerals.

Our contract states that we have to take delivery between 1 and 5 August, so we will need a ship that will be able to load during those dates. Please advise us if you can get a vessel and let us know the terms.

Yours faithfully,
Paul Gans
Paul Gans

Director

Shipbroker's reply

Dear Mr. Gans,

You should have already received our fax in which we said that we had an option on a vessel, the SS Shark, which is docked in Hong Kong, at present. She has a cargo capacity of 10,000 tons and although she is larger than you wanted, her owners are willing to offer a part charter of her.

They have quoted £ 2.30 per ton which is a very competitive rate considering you will be sharing the cost. Please will you cable your decision as soon as possible? Thank you.

Yours sincerely,
H. Weldon
H. Weldon
Charter Department

USEFUL WORDS & EXPRESSIONS

road/rail/air transport	公路/铁路/航空运输
transhipment (= transshipment)	转运，转船
haulage (trucking)	拖运
a freight company	货运公司
a forwarding agent	运送经理人，运输行/商，转运公司
a clearing agent	清算代理人
clearing agency	票据交换所，清算代理处
private company	私人公司，股权不公开公司
a private carrier	私人货运公司
a consignor	委托者，发货人，寄件人，交付人
a consignee	受托者，收件人，代销人
a checker	检验员

a packer	包装工人，打包机，包装食品生产厂
in transit	运送中的
a lorry	卡车，铁路货车
a van	有篷货车
a container	集装箱
a passenger liner	定期客船
a passenger/cargo/vessel	客轮
a tramp	（货船)不定期航行
a tanker	油轮
a bulk carrier	散装货轮
a container vessel	集装箱船
roll-on-off cargo	滚装货
roll-on-off facilities	滚装设备
a ferry	渡船，渡口
a barge	驳船，游艇
a lighter	驳船
a goods depot	货物库房/ 仓库
a terminal	终点站，终端，接线端
a consignment	（货物的）交托，交货，发货，运送，托付物
a shipment	装船，出货
a bulk commodity	散装商品/物品
perishable	易坏的；易腐败的；不经久的；脆弱的；
volume	体积；容量
a dispatch note	发货通知
a consignment note	托运单，寄售挑战书
an air waybill	空运单
an advice note	通知(书/单)
freight charges	货运费

customs clearance and handling charge	报关和手续费
to charter a ship	租船
a shipbroker	船舶经纪人
voyage charter charges	程租(船)费;航次租船费
time charter charges	定期租船契约费
mixed charter	混合租赁
charter party	租船契约,(船只的)租赁
tonnage value	登记吨位/排水量估价
export cargo shipping instruction	出口货装载/发送指示
export cargo packing instructions	出口货包装指示
a shipping mark	发货(装船)标记,运输标志,唛头(货品包装外面注明的标记)
clean bill of lading	清洁提单
dirty bill of lading	不洁提单
to order unto order	指定收货人,指定货单
a shipped bill	已装船提单
a shipping note	船货清单,装货通知单
a dock receipt	码头收据
a wharfinger's receipt	码头管理员收据
all risks	综合保险
negligence	疏忽
to inspect goods	检查货物
fragile	易碎的,脆的
Hague Rules	海牙规则
Acts of War	战争行为,侵略行为
Force majeure	不可抗力

EXERCISES

I. Write a letter to your customer informing him what arrangements you have made for the transport of a consignment of oil.

II. Write a letter according to the following particulars:

As the direct steamer to London is unavailable at the moment, transhipment at Liverpool is therefore compulsory. Request your customer to amend the L/L allowing transhipment and extend the date of shipment and validity to October 18 and 20 respectively.

III. Translate the following letter into English.

贵公司开来的第 118 号信用证已收到，订购的货物将于 11 初由 "和平" 轮装出。因 "海伦" 轮的舱位已满，无法装运，甚歉。一俟装妥即电告船名和开船日期。

IV. Writer a letter, asking a shipping agent to collect a consignment from your warehouse and make all arrangements for transport to Amsterdam. Give imaginary particulars as to name of commodity, names of consignee and say who will take delivery of the consignment upon arrival.

CHAPTER 9

CREDIT

Whether you're the creditor or the applicant, a well-written credit letter is a must.

FORMS OF CREDIT

Credit arrangements between trading firms take two forms:

Bills of exchange, or drafts, by which the seller gives credit to the buyer for the period specified on the bill, e. g. 30, 60 or 90 days.

Open account facilities by which the buyer is allowed to pay for his goods against monthly or quarterly statements.

Requirements for granting credit

Credit facilities will only be granted by a supplier if the customer can satisfy one or more of certain requirements.

1. Reputation

Credit may be given to firms which have an established reputation, i. e. are well-known nationally or internationally.

2. Long-term trading association

If a customer has been trading with a supplier over a period of time and has built up a good relationship with the supplier by, for example, settling accounts promptly, he may be able to persuade his supplier to grant him credit facilities on this basis alone.

3. References

Normally, however, when asking for credit, a customer will supply references, i. e. the names of the concerns or companies which will satisfy the supplier that the customer is reputable and creditworthy. Banks will supply references, though these tend to be brief, stating what the company's capital is and who its directors are. Trade associations, i. e. organizations which represent the company's trade or profession, also tend to give brief references telling the enquirer how long the company has been trading and whether it is a large or small firm. References can also be obtained from the customer's business associates, the commercial departments of embassies, and so on.

Effective Writing of Credit Letters

1. Keep a courteous tone, no matter the circumstances

If you must deny a person credit, discontinue credit, or begin the collection process, maintain a professional tone as you explain your reasons for taking this action. Remember, you'll probably want to keep this customer's business, even if you must ask for cash payments.

If you must deny a request for credit, leave the door open to future applications from the same party.

If payment is more than a month later, encourage the customer to contact you to discuss the lapse in payment.

If a payment is more than 60 days overdue and the customer has shown no move toward making the payment or discussing why he or she has not made payment, let him or her know exactly what the penalty will be unless he or she responds immediately with the payment. Don't make an empty threat, however. You must be prepared to follow through.

2. Be clear and include enough information to clearly convey your request or offer to your client or potential customer

3. Tailor your letter to your audience

Be brief; credit letters should be straightforward and businesslike. Be confident and persuasive. Be assertive but not overbearing. Assure your reader that any information he or she gives you will remain confidential.

4. Credit letters allow you to
- Approve/deny a loan or application for a credit card or increased line of credit.

- Invite a customer or potential client to apply for a loan or line of credit.
- Promise a delayed payment to a creditor.
- Acknowledge payment toward a credit balance or for an overdue balance.
- Explain your reasons for withdrawing the customer's credit option.
- Announce intentions to begin the collection process if a client does not make payment.
- Request that a customer make his or her loan or credit card payment.
- Offer alternative payment plans if a client is unable to meet the current payment obligation.
- Write a letter to a credit bureau stating that they have included inaccurate information on your credit report and ask that this information be corrected or removed, and request that corrected statements be sent to everyone who has been misinformed.
- Work to maintain goodwill and trust.

ASKING FOR CREDIT

Opening

In the opening paragraph of a letter asking for credit facilities, it is best to go straight to the point and specify what form of credit you are looking for.

I am writing to ask if it would be possible for us to have credit facilities in the form of payment by 60-day bill of exchange.

Thank you for your catalogue and letter. As there was no indication of your credit terms, could you let me know if you would allow us to settle on monthly statements?

We appreciate your answering our enquiry so promptly. As I pointed out in my letter to you, our supplier usually allow us open account facilities with quarterly settlements, and I hope that this method of payment will be acceptable to you also.

Convincing your supplier

As mentioned above, your supplier will only grant credit if he is convinced that you will not default. So mention your previous dealing with the supplier.

We believe we have established our reliability with you over the past six months and would now like to settle accounts on a quarterly basis.

During the past few months of our transactions we have always settled promptly, and therefore we feel we can ask for better credit facilities from you.

Mention your reputation, and, of course, offer references.

We are a well-established firm and can offer references if necessary.

We can certainly pay on the due dates, but if you would like confirmation concerning our creditworthiness then please contact any of the following who will act as our referees:...

We deal with most of our suppliers on a quarterly settlement basis and you may contact any of those listed below for a reference.

Closing

We hope you will consider our request favourably and look forward to your reply.

Please follow up the references we have submitted. We look forward to your confirmation that payment by 30-day bill of exchange is acceptable.

As soon as we receive your confirmation that you will allow the open account facilities we have asked for, we will send our next order.

REPLYING TO REQUESTS

Agreeing to credit

If the supplier does not think it necessary to take up references, he may grant credit immediately.

As we have been trading for over a year, references will not be necessary and you may clear your accounts by 30-day bill of exchange which will be sent to Burnley's Bank (Queens Building, Cathays Park, Cardiff CF1 9UJ) with shipping documents for your acceptance.

We are pleased to inform you that the credit facilities you asked for are acceptable, and knowing the reputation of your company there will be no need for us to contact any referees. Just to confirm what has been agreed—settlement will be made against monthly statements. We look forward to receiving your next order.

If references are considered necessary, however, the supplier will acknowledge the request and then reply in full when references have been received.

We have now received the necessary references and are pleased to say that from your next order payment can be made on a quarterly basis against statements.

The referees you gave us have replied and we are able to tell you that from next month you may settle your account on a documents against acceptance basis by 60 d/s B/E.

Refusing credit

When refusing credit facilities, the writer must explain why he is turning the request down. There may be a number of reasons for this. It may be uneconomical for him to offer credit facilities; he may not trust the customer, i. e. the customer has a bad reputation for settling accounts; or it might just be a policy of his company not to give credit. Whatever the reason, the reply must be worded carefully so as not to offend the customer.

Thank you for your letter of 9 November in which you asked to be put on open account terms. Unfortunately we never allow credit facilities to customers until they have traded with us for over a year. We really are sorry that we cannot be more helpful in this case.

We regret that we are unable to offer open account terms to customers as our products are competitively priced and with small profit margin it is uneconomical to allow credit facilities.

We are sorry that we cannot offer credit facilities of any kind at present due to the economic climate viz. rising inflation. However, perhaps if things settle in future we may be able to reconsider your request.

We have considered your request for quarterly settlements, but feel that, with our competitive pricing policy which leaves only small profit margins, it would be uneconomical to allow credit on your present purchases. However, if you can offer the usual references and increase your purchases by at least fifty per cent perhaps we can reconsider the situation.

Negotiating

Sometimes a supplier will not offer as much credit as the customer wants but will negotiate a compromise.

I regret that we cannot offer you credit for as long as three months, since this would be uneconomical for us. However, I am prepared to offer you settlement against monthly statements, and perhaps you will let me know if this would be acceptable.

Though we do not usually offer credit facilities, we would be prepared to consider partial credit. In this case you would pay half your invoices on a cash basis, and the rest by 30-day bill of exchange. If this arrangement suits you, please contact us.

Reply while waiting for references

In some cases you will not be able to grant credit without making further investigations. In particular, you may want to take up the references your customer has offered. In these cases, your reply will be little more than an acknowledgement of the request.

Thank you for your letter in which you asked for credit facilities. At present we are writing to the referees you mentioned and will let you know as soon as we hear from them.

In reply your letter of 8 June we will consider your request to pay by 30-day bill of exchange and will contact you as soon as we have reached a decision.

I received your letter of 15 March, yesterday, in which you asked for open account facilities. As soon as the usual enquiries have been made, I will contact you.

SPECIMEN LETTERS

Request for open-account facilities

Mr. Hughes asks his supplier if he will allow him open facilities. He makes his request while sending an order rather than making his next order conditional on Mr. Cliff's acceptance.

R. Hughes & Son Ltd.

21 Mead Road, Swansea, Glamorgan 3ST 1DR

Telephone: Swansea 58441   VAT No. 215 2261 30
Fax: 881821

Mr. R. Cliff,
Homemakers Ltd. ,
54 – 59 Riverside,
Cardiff CF 1 1JW

Dear Mr. Cliff,

I have enclosed an order, No. B1662, for seven more 'Sleepcomfy' beds which have proved to be a popular line here, and will pay for them as usual on invoice. However, I wondered if in future you would allow me to settle my accounts by monthly statement which would be a more convenient method of payment for me.

As we have been dealing with one another for some time, I think you have enough confidence in my firm to allow open account facilities, but of course I can supply the necessary references.

Yours sincerely,

R. Hughes

R. Hughes

Encl. Order No. B1662

Replying granting open-account facilities

In the following reply, Homemakers are prepared to give credit even though they feel it may not be in the best interests of their customer.

HOMEMAKERS Ltd.
54 – 59 Riverside, Cardiff CF 1 1JW

Telephone (0222) 49721   Registered No. C135162
Fax: 38217

24 July 2005

Mr. R. Hughes
R. Hughees & Son Ltd.
21 Mead Road
Swansea
Glamorgan 3ST 1DR

Dear Mr. Hughes,

Thank you for your order, No. B1662, which will be sent to you tomorrow. I have taken the opportunity to enclose the invoice, DM113, with this letter.

With regard to your request for open account facilities, settlement against monthly statement, I feel there would be more advantage for you in claiming the 3% cash discounts offered for payment within seven days of receipt of invoice. Nevertheless, I am quite prepared to allow monthly settlements, and there will be no need to supply references as you are a long-standing customer.

The enclosed invoice will be included in your next statement.

Yours sincerely,
R. Cliff
R. Cliff

Enc. Invoice DM1113

Request for general credit facilities

A&C (Records) Ltd.

41 – 43 Broadway, Manchester M2 5BP

Directors: J. Allen, P. D. Robins M. A., RC. Frial

Reg. No. 901107
VAT No. 821 621531

Telephone: 061 832 4397

Your ref: JA/MR

3 December 2005

Mr. B. Lyndon
Southern Importers Ltd.
Dane street
Northam
Southampton SO9 4 YQ

Dear Mr Lyndon,

I intend to place a substantial order with you in the next few weeks and wondered what sort of credit facilities your company offered.

As you know, over the past months I have placed a number of orders with you and settled promptly, so I hope this has established my reputation with your company. Nevertheless, if necessary, I am willing to supply references.

Please let me know if I could settle future accounts on, say, quarterly terms with payments against statements. Thank you.

Yours sincerely,

J. Allen

J. Allen

Refusal of credit facilities

In the following reply, Southern Importers turn the request down, even though the two companies have traded for some time.

Southern Importers Ltd.

Dane Street, Northam, Southampton SO9 4 YQ

Directors: B. Lydon, D. C. Crown.

Telephone: 0703 16625

Fax: 312591

Reg. No. England 282533

VAT No. 243 7610 27

Your Ref.

Mr. J. Allen

A&C (Records) Ltd.

41 – 43 Broadway

Manchester M2 5BP

8 December 2005

Dear Mr. Allen,

Thank you for your letter of December 5 in which you enquired about credit facilities.

We appreciate that you have placed a number of orders with us in the past, and are sure that you can supply the necessary references to support your request. However, as you probably realize, our tapes and records are sold at extremely competitive prices which allow us only small profit margins, and this prevents us offering any of our customers credit facilities.

We are very sorry that we cannot help you in this case, but are sure you can understand our reasons.

Once again, thank you for writing, and we look forward to hearing from you soon.

Yours sincerely,
B. Lyndon
B. Lyndon

Request for a change in the terms of payment

MacKenzie Bros. of Canada, as we have seen in previous units, import chinaware from Glaston Potteries in England, they currently pay by letter of credit, but now want to pay on quarterly statements by international banker's draft. This involves fairly long-term draft, so they supply references.

MACKENZIE BROS. LTD.
1 – 5 Whale Drive, Dawson, Ontario, Canada
Branches: Ottawa, Vancouver, New York, Chicago.
Tel: (613) 238 1492 Cable: MAKIE Fax: 315515

Mr. J. Merton   *9 February 2005*
Glaston Potteries Ltd.
Clayfield
Burnley BB10 1RQ
UNITED KONDOM

Dear Mr. Merton,

Our bank has advised us that the proceeds of our letter of credit against your invoice, No. G1197/S, have now been credited to your account.

We have been paying you for some time on this basis, which does not really suit our accounting system, and as we feel you know us well enough by now, we think you would not object to our paying on quarterly statements by international bankers draft.

If you require a reference, you can contact our other suppliers, Pierson & Co., Loius Drive, Dawson, Ontario, who will vouch for us. Write to either Mr. M. Pierson or Mr. J. Tane.

Please confirm that these new terms are acceptable.

Yours sincerely,

R. Mackenzie
R. Mackenzie

Notification of taking up references

Glaston Potteries are sympathetic to Mackenzie Bros. 's Request, but decide to take up the reference offered.

GLASTON POTTERIES Ltd.

Clayfield, Burnley BB 10 1 RQ

Tel: 0315 46125	*Registered No. 716481*
Fax: 8801773	*VAT Registered No. 133 5341 08*

Mr. R. MacKenzie   *14 February 2005*
MacKenzie Bros. Ltd.
1 – 5 Whale Drive
Dawson
Ontario
CANADA

Dear Mr. MacKenzie,

Thank you for your letter of 9 February in which you asked to change your terms of payment to settlement by bankers draft on quarterly statements.

We are taking up the references you offered, and provided it is satisfactory you can consider the new arrangement effective from your next order.

Yours sincerely,
J. Merton
J. Merton
Sales Manager

ASKING ABOUT CREDIT

The guide below gives you an outline on how to take up references and to ask about a company's credit rating.

Opening

Say who you are and why you want the information. Make it clear that the name of the company you are writing to has been given to you as a reference by your customer.

We are a furniture wholesalers and have been asked by L. R. Naismith & Co. Ltd. of 21 Barnsley Road, Sheffield to offer them open account facilities, with quarterly settlement terms. They have given us your name as a reference.

As you will see from the letter heading, we are a glass manufacturers and have recently begun to export to the UK. D. R. Mitchell & Son, who are customers of yours, have placed an order with us, but want to pay by 30-day bill of exchange, and informed us that you would be prepared to act as their referees.

Your branch of the Eastland Bank was given to us as a reference by I. T. S. Ltd. Who have placed a substantial order with us, but want to settle by 40-day draft. As we are a Yugoslavian company, we have little knowledge of British companies and their credit ratings.

Details

Say exactly what you want to know.

We would like to know if the firm is creditworthy and has a good reputation. We would be grateful if you could tell us if the firm is reliable in settling its accounts promptly.

Could you let us know if this firm is capable of repaying a loan of this size within the specified time?

Could you tell us if the firm has a good reputation in your country; whether they can be relied on to settle promptly on due dates, and what limit you would place or have placed on credit when dealing with them?

If the amount of credit is unknown, it is usually mentioned.

The credit will be about £ 2,000. 00.

We do not expect the credit to exceed £ 500. 00.

The draft is for £ 226. 00.

It is unlikely that they will ask for more than a £ 1,000. 00 credit at this stage.

Closing

Thank the firm in advance for giving you the information, and tell them you will reciprocate if the opportunity arises. Also let them know that whatever they say in their letter will be treated in the strictest confidence.

We would like to thank you in advance for the information and can assure you that it will be treated in the strictest confidence.

Your help will be appreciated, and the information will be held in confidence. We will return the service should the opportunity arise.

You can be sure that the information will not be disclosed. Thank you for your assistance, and we will reciprocate in a similar situation in the future.

Using an enquiry agency

We have seen that banks and trade associations will usually only give brief references. Business associates may give more information, but see below an Enquiry Agency will give much more detail about a firm's activities, and for a fee, will research the firm's financial background, its standing, creditworthiness and ability to repay loans or fulfill obligations. When writing to an Enquiry Agency, therefore, you can ask for more.

We have been asked by D. F. Rowlands Ltd. of Milton Trading Estate, Peterborough, to allow them a credit up to £ 5,000. 00 in allowing them to settle by quarterly statements. As we have no knowledge of this firm, would it be possible for you to give us detailed information of their trading activities over, say, the past three years?

The firm named on the enclosed slip has written to us asking if we would allow them to settle by 60-day bill of exchange. Our trading with them so far has only been up to £ 500. 00. But as we know nothing about them or their creditworthiness, would it be possible for you to investigate their business activities over the past few years and give us a detailed report?

Replying to Enquiries about Credit Rating

In most countries there are laws which protect a firm from having its reputation damaged by another company saying or writing things that could harm the firm's good name, and this should be considered when giving details of a company's creditworthiness, or commenting on its standing.

Refusing to reply

There are a number of reasons why you may not wish to reply to an enquiry about one of your customers. If, for example, the company writing to you does not state that you have been named as a referee by their customer, and you do not want to risk offending them, it would be better not to make any comment.

Thank you for your letter concerning our customer, but we cannot give you any information until we get permission from the customer himself. So if you can get the person mentioned in your letter to write to us asking us to act as referees we will give you the necessary information.

As we have not been asked by the person mentioned in your letter to write a reference on their behalf we cannot supply any information about them.

If you do not know enough about the company to comment, then it is better to say so.

With reference to the company you mentioned in your letter of 9 October, we are sorry to say we know little about them as we have only supplied them on a couple of occasions. Therefore we cannot give you any details of their trading record or credit standing.

Thank you for your letter which we received today. Unfortunately we know nothing about the firm you are enquiring about as our only dealings with them have been on a cash basis. We are sorry that we cannot be of help to you in this matter.

Sometimes you may simply not want to give any information about a customer whether you know their reputation or not. In this case a polite refusal, generalizing your statements, is the best course of action.

With reference to your letter of October 16 in which you asked about the credit standing of one of our customers, we are sorry to say that we never give any information about customers to inquirers, and as business associates of ours we are sure you will appreciate that confidence. Perhaps an enquiry agen-

cy could be of more help to you in this.

Replying unfavourably

If you have to write an unfavourable reply, it is better not to mention the name of the company. Give only the few facts as they concern you. Do not offer opinions and remind the firm you are writing to, that the information is strictly confidential.

With reference to your letter of 19 April where you asked us to act as referees for the customer mentioned, we have only dealt with this firm on a few occasions but found they tended to delay payment and had to be reminded several times before their account was cleared. But we have no idea of their trading records with other companies. We are sure you will treat this information in the strictest confidence.

In reply to your letter of 14 September concerning the customer you enquired about, we are sorry to say that we cannot recommend the firm as being reliable in their credit dealings, but this is only based on our own experiences of trading with them. We offer this information on the strict understanding that it will be treated confidentially.

Replying favourably

If giving a favourably reply it is still wise not to mention the customer's name if possible. You can quote that you have yourself allowed credit facilities and also mention that the customer has a good reputation within your trade. In the examples you will see that the reference should still be considered confidential and that the referee takes no responsibility as to how the information is used.

We are pleased to inform you that the firm mentioned in your letter of November is completely reliable and can be trusted to clear their balances promptly on due dates. We find no reason at all for you not offering the facilities they have asked for. However, we take no responsibility as to how this information is used.

With regard to the company mentioned in your letter of 8 December, we are willing to assure you that they have an excellent reputation in dealing with their suppliers, and though we have not given them the credit they have asked you for, we would allow them those facilities if they approached us. Please treat this information in confidence.

Letter to a referee

As notified in previously, Glaston Potteries take up the reference offered by MacKenzie Bros.

GLASTON POTTERIES Ltd.
Clayfield, Burnley BB10 1RQ

Tel: *0315 46125*   *Registered No. 716481*
Fax: *8804773*   *VAT Registered No. 138 5341 08*

Mr. M. Pierson   *16 February 2005*
Pierson & Co.
Louis Drive
Dawson
Ontario
CANADA

Dear Mr. Pierson,

We are suppliers to MacKenzie Bros. Ltd., 1 – 5 Whale drive, Dawson, Ontario, who have asked us to give them facilities to settle their statements on a quarterly basis.

They told us that you would be prepared to act as their referees, and while we have little doubt about their ability to clear their accounts, we would just like confirmation that their credit rating warrants quarterly settlements of up to £ 4,000.00.

We would be extremely grateful for an early reply, and can assure you that it will be treated in the strictest confidence. Thank you.

Yours sincerely,
J. Merton
J. Merton
Sales Manager

Referee's reply

Pierson & Co.
Louis Drive, Dawson, Ontario, Canada.
Tel: (614) 295 1682 Telex: 383172

Mr. Merton   Date: 28 February 2005
Glaston Potteries Ltd.
Burnley BB 10 1RQ
UNITED KINGDOM

Dear Mr. Merton,

I am replying to your enquiry of the 16 February in which you asked about MacKenzie Bros. of Dawson, Ontario.

I contacted them yesterday and they confirmed that they wanted us to act as their referees, and I am pleased to be able to do so.

The firm has an excellent reputation in North America for both service and the way they conduct their business with their associates in the trade.

We have given them credit facilities for years and always found that they paid on due dates without any problems. I might also add that our credit is in excess of the one mentioned in your letter.

I am sure that you can have every confidence in this firm and offer them the facilities asked for.

Yours sincerely,

M. Pierson
M. Pierson

Letter to a referee

Here is another example of taking up references, this one from Satex, the Italian sweater manufacturer we met in previous units. In the letter previous, their customer, F. Lynch, asked to be allowed to settle their accounts by 40-day bill of exchange, documents against acceptance. Lynch offered references which Satex are taking up.

Satex S. P. A.
Via di Pietra Papa, 00146 Roma
Telephone: Roma 769910

Mr. T. Grover   4 July 2005
Grover Menswear Ltd.
Browns Lane
Rugeley
Staffordshire WS15 1DR

Dear Mr. Grover,

Your name was given to us by Mr. L. Crane, the chief buyer of F. Lynch & Co. Ltd, Nasson Hopuse, Newell Street, Birmingham B3 3EL, who have asked us to allow them to settle their account by 40-day draft.

They told us that you would be prepared to act as their referee. We would be grateful if you could confirm that this company settles promptly on due dates, and are sound enough to meet credits of up to £ 3,000.00 in transactions.

Thank you in advance for the information.

Yours sincerely,

D. Causio

D. Causio

Referee's reply

Note how Mr. Grover says he will take no responsibility for how then information is used, and reminds Satex that the letter is confidential.

Grover Menswear Ltd.

Browns Lane, Rugeley, Staffordshire WS 15 1DR
Telephone: 08894 31621 Fax: 246181

Mr. D. Causio   9   July 2005
Satex S. p. A.
Via di Pietra Papa
011146 Roma
ITALY

Dear Mr. Causio,

We have had confirmation from F. Lynch & Co. Ltd. that they want us to act as referees on their behalf, and can give you the following information.

We have been dealing with the firm for ten years and allow them credit facilities of up to £ 2,000 00 which they only use occasionally as they prefer to take advantage of our cash discounts. However, we would have no hesitation in offering them the sort of credit you mentioned, viz. £ 3,000.00, as they are a large reputable organization and very well known in this country.

Of course, we take no responsibility for how you use this information, would remind you to consider it as confidential.

Yours sincerely,
T. Grover
T. Grover

Negative replies to enquiries about credit rating

1. In this letter, the writer refuses to reply because he does not have the company's permission.

Dear Mr. Stevens,

I am replying to your letter of 10 August in which you asked about one of our mutual business associates.

I am afraid I cannot give you the information you asked for as it would be a breach of confidence, and you, as one of our customers would appreciate this. If however, you can get the firm to write instructing us to act as their referee, then we may be able to help you.

Yours sincerely,

2. The reply in this case is unfavourable. Notice how the writer does not refer to the company by name.

Dear Mr. Scrutton,

I am answering your enquiry about the company mentioned in your letter to me of 3 May.

We have in the past allowed that company credit, but nowhere near the amount you mentioned, and we found they needed at least one reminder before clearing their account.

This information is strictly confidential and we take no responsibility as to how it is used.

Yours sincerely,

3. The writer of this letter is unable to reply because he has little knowledge of the company.

Dear Mr. Cox,

In reply to your letter of 10 August, we cannot offer you any information concerning the firm you asked about in your letter.

We have had very little dealing with them and they have never asked for credit of any kind. Therefore any information we gave would be of no relevance.

Yours sincerely,

Letter to enquiry agent

Checking on a customer's credit rating with an Enquiry Agency allows the seller to be more specific about the details he wants concerning his customer.

P. Marlow & Co. Ltd.

31 Goodge Street, London EC 49 4 EE

Telephone: 01 583 6119   Registered in England 221359

VAT 240 7225 03

Mr. S. Spade   9 April 2006

Credit Investigations Ltd.

1 Bird Street

London E1 6TM

Dear Mr. Spade,

I was recommended to you by a previous client of yours, S. Greenstreet & Co. Ltd.

I would like information about Falcon Retailers Ltd. who have asked us to allow them open account facilities with quarterly settlements and credits of up to £ 5,000.00.

Would you please tell us if this firm has had any bad debts in the past; if any court action has been taken against them to recover overdue accounts; what sort of reputation they have amongst suppliers in the trade; whether they have ever traded under another name, and if they have, whether that business has been subject to bankruptcy proceedings?

Please would you make the necessary enquiries, and let us have your fee, so that we can send you a check?

Yours sincerely,

P. Marlow

P. Marlow

Enquiry agent's reply

CREDIT INVESTIGATIONS Ltd.

1 Bird Street, London E1 6 TM
Telephone: 01 623 1494   Reg. London 3121561

Mr. P. Marlow   26 April 2006
P. Marlow & Co. Ltd
31 Goodge Street
London EC 49 4 EE

Dear Mr. Marlow,

We have completed our investigation into Falcon Retailers Ltd. , who you enquired about in your letter dated 9 April 2006.

The firm is a private limited company with a registered capital of £ 1 ,000. 00 and consists of two partners, David and Peter Lorre. It has an annual turnover of £ 50 ,000. 00 and has been trading since October 1971. As far as we know neither the company nor its directors have ever been subject to bankruptcy proceedings, but the firm was involved in a court case to recover an outstanding debt on the 17 January 2004. The action was brought by L. D. M. Ltd. and concerned the recovery of £ 2 ,150. 00 which Falcon eventually paid. But we ought to point out that L. D. M. broke a delivery contact which accounted for the delayed payment.

From our general enquiries we gather that some of Falcon's suppliers have had to send them second and third reminders before outstanding balances were cleared, but this does not suggest dishonestly so much as a tendency to overbuy which means the company needs time to sell before they can clear their accounts.

We hope this information proves useful, and you have any further enquiries, please contact us.

You will find our account for £ 60. 00 enclosed.

Yours sincerely,

S. Spade

S. Spade

Credit Investigations Ltd.
Encl. Account

USEFUL WORDS & EXPRESSIONS

credit	信任,信用,声望,荣誉,[财务]贷方,银行存款
credit facilities/terms	银行对同业提供信用,信用透支,信贷组织,融通便利
credit-worthy	信誉卓著的,有信誉的
credit rating	贷款分配/信用配给
to ask for credit	申请贷款
to grant credit	发放贷款
a reference	证明书,介绍书;证明人,介绍人
a referee	仲裁人,调解人
to offer/take up references	提供证明人
to treat something in confidence	对某事严格保密
confidential	秘密的,机密的
a due date [date of maturity]	到期日,期头,支付日
to settle an account	结清账款
to clear a balance	结清余额
a bad debt	呆账(收不回的账)
to default	疏怠职责,缺席,拖欠,默认
bankruptcy proceedings	破产
a bill of exchange	汇票
a banker's draft	银行汇票
open account facilities	未清结的账目,往来账户设备

documents against acceptance	承兑交单
documents against payment	付款交单
profit margins	利润率
profit on sales	销售利润
profit maximization	利润最大/极大化
profit motive	谋利动机

EXERCISES

I. Translate the following terms into Chinese.
   a bill of exchange
   a banker's draft
   documents against acceptance
   60d/s
   D/P at sight
   rate of exchange
   confirmed, irrevocable L/C
   down payment
   D/A
   amendment to L/C
   revolving L/C
   debit note
   time (usance, term) draft
   financial standing
   credit rating
   open account facilities
   bank reference

II. Write a letter to Bank of China, Shanghai Branch, asking for financial standing concerning Shanghai Textile Import & Export Corp. with whose branch office in Kunming you are doing business.

III. Write a letter to Messrs. R. Hughes & Son Ltd. '21 Mead Road, Swansea, Glamorgan 3ST 1DR, Britain requesting them to amend L/C No. 58183 covering 50,000 dozen of men's shirts by allowing transshipment, and packing in half-dozen carton boxes instead of in one-dozen ones.

CHAPTER 10

BANKING

Banks can be divided into two groups: merchant banks and commercial banks. Merchant banks tend to encourage larger organizations to use their services, and while the facilities they offer are similar to those of the commercial banks, the former specialize in areas of international trade and finance, discounting bills, confirming credit status of overseas customers through confirming houses, acting in the new issue market (placing shares), and in the bullion and Eurobond market. They are, in addition, involved in shipping, insurance, and foreign exchange markets.

Commercial banks offer similar services but are particularly interested in private customers' accounts, encouraging them to use their current account, deposit account, saving account and credit facilities. They will lend money, against securities, in the forms of overdrafts and loans, pay accounts regularly by standing orders, and transfer credits through the bank Giro (直接转账, 汇划) system.

In Great Britain, the difference between the merchant and commercial banks is the latter's availability to customers with their numerous branches through the UK, their low charges, and the laws which govern the way each organization handles its affairs.

COMMERCIAL FACILITITES IN THE UK

Current accounts

Current accounts can be owned by anyone in the UK provided they can supply a reference or references. The advantages of this sort of account includes the facility to pay anyone, anywhere, at any time, by check, provided there are funds in the account. As a matter of extra security the customer, when paying by check, is usually required to provide a check card, which as a rule makes the bank responsible for the check he passes up to the limit stated on the card.

Although checks can be drawn immediately without notice to the bank, they will take three working days to pass before the amount will be debited or credited to an account.

When depositing cash or checks, a paying-in slip is used to record the deposit, its counterfoil, with the bank's stamp and cashier's initials, being proof that the deposit was made.

It is possible to overdraw the account, i. e. take out more money that there is in credit, but this can only be done with the bank manager's agreement, otherwise any checks exceeding the customer's credit may not be honoured.

There is usually no interest paid on current account credit balances, and charges are made for transactions.

Many firms have more than one current account, e. g. a No. 1 account for paying wages and overheads, and a No. 2 account for paying their suppliers.

Deposit accounts

Deposit accounts pay interest at a rate that is linked to the Bank of England's minimum lending rate to a maximum established by the bank, but the customer can be asked to give notice of withdrawal, and can only withdraw on a slip given to him at the counter. Naturally no check book is supplied, and there are no overdraft facilities on these accounts.

A special type of deposit account, on which no interest is paid, is a budget account, in which funds are held by the bank to pay domestic bills on behalf of the customer. The bank will spread the bills over twelve months so that the customer will not have to face one large amount at the end of the year.

Credit cards

Credit cards, can serve as identification when paying by check, but they also offer credit facilities up to the amount stated on the card. Customers are not usually charged interest for up to 25 days, after which they are charged at the rate of 2% per month.

Standing orders

Standing orders are periodic payments made by the bank on behalf of its customer and debited to the customer's account. They are used to pay rent on mortgage payments, subscriptions to clubs and associations etc.

Direct debits

Another type of order to pay, similar to a standing order, is a direct debit. With this form of payment the customer cannot cancel the order, as he can with a standing order, unless the payee agrees. This therefore guarantees payment to the payee for the period stated. A seller making a hire-purchase payment might demand a direct debit to ensure the customer does not cancel payment.

Loans and overdrafts

Loads secured from banks are usually based on a formal agreement between the bank and the customer with the loan being covered by a negotiable security, e. g. shares, and with repayment specified on the agreement. Interest is usually calculated half-yearly and is not controlled by law, but by current market rates. The money for the loan is immediately deposited in the customer's account.

Overdrafts, unless for a very small amount, require some security, and are charged at 2% above the minimum lending rate. Banks reserve the right to call in the overdraft whenever they think necessary. Unlike loans, they are not deposited in a customer's account, but are permission to overdraw an account by a stipulated amount.

A bank may refuse a loan or overdraft for a number of reasons:
- The customer cannot support the loan with security or find a guarantor.
- The bank feels the customer would be a bad risk, e. g. he had not kept a steady balance on his current account, and has been overdrawn.
- The bank has been instructed by the Bank of England (who is their banker) to restrict credit as the government wants to contract the economy to fight inflation, or it has been directed to lend only to particular areas of the economy, e. g. the export market or industry, and not to the service section of the economy (i. e. retailers, professions etc.)

SPECIMEN LETTERS

Opening a current account

The owner of a fashion shop applies to open a current account. The bank manager will acknowledge the letter, telling the customer that the account has been opened and the money credited, and either enclose a check book or let her know that one is being made up for her.

Dear Mr. Day,

I am writing to you with reference to our conversation three days ago when we discussed my opening a current account with your branch.

I would appreciate it if you could open a current a/c for me under my trading name R & S Fashions Ltd, 915 East Street, Brighton, Sussex. Enclosed you will find two specimen signatures, my own and my partner's, Miss Catherine Sidden, and both signature will be required on all checks. I have included a reference from Mr. Young, who banks with your branch, a check for £ 57. 00 from a customer, and a paying-in slip which I picked up in the bank the other day.

Yours sincerely,

Change of signature

The bank must be informed of any change of address and, as here, of a change in the signatures required on checks.

Dear Mr. Winston,

Will you please note that as from 11 August 2005 the two signatures that will appear on checks for our number 1 and 2 accounts will be mine and our new accountant Mr. Harold Lloyd who is taking over from Mr. David Story?

I enclose a specimen of Mr. Lloyd's signature and look forward to your acknowledgement.

Yours sincerely,

Request for a standing order

Dear Sir,

Account No. 33152 1109601

We have just moved to new premises at the above address and would like to pay our monthly rent of £ 574. 00 to our landlords, Richards & Long; 30 Blare Street, London SW7 1LN, by standing order.

Would you please arrange for £ 574. 00 to be transferred from our No. 2 account to their account with Dewlands Bank, Leadenhall Street, London EC2, on the lst of every month, beginning 1 May this year?

Please confirm that the arrangement has been made.

Yours faithfully,

Cancellation of a check

Cancelling a check must be done in writing, not on the phone. Banks are obliged to pay checks if the payer has funds in his current account, so the bank will want written proof to protect them.

Dear Sir,

Please would you cancel check No. 178921 65001 for £ 1,672.00 in favour of B. Gelt Ltd? The check appears to have been lost in the post and I am sending another in its place.

Yours faithfully,

Transfer of money from current account to deposit account

Dear Mr. Collis,

Please would you transfer £ 2,500.00 from my current account to my deposit account? The account numbers and details are on the enclosed transfer slip, and I would be grateful if you could stamp the counterfoil and return it to me.

Yours sincerely,

Advice of an overdrawn account

Banks prefer not to stop payments because of the embarrassment it can cause the customer, but if there has not been an arrangement for overdraft facilities, and the check, in the bank manager's opinion, is too large, he will stop it. In the case of Mr. Hughes, however, the bank manager lets the credit transfer go through.

Welsh Co-operative Bank

Chairman: A. C. M. Conway   *Directors:* R. M. Lloyd, C. R. Gymre A. I. S

Seaway house, Glendower Road, Swansea, Glamorgan 8RN 1TA

Reg. No.: Swansea 385 1623   Telephone (0792) 469008
Telex: 84903

Mr. R. Hughes   8 August 2005
R. Hughes & Son Ltd.
21 Meads Road
Swansea
Glamorgan 3ST 1DR

Dear Mr. Hughes,

<u>Account No. 0566853 01362</u>

I am writing to inform you that you now have an overdraft of £ 158. 63 on current account.

I allowed your last credit transfer to Homemakers Ltd. to pass as you have a large Credit balance on your deposit account. But I would point out that we cannot allow overdraft facilities unless you make a formal arrangement with the bank. If you would like to do this, please contact me and we can discuss it. Alternatively, would you make sure that your current account is in credit? Thank you.

Yours sincerely,

D. Collis

D. Collis
Manager

Reply to advice of an overdrawn account

Mr. Hughes is aware that the credit transfer could have been stopped, which would have been embarrassing to him, especially as he had arranged monthly settlements with Homemakers only recently and there had earlier been a problem over a credit transfer.

R. Hughes & Son Ltd.

21 Mead Road, Swansea, Glamorgan 3ST 1DR
Telephone: Swansea 58441   VAT no. 215 2261 30
Fax: 881821

The Manager   10 August 2005
Welsh Co-operative Bank Ltd.
Seaway House
Glendower Road
Glamorgan 8 RN 1TA

Dear Mr. Collis,

Thank you for your letter of 8 August. Please allow me to apologize for my oversight in not realizing I had a debit balance on my current account.

The reason I did not realize I had overdrawn my account was that I had received a post-dated check for £ 300. 000 from a customer which had not been cleared. However, to avoid a repletion I have transferred £ 5 ,000. 00 from my deposit account and this should ensure against overdrawing in the future.

Thank you for allowing the credit transfer to Homemakers to go through despite the debit balance it created.

Yours sincerely,
R. Hughes

R. Hughes

Request for an overdraft or loan

In this letter Mr. Cliff of Homemakers Ltd. wants to obtain either an overdraft or loan to expand his furniture factory. He asks for an appointment to discuss the matter, and explains why he needs the money.

HOMEMAKERS Ltd.

54 – 59 Riverside, Cardiff CF 1 1JW
Telephone: (0222) 49721   Registered No. C135162
Fax: 382176

The Manager   18 September 2005
Barnley's Bank Ltd.
Queens Building
Cathays Park
Cardiff CF 1 9UT

Dear Mr. Evans,

I would like to make an appointment to see you to discuss either a loan or overdraft to enable me to expand my business.

Over the past year I have been testing the market with a new line—furniture assembly kits—and have found that demand for these kits, both here and overseas, has exceeded my expectations. In the past six months alone I have had over £ 60,000 worth of orders, half of which I could not fulfill because of my limited resources.

I will need a loan for about £ 8,000. 00 to buy additional equipment and raw materials. I can offer £ 2,000. 00 in IBM ordinary shares, and £ 3,000. 00 in local government bonds as part security for the loan, which I estimate it will take me about nine months to repay.

I enclose an audited copy of the company's current balance sheet, which I imagine you will wish to inspect, and I look forward to hearing from you.

Yours sincerely,
R. Cliff
R. Cliff

Encl.

Grant of a loan

The bank manager has now seen Mr. Cliff and checked his accounts to make sure that the business has been doing as well as the owner said. He has considered the matter of the overdraft or loan, and is now replying.

BARNLEY'S BANK Ltd.

Chairman B. Davenport F. I. D   Telephone: (0222) 825316   *Head Office*
Directors: *B. R. Lewin V. C. D. F. C. C. I. S.* Fax: 841132   *Queens Building*
  A. L. Bradwin A. I. C. A.   *Cathays Park*
  N. CHARDIS   Reg. No Cardiff 3516614   *Cardiff*
  CF1 9UJ

Mr. R. Cliff   Date: 27 September 2005
Homemakers Ltd.

54 – 59 riverside
Cardiff CF 1 1 JW

Dear Mr. Cliff,

With reference to our meeting on 23 September, I am pleased to tell you that the credit for
£ 8,000.00 which you requested has been approved.

I know we discussed an overdraft, but I think it would be better if the credit were given in the form of
a loan at the current rate of interest which is 15 per cent, and which will be calculated on half-yearly
balances.

The loan must be repaid by June 2005 and we will hold the £ 2,000.00 IBM ordinary shares and
£ 3,000.00 local government bonds you pledged as security. We agreed that the other £ 3,000.00
was to be guaranteed by Mr. Y. Morgan. Your business associate, and I would appreciate it if you
could ask him to sign the enclosed guarantor's form, and if you would sign the attached agreement.

The money will be credited to your current account and available from September 30 subject to your returning both forms by that time.

I wish you luck with the expansion of your business and look forward to hearing from you.

Yours sincerely,
T. Evans
I. Evans
Manager

Encls.

Refusal of an overdraft

Mr. Ellison's company owns a chain of petrol stations and garages. He is also a customer of
Barnley's Bank and has also asked for an overdraft, but in his case the bank is not willing to lend
him the money.

BARNLEY'S BANK Ltd.

Chairman B. Davenport F. I. D   Telephone: (0222) 825316   Head Office
Directors: B. R. Lewin V. C. D.. F. C. C. I. S.   Fax: 8411325   Queens Building
      A. L. Bradwin A. I. C. A.   Cathays Park

Mr. P. Ellison   Date: 19 November 2005
Ellison & Co. Ltd.
Bridgend Road
Bridgend 1F31 3DF

Dear Mr. Ellison,

I am sorry to inform you that we will not be able to offer the credit you asked for in your letter of 14 November.

You have had an overdraft in the past year which partly influenced our decision, but there is also a credit squeeze at present which has particularly affected loans to the service section of the economy. I sympathize with you when you say that you have been offered a rare opportunity to expand your business if you can secure the £ 5,000.00 additional capital. With regard to this, may I suggest that if there are no other possibilities for you to raise the money, perhaps you could approach a Finance Corporation who might be willing to help.

I am sorry that we have to disappoint you in this matter, and hope that we may be of more help in the future.

Yours sincerely,

J. Evans
I. Evans
Manager

INTERNATIONAL BANKING

In previous chapters we looked at various methods of payment used in foreign trade. In this section we look in detail at two methods of payment, bills of exchange and documentary credits, and the way in which they involve banks at home and abroad.

Bills of exchange

A bill of exchange is an order sent by the drawer (the person asking for the money) to the drawee (the person paying) stating that the drawee will pay on demand or at a specified time the amount shown on the bill. If the drawee accepts the bill, he will sign his name on the face of it and date it.

The bill can be paid to a bank named by the drawer, or the drawee can name a bank he wants to use to clear the bill. If this is the case, the bill will be kept in the drawer's bank until it is to be paid. When the bill is due it is presented to the paying bank. Such bills are said to be domiciled with the bank holding them.

A sight draft, or sight bill is paid on presentation. In a documents against payment (D/P) transaction, the sight draft is presented to the importer with the shipping documents, and the importer pays immediately, i. e. "on presentation" or "at sight".

A bill paid "after date" or "after sight" can be paid on or within the number of days specified on the bill. Therefore, "30 days after sight" means that the bill can be paid 30 days after it has been presented.

Overseas bills in the UK are known as foreign bills, and those used within the UK as inland bills. A clean bill is one that is not accompanied by shipping documents.

The advantage for the exporter of payment by bill is that the draft can be discounted, i. e. sold, to a bank at a percentage less than its value, the percentage being decided by the current market rates of discounting. So even if the bill is marked 90 days, the exporter can get his money immediately. The advantage for the importer is that he is given credit, provided the bill is not a sight draft. The bank, however, will only discount a bill if the buyer has a good reputation.

Bills can be negotiable if the drawer endorses the bill. If the beneficiary wants to pay another manufacturer, he could write on the back of the bill, i. e. endorse it, and the bill would become payable to the person who owns it.

It is possible to send the bill direct to the importer, if he is well known to the exporter, or if not, to his bank which will hand it to him with the documents for either acceptance or payment.

A dishonoured bill is one that is not paid on the due date. In this case the exporter will protest the bill, i. e. he will go to a notary, a lawyer, who will, after a warning, take legal action to recover the debt.

The abbreviations B/E for bill of exchange and d/s for days after sight are often used. And you are now familiar with D/P, documents against payment and D/A, documents against acceptance.

SPECIMEN LETTERS AND FORM: BILL OF EXCHANGE
TRANSACTION

Letter advertising dispatch of a bill

Panton Manufacturing Ltd. have completed an order for a Dutch customer. They now advise him that the agreed bill of exchange has been sent off.

Panton Manufacturing Ltd.

Panton Works, Hounslow, Middlesex, TW6 2 BQ

Tel: 353 0215   *Registered No: England 266135*
Fax: 353 0215

Mr. B Haas,   2 March 2005
A. Haas B. V.
Heldringstraat 280 – 2
Postbus 5411,
Amsterdam 1007,
NETHERLANDS

Dear Mr. Haas,

Order No. 8842

Thank you for your order which has now been completed and is being sent to you today.

As agreed we have forwarded our bill, No. 1671 for £ 860. 00 with the documents to your bank, Nederlandsbank, Heldringstraat, Amsterdam. The draft has been made out for payment 30 days after sight, and the documents will be handed to you on acceptance.

Yours sincerely,

D. Panton
D. Panton

Managing Director

Bill of exchange

Here is the bill mentioned in the previous letter. The bill has already been accepted by the drawee, who has named a bank in London which he wants to use to clear the bill.

<u>B/E No. 1671</u>   *5 March 2005*

30 days after sight pay to the order of
Panton Manufacturing Ltd. London
<u>*Eight hundred and sixty pounds only*</u>
value received payable at the current rate exchange for Banker's
sight drafts on London.

To. B. Haas B. V.
Heldringstraat 180 – 2
Amsterdam 1007

Signed: *D. Panton*
Managing Director

Letter advising dispatch of a sight draft

If a supplier wants immediate payment or does not have time to check the customer's creditworthiness, he may send a sight draft, as in the following example.

Panton Manufacturing Ltd.

Panton Works, Houslow, Middlesex, TW6 2 BQ

Tel: *353 0215*
Fax: *353 0215*

Registered No: *England 266135*

Mr. J. Lindquvist,
Lindquvist A. S.,
Vestergade 190 – 2,
DK 1171,
Copenhagen K,

10 June 2005

DENMARK

Dear Mr. Lindquvist,

We have made up your order, No. 8540, which is now abroad the <u>SS Leda</u> which sails for Copenhagen tomorrow.

We are sure you will be pleased with the selection of items that we were able to get from stock. As there was no time to check references, we have drawn a sight draft which will be sent to Nordbank, Garnes Vej, Copenhagen, and will be presented to you with the documents for payment.

If you can supply two references before placing your next order, we will put the transaction on a documents against acceptance basis with payment 30 days after sight.

Yours sincerely,

D. Panton

D. Panton
Managing Director

Request to a bank to forward a bill

Exporters sometimes ask their banks to forward bills to importers' banks.

Panton Manufacturing Ltd.
Panton Works, Houslow, Middlesex, TW6 2 BQ

Tel: 353 0215
Fax: 353 0215

Registered No: England 266135

The manager,

4 July 2005

Midland Bank Ltd. ,
Portman House,
Great Portland Street,
London WIN6 LL

Dear Sir,

Please would you send the enclosed draft on J. K. B. Products Pty. and documents to the National Australian Bank, 632 George Street, Sydney, Australia, and tell them to release the documents on acceptance?

Yours sincerely,

D. Panton
D. Panton

Managing Director

Encl.

Request to a bank to accept a bill

The Australian importer mentioned in the previous letter now writes to his bankers to tell them to accept the bill.

J. K. B. Products Pty.

President: D. Bruce   Managing Director: L. Thompson   Directors: I. R. Marsh, T. L. Bradman
Bridge House, 183-9 Kent Street, Sydney NSW 2000

Telephone: 02 279611
Fax: 2121608

Date: 18 July 2005

The Manager
National Australian Bank
632 George street
Sydney NSW 2000

Dear Sir,

You will shortly be receiving a bill of exchange for £ 2,163. 00 and relevant documents from Panton Manufacturing Ltd. , England. Would you please accept the draft on our behalf, send us the documents, and debit our account?

Yours faithfully,
L. Corey

L. Corey

J. K. B. Products Pty.

Non-payment of a bill

If a customer cannot pay a bill, he must inform his supplier immediately. When a bill is not paid and no notice has been given, the supplier usually writes to the customer before protesting the draft, as here. Note the expression "Refer to Drawer" which means the bank is returning the bill to the drawer. (This expression is also used when a dishonored check is returned.) Also notice that a formal protest is to be made, which means that the drawer will contact a lawyer to handle the debt, if payment is not made within the specified time.

Panton Manufacturing Ltd.

Panton Works, Houslow, Middlesex, TW6 2 BQ

Tel: 353 0215
Fax: 353 0215

Registered No: England 266135

Mr. B. Haas,
B. Haas B. V. ,
Heldringstraat 180 – 2
Postbus 5411
Amsterdam 1007
NETHERLANDS

10 April 2005

Dear Mr. Haas,

B/E No. 1671

The above bill for £ 860. 00 was returned to us from our bank this morning marked "Refer to Drawer".

The bill was due on the 5 April and appears to heave been dishonoured. We are prepared to allow you a further three days before presenting it to the bank again, in which time we hope that the draft will have been met.

If the account is still not settled, we will have to make formal protest, which we hope will not be necessary.

Yours sincerely,

D. Panton

D. Panton

Managing Director

USEFUL WORDS & EXPRESSIONS

a merchant bank	商业银行
to open an account	开立账户
a current account	经常账户
a deposit account	有息存款；储蓄存款
a savings account	储蓄存款账户
a budget account	［科目］预算账户
a specimen signature	签字样本，印鉴样本
a balance	收支差额，结余，余额
a transaction	交易
Giro system	直接转账制度
a traveller's check	旅行支票
Eurocheck	欧洲货币支票（一种在若干欧洲国家通用的信用卡）
a check card	英国银行发行的支票卡
a credit card	信用卡，签账卡
to honour a check	兑付支票
to cancel a check	取消支票
to stop a check	停付支票
a paying-in slip	缴款凭单，存款单据
a withdrawal slip	提款单
a transfer slip	拨单，转账传票
notice of withdrawal	收回/退回/取消通知

a counterfoil	支票存根，票根，存根
a cashier	（商店等的）出纳员，（银行或公司的）司库
negotiable securities	流通证券，有价证券
a guarantor	[律]保证人
a loan	（借出的）贷款，借出
an overdraft	透支，透支之款项
to overdraw	透支
overdraft facilities	透支贷款
minimum lending rate（MLR）	最小值贷款/借款利率
inflation	通货膨胀，（物价）暴涨
bank charges	银行收费
a standing order	委托书，现行命令
credit status	信用评价/评价
confirming houses	保付行，保付公司
bullion	金条，金块；银条，银块
Euro-bond market	欧洲债券市场
foreign exchange market	外汇市场
a bill of exchange	汇票
a drawer	出票人
a drawee	收票人，付款人
a sight draft	即期汇票，见票即付票据
a sight bill	即期票据，见票即付票据
days after sight（d/s）	见票后……日（付款）
documents against payment（D/P）	付款交单
documents against acceptance（D/A）	承兑交单
a foreign bill	外汇汇票
an inland bill	国内汇票
a clean bill（of exchange）	光票

to discount a bill	扣兑汇票，贴现承兑汇票
to endorse a bill	票据背书
a dishonoured bill	退票，拒付票据
to protest a bill	拒付汇票
a revocable letter of credit	可撤销信用证
an irrevocable letter of credit	不可撤销信用证
confirmed credit	保兑信用证
commission	佣金

EXERCISES

I. Translate the following terms into Chinese：
 a merchant bank
 to open an account
 a current/deposit/savings/budget
 Giro system
 A check/ Eurocheck/ traveller's
 a credit card
 to honour a check
 to cancel a check
 to stop a check
 a paying-in/withdrawal/ transfer slip
 notice of withdrawal
 a counterfoil
 a cashier
 to overdraw
 overdraft facilities
 minimum lending rate （MLR）
 a standing order
 credit status
 a bill of exchange
 a drawer
 a drawee
 a sight draft/ bill
 days after sight （d/s）

documents against payment (D/P)
documents against acceptance (D/A)
a foreign bill
an inland bill
a clean bill
to discount a bill
to endorse a bill
a dishonoured bill
to protest a bill
a revocable/ irrevocable letter of credit
confirmed credit

II. Write to Citibank asking them to open an irrevocable letter of credit for £ 5,000 in favour of H & G Co. Ltd. to cover a consignment of PC Computers. The credit is to be available for four months from the date of your letter. The supplier's draft at 90 days will be accepted by the bank 's branch office in China.

III. Write a letter for H & G Co. Ltd. to the correspondent bank giving details of the shipment and enclosing shipping documents together with draft for their acceptance.

IV. Write a letter in English asking for amendments in the following letter of credit by checking it with the given contract terms:

The Standard Chartered Bank

No. 2005/088

Date: October 28, 2005

Irrevocable Credit

To: Kunming Garments I/E Corp.

Gentlemen,

You are authorized to draw on us for account of Chinatown Company for a sum not exceeding USD 96,000 (Say US Dollar Ninety-six Thousand Only) available by draft drawn in duplicate at sight accompanied by the following documents:

1. Signed Commercial Invoice in duplicate, indicating S/C No. 2005/182.
2. Full set of Clean on Board Bills of Lading made out to order and blank endorsed, marked "freight prepaid" covering 100 dozen silk blouses.
3. One original insurance policy/certificate covering Marine and War risks for 130% of the invoice value.

   Shipment from China port to San Francisco, USA.

   Shipment to be effected before Nov. 29, 2005.

This credit is valid at our end until Dec. 10, 2005.

No. 2005/182 合同的主要内容：

卖方：昆明服装进口公司

买方：Chinatown Company

1000 打真丝衬衫，每打 CIF San Francisco USD 96；由卖方按发票金额 110% 投保综合险和战争险；信用证可转让。

CHAPTER 11

AGENTS AND AGENCIES

Agents and agencies are appointed by firms to represent them. There is a wide range of activities concerning representation and although in this chapter we will mainly be dealing with buying and selling agencies, it would be useful to look at other areas where companies act on behalf of their clients, as they will be referred to later.

TYPES OF AGENCIES

Brokers

Brokers usually buy or sell goods for their principals (the firms they represent) and sometimes never handle the consignment themselves. There are various types of brokers, and the list below will give you an idea of the sort of broking facilities that exist.

Stockbrokers on the Stock exchange buy and sell shares for their clients, who cannot go on to the "floor" of the Exchange and deal for themselves if they are not members. The client asks the broker to buy or sell shares for him, and the broker takes a commission on the purchase or sale.

Ship brokers arrange for ships to transport goods for their clients.

Insurance brokers arrange insurance cover with underwriters who pay compensation in the event of a loss.

The Commodity Markets. In these markets brokers buy and sell commodities, e. g. cocoa, tea, coffee, rubber etc. , on behalf of their clients.

The Metal Exchange, i. e. the market for buying and selling ores and metals in bulk, also employs brokers to deal on behalf of companies.

Confirming houses

These agents often receive orders from abroad, place them, arrange for packing, shipment, insurance and sometimes finance or purchase the goods themselves, then resell them to the client. They may act on a commission, but if buying on their own account will make a profit on the difference between the ex-works price and the resale price they quote the importer.

Export managers

If a firm does not have a branch in the country it is exporting to, they can appoint an Export Manager. He will deal under his own name, but use the address of the company he represents. His job is primarily to develop the market for the exporter, and for his services he may charge a fee, or arrange for a profit-sharing scheme between himself and the exporter.

Factors

These agents can buy and sell in their own names, i. e. on their own account, receive payment, and send accounts to their principals. They often represent firms exporting fruit or vegetables.

Manufacturing agents

This agent represents a manufacturer and obtains goods, then resells them. The agent may work on a commission, i. e. buying the goods on consignment, or, if described as a member, he will buy the goods from the manufacturer on his own account, that is to sell them for his own profit. If he is a sole agent, he agrees only to sell his principal's products, and not those of a competitor, and the manufacturer would probably agree not to supply the sole agent's rivals in his country.

Buying agents

Buying Agents, or Buying Houses, buy products on behalf of a principal and receive a commission. The agency is employed to get the best possible terms for their principal, and will try to find the most competitive rates in shipping and insurance for them. Buying Houses often act on behalf of large stores.

FINDING AN AGENT

It is possible to find an agent through a number of sources: advertising; in Trade Journals; contacting government departments of trade in your own country or the country you wish to export to; consulting Chambers of Commerce, Consulates, Trade Associations and banks. Letters to these organizations are routine, and the guide below gives you an indication of how these letters are laid out.

Opening

Tell the organization who you are.

We are a large manufacturing company specializing in...

We are one of the leading products of ...

You probably associate our name with the manufacture of chemicals/textiles/ business machines /heavy/ engineering...

Explaining what you want

We are looking for an agent who can represent us in...

We would like to appoint a sole agent in Scotland to act on our behalf selling...

We are trying to find an established firm who will represent us in selling our products.

Closing

Close by saying that you would be grateful for any help that can be given.

We would be grateful if you could supply us with a list of possible agents.

We hope you can help us, and look forward to hearing from you.

Thank you in advance for your help, and we look forward to receiving your recommendations.

OFFERING AN AGENCY

Once you have found out the names and addresses of prospective agents, you can write to them direct. Below is a guide for manufacturers offering terms to a prospective agent.

Opening

Tell the agent how you obtained his name.

You were recommended to us by the Saudi Arabian Trade Commission in London.

Mr. Milos Petric of the Jugobank Export Department wrote to us telling us that ...

We are writing to you because we were told by the London Chamber of Commerce that you might be interested in a sole agency to handle our products.

Explain who you are.

We are an established company manufacturing ...

We are the leading exporters of ...

We are one of the main producers of chemicals/ steel/kitchenware/ furniture/chinaware/industrial equipment etc.

Convincing the prospective agent

Convince the agent that the products you make are worth taking and will sell in his market.

As you can see from our catalogue, we can offer a wide range of products which have attractive designs, are hard-wearing, light, easy to use, and fully guaranteed for one year.

You will notice that the prices quoted are extremely competitive for a product of this quality. We know there is a growing demand for this product in your country and are sure that once our brand is established, it will lead the market.

Exclusive or non-exclusive agency

There are two types of agency: a sole or exclusive agency, when your agent will only be supplied by you in a particular area, and when he will not sell products that compete with yours; and a non-exclusive agency where there is no such undertaking. The agency contract explains the conditions on which the agency will be operated and what the rights and obligations of the agent and principal are.

We will not restrict the agent by offering a sole agency as we have found that this limits our own sales, and is sometimes awkward for the agent himself.

We are offering a sole agency which will mean that you will not have competition from our products in the area specified in the contract.

We cannot offer an exclusive agency for Zambia at present. However, if the agency is successful we may reconsider a sole agency in the future.

It should be established whether you are going to deal with your agent on a consignment basis, when the agent will not own the products you send, but will sell them on a commission basis; or whether you want to supply the agent for him to re-sell to customers on his own account, in which case he will decide on resale prices and take the profits from his sales.

We generally do not deal on a consignment basis, but prefer our agents to buy our products on their own account. They usually prefer this method as it proves more profitable for them and allows them greater freedom in determining prices.

Area to be covered

Make it clear what region or area the agency is for.

You will have sole distribution rights for the whole of Shanghai, which will give you an excellent opportunity to establish a wide range of customers.

Initially we will give you a sole agency for the Guangzhou region, but if sales are successful, we will extend that to other regions.

As sole agents you will have no competition from our products in South Africa, therefore with effective selling you would be able to get a large return.

Commission

Some firms offer terms in an initial enquiry, others wait until they have had a reply from the prospective agent. If offering terms, however, you should make them sound as inviting as possible.

The agency we are offering will be on a commission, and as we are very interested in getting into the Australian market, we are prepared to off a 15% commission to our agent, plus a substantial advertising allowance.

As the agency will be a sole agency, to prevent a competitive product being sold, we are prepared to offer a generous commission as compensation, and a reasonable allowance for expenses.

As an inducement to the agent we appoint, we will be offering a 12 per cent commission on net prices.

Settlement of accounts

Orders should be sent to us direct for shipment, and we will arrange for customers to pay us. You may issue us with quarterly/monthly statements of account which will be paid sight draft at the bank of your choice.

We would expect you to supply orders from your stock, or we will ship consignments as soon as you send the order to us.

Customers should pay us direct by letter of credit, on each sale, and we will remit your commission by bill once you have submitted your monthly/quarterly account. Credit is not to be offered without our express consent.

Support from the principal

The prospective agent will want to know what support you will give him in his efforts to sell your goods.

Our products of course carry a one-year guarantee and we will replace any faulty item carriage paid.

As you know, our company offers a full after-sales service, which is essential in establishing the reputation of our brands, and your customers need have no worries about spare parts or maintenance.

We will offer you additional expenses of £ 5,000.00 per annum for any advertising that you think will help sell the products. This will be increased after a year if we think sales warrant it.

Delivery

Providing there are no unforeseen delays we will be able to deliver six weeks from receipt of order.

We would hope that you will keep large stocks of our three main ranges, however, we will be able to deliver within a month of receiving orders.

Delivery should not take longer than three weeks providing we have the items in stock.

Duration of the contract

The length of time for the contract is usually discussed after the agency has been agreed. Nevertheless, it would be as follows.

The contract will be from 1 October for one year, and, provided both parties agrees, will be renewed for a further year.

We feel that nine months should be ample time to decide whether it is worth continuing with sales, and will make out the first contract accordingly.

Subject to our mutual agreement, the contract will be renewed annually.

Disagreements and disputes

A provision is usually made for disagreements and disputes. This too, would not usually appear in an opening letter, but in correspondence confirming the agency.

In the case of disagreement over conditions or payments, the matter will be settled by arbitration.

As a rule we follow American law to determine legal disputes over contracts.

Special terms

In some cases agents are offered special terms if they are prepared to hold themselves liable (responsible) for their customers' debts. These agents receive a 'del credere commission', which is a special commission to compensate them for the risk they take.

We are prepared to offer an extra $2\frac{1}{2}$% del credere commission if you are willing to be responsible for customers' debts.

In addition to the 12% commission on net sales, we will offer a further 3% del credere commission, if you are willing to deposit £ 5,000.00 as a security to guarantee all customers' debts.

ASKING FOR AGENCY

Here is a guide to the kind of letter you should write if you want to offer your services as an agent to a manufacturer.

Opening

Explain who you are and how you saw or heard of the manufacturer's product.

We are a large importing agency situated in Bangkok dealing in agricultural equipment. Last month at the International Farming Equipment Exhibition, in Bombay, we saw a selection of your products and were impressed with them.

You were recommended to us by our associates Lindus Products Ltd. , of Lagos, who told us that you were looking for an agent to represent you in oil-drilling equipment in China.

Convincing the manufacturer

You have to convince the supplier first that there is a market for his product in your country or area, and second that you are the best person to develop the market and sell his goods.

As you know China is extending its farming areas with the aid of government grants to farmers and this expansion is creating a demand for all forms of motorized agricultural machinery, particularly with regard to your products which are geared to jungle-clearing and reclamation programmes. We ourselves have many contacts in the government who will direct us to large-scale farms and enterprises who are in the market for your products.

We have an established reputation in Canada for supplying oil companies here with excavation and drilling equipment and are quite willing to offer you references. We can also assure you of excellent sales prospects as the oil industry is rapidly expanding.

Because we have already established business relationships with hospitals and clinics here in Saudi Arabia we are sure that we would be the best company to represent you here. And as you are probably aware, the development of the health service here means that generous grants to clinics and hospitals have increased the demand for the more sophisticated equipment that you manufacture.

Suggesting terms

You may want to leave discussion of terms until after you know that the supplier is interested in your request. But there is no harm, even at this stage, in describing the terms on which you normally operate and asking if they would be acceptable in the present case.

May we suggest the terms we usually operate on to give you an idea of the sort of agency contract we are considering? We generally represent our principals as sole agents for France buying products on our own account, with an initial contract to run for one year, renewable by mutual agreement. We expect manufacturers to offer advertising support in the form of brochures—in France and English—and catalogues, and in return we promise our customers a full after-sales service and two-year guarantees on all products. Therefore we would expect a first class spare-parts service with delivery for both manufactures and spare parts within six weeks of receipt of order. We would pay you direct by 40-day bill of exchange, documents against acceptance. If this type of agency interests you, please contact us so that we can draw up a draft agreement.

SPECIMEN LETTERS AND FORMS

Offer of an agency

In this set of three specimen letter, the manufacturer offers an agency, the prospective agent discusses terms, and the manufacturer replies by adding more details and sending a copy of an agency agreement.

BRITISH CRYSTAL Ltd.

Glazier House, Green Lane, Derby DE 1 1RT

Telephone: 0332 45690

S. A. Importers Ltd.   *4 May 2005*
Al Manni Way
Riyadh
SAUDI ARABIA

Dear Sirs,

Mr. Mohammed Al Wazi, of the Saudi Arabian Trade Commission in London, informed us that you may be interested in acting as our agent in your country.

As you will see from the catalogue enclosed, we are manufacturers of high quality glassware and produce a wide selection of products from moderately-priced tableware in toughened smoked glass to ornate Scandinavian and Japanese-designed light coverings.

We already export to North and south America and the Far East, and would now like to expand into the Middle Eastern market where we know there is an increasing demand for our products.

The type of agency we are looking for will have resources to cover the whole area of Saudi Arabia in selling our products, and as an incentive we are offering a 10% commission on net list-prices, plus advertising support. There would be an additional $2\frac{1}{2}$% del credere commission if the agent is willing to guarantee his customer's accounts, and he may offer generous credit terms once we have approved of the account.

This is a unique opportunity for someone to start in an expanding market and grow with it. Therefore, if you believe you have the resources to handle a sole agency covering the area mentioned, and feel that you can develop this market, please write to us as soon as possible.

Yours faithfully,

N. Jay

N. Jay
Director

Enc. Catalogue

Agent's reply, asking for more details

Mr. Kassim, of SA importers Ltd., is interested but wants more information.

S. A. Importers Ltd.
Al Manni Way, Riyadh
Telephone: 4356698 Fax: 9915467

Mr. N. Jay   Your ref: 4May 2005
British Crystal Ltd.   Our ref: SA/8016

Glazier House
Green Lane
Derby De1 1RT
UNITED KINGDOM

Date: 17 May 2005

Dear Mr. Jay,

Thank you for your letter of 4 May in which you offered us a sole agency for your products in Saudi Arabia.

First, let me say that we can handle an agency of the type you described, and that we agree that the demand for Western goods here is increasing. However, there are some points we would like to be answered before we make a decision.

Payment of accounts. Would customers pay you direction the U. K. , or will they pay us and we in turn would settle with you deducting our commission? How would payment be arranged? Bill of exchange, letter of credit, or bank draft?

Delivery. Would we be expected to hold stocks or will you supply from stock? If you supply the customers direct, how long will it take an order to be made up and shipped once it has been received?

Advertising. You mentioned that you would be willing to help with advertising. We would like more details about the type of assistance you would give us.

Disputes. If a disagreement arises over the terms of the contract, which law would be referred to in arbitration?

Length of contract. Finally, how long would the initial contract run? I think a year would allow us to see how your products sell in this market.

If you can send us this information, and possibly enclose a draft contract, we could give you our answer within the next few weeks.

Yours sincerely,

M. Kassim
M. Kassim

Manufacturer's reply, giving more details

Mr. Jay provides the information and encloses a draft contract.

BRITISH CRYSTAL Ltd.
Glazier House, Green Lane, Derby DE1 1RT
Telephone: 0332 45790 Fax: 9016148

Mr. M Kassim   6 June 2005
S. A. Importers Ltd.
Al Manni Way
Riyadh
SAUDI ARABIA

Dear Mr. Kassim,

Thank you for your letter which we received today. As you requested, we have enclosed a draft contract of the agency agreement.

You will see that we prefer our customers to pay us direct, and usually deal on a letter of credit basis, unless we can obtain references or your guarantee if you take the del credere commission.

You would not be required to hold large stocks of our products, but a representative selection of samples, and we can meet orders from the Middle East within four weeks of receipt.

Leaflets and brochures will be sent to you to handle out to your customers as one method of advertising, but we will also allow £ 3,000.00 in the first year for publicity which can be spent on the type of advertising you think suitable for glassware. We find that newspapers and magazines are the best media.

The initial contract will be for one year, subject to renewal by mutual agreement, and that disputes will be settled with reference to Dutch law, as our relative legal systems are different.

If you have any further questions with regard to the contract, or anything else, please contact me. I look forward to hearing from you.

Yours sincerely,
N. Jay
N. Jay

Enc: Draft contract

Reply to an offer of an agency

This letter is a reply to an offer of an agency, but the prospective agent is asking for the terms to be changed.

Alliso & Locke Importers Ltd.

Rooms 21 – 8, Rothermede House, Eastgage Street, London WC1, 1AR

Directors: M. Allson, B. Locke

Telephone: 01 636 9010/1/2/3/4   *Reg. No. : London 8970323*

Fax: 9816172   *VAT No. : 232 616573*

Mr. F. Iglasis   *17 October 2005*

Iglasis Leather Manufacturing SA

Enrique Granados 109

Barceona

Spain

Dear Mr. Iglasis,

We are interested in the offer you made to us in your letter of 8 October to act as sole agents for your leather goods in this country.

We think that the annual turnover you suggested was rather optimistic, and while we agree that there is a demand for leather cases and bags here, we think that half the figure you quoted would be more realistic. In view of this, the commission you offer viz. six per cent, is rather low, and we would expect a minimum of ten cent on net invoice totals.

As sole agents, the territory you offer, viz. London, would be too restrictive for sales, and this would have to be extended to the home countries. We also feel it would be better for customers to settle with us direct, and we would remit quarterly account sales deducting our commission, but we are prepared to leave this matter open for discussion.

Finally, we will hold the stock you suggested, but if there is a rush of orders, as there may be now we are nearing Christmas, you would have to shorten the delivery date you quoted, from six weeks to three from receipt of order.

If these conditions are suitable, then we would certainly accept an initial one year contact to act as your agents.

Yours sincerely,

M. Allison

M. Allison

Request for an agency

In this letter a British retailer is asking an American manufacturer if he can represent him in the UK. Notice that he explains who he is, tells the manufacturer where he saw the product, convinces him that there is a market, and suggests terms.

Glough & Book Motorcycles Ltd.

31 – 37 Traders Street, Nottingham NG 1 3AA

Directors: B. Glough, T. Book

Telephone: 0602 77153　　　　　　　　　　　*Registration: 733152*

Fax: 3455138

Sales Manager

Hartley-Mason Inc.

618 West and Vine Street

Chicago

Illinois

U. S. A.

Dear Sir,

We are a large motorcycle retail chain, with outlets throughout the UK, and are interested in the heavy touring bikes displayed on your stand at the Milan Trade Fair recently.

As you are probably aware there is an increasing demand in this country for machines of this type due to the rises in oil prices and the acceptance of the motorcycle as a common means of transport, rather than just a teenage phase. And sales of large machines have increased by more than 70 per cent in the last two years.

We are looking for a supplier who will offer us a sole agency to retail heavy machines. At present we re-

present a number of manufacturers, but only sell machines up to the 600cc range, which would not compete with the 750cc, 1,000cc, and 1,200 models you make.

We operate on a 10% commission basis on net list-prices, with an additional 3% del credere commission if required, and we think you could expect an annual turnover of more than £ 200,000.00. With an advertising allowance we could probably double this figure.

Our customers usually settle with us direct, and we pay our principals by bill of exchange on a quarterly basis.

You can be sure that our organization will offer you first class representation and excellent sales to guarantee the success of your products in this country.

Yours faithfully,
B. Glough
B. Glough

Reply to a request for an agency

The American manufacturer is interested in Mr. Glough's proposal, but does not agree to the terms.

Hartley-Mason Inc.

President: J. R. Mason D. F. A.   Directors: P. Hartley Snr., A. Hartley Jnr.
Telephone: 216 8188532 Fax: 6773128

Mr. B. Glough   14 March 2005
Glough & Book Motorcycles Ltd.
31 – 37 Traders Street
Nottingham NG1 3AA
ENGLAND

Dear Mr. Glough,

We were pleased to receive your letter of March 1 and to see that you were interested in the machines we produce.

The United States, like Great Britain, has also experienced an increase in motorbike sales, and like you we think that there is a vast market to be tapped for the heavy touring bike.

With regard to your offer, I should tell you straight away that we never use sole agencies anywhere in the world, but rely on merchant buying our products on their own account, then retailing them at market prices in their country. We, of course, offer a 30% trade discount off net list-prices and a further 5% quantity discount for sales above $ 100,000.00. We have found sole agencies tend to be rather restrictive both for ourselves and our customers.

As far as advertising is concerned, you will be pleased to hear that we have arranged for an extensive campaign which begins next month and features our heavy machines. We are sending dealers throughout Europe brochure, leaflets and posters to hand to their customers, and this will be followed up by television advertising in May.

Our terms of payment are 60d/s bills, documents against acceptance if the customer can provide references.

Once again, thank you for writing to us, and please contact us if you have any more enquiries.

Yours truly,
J. R. Mason

J. R. Mason
President

Request from a buying agent

This letter is from a buying agent in the UK asking a Canadian store if he could represent them. Buying agents have a first-class knowledge of the country, its products, the most competitive prices on the markets for goods, freight and insurance, and that is why they often take a commission on c. i. f. invoice values rather than net invoice values.

L. Dobson & Co. Ltd.

Royal Parade, Plymouth PL1 4BG

Telephone: 0752 31261
Fax: 8810758

Reg. No. 81 561771

H & D Stores Ltd
131 – 5 High Street
Montreal
Canada

8 June 2005

Dear Sir,

I am replying to your advertisements in the trade magazine "Housecare" in which you said you were looking for a buying agent in the UK to repent your group of stores in West Africa.

My company already acts for several firms in Europe and America and we specialize in buying domestic appliances and other household goods for these markets.

We have contacts with all leading brand manufacturers so we are able to obtain specially reduced export prices for their products and we can offer excellent terms for freight and insurance.

Our usual commission is 5 per cent on c. i. f. invoiced values, and we make purchases in our principal's names, sending them accounts for settlements.

We will keep you well informed of new products that come on to the market, sending you any information or literature that we think will be helpful.

I have enclosed our usual draft contract for you to consider, and if you are interested, I would be pleased to hear from you.

Yours faithfully,

L. Dobson
L. Dobson

Enc.

Reply to a buying agent's request

The Canadian company is not happy with Mr. Dobson's proposal to change 5% commission on c. i. f. invoiced values.

H & D Stores Ltd.

131 – 5 High Street, Montreal
Telephone: 5164789   Fax: 3415518

L. Dobson & Co. Ltd.

Royal Parade
Plymouth PL1 4BG
UNITED KINGDOM   *23 June 2005*

Dear Mr. Dobson ,

Thank you for your letter in reply to our advert in "Homecare". Although we are interested in your proposition , the five per cent commission you quoted on c. i. f. invoice values is higher than we considered paying. However , the other terms quoted in your draft contract are quite suitable.

We accept that you can get competitive rates in freight and insurance , nevertheless we do <u>not</u> envisage paying more than three per cent commission on net invoice values , and if you were willing to accept this rate we would sign a one-year contract to be effective as from 1 August. We can assure you that the volume of business would make it worth accepting our offer.

Yours sincerely ,

M. Habib
M. Habib

USEFUL WORDS & EXPRESSIONS

an agent	代理(商)
an agency	代理处，行销处，代理，中介
a broker	掮客，经纪人
a principal	本金
a competitor	竞争者
a rival	竞争者，对手
sole/exclusive agency	独家代理
non-exclusive	非独家的
"del credere" commission	保付货价佣金
c. i. f invoice values	c. i. f 发票价值
net invoice values	净发票价值

a stockbroker	股票经纪人
the Stock Exchange	证券交易所/证券交易
shares	份额，参股
commodity markets	商品市场
bullion	金条，金块；银条，银块
foreign currency	外币
insurance cover	安排必要的保险
underwriters	保险商
a confirming house	保付行，保付公司
an export manager	出口部经理
a manufacturer	制造业者，厂商
a supplier	供应者/厂商/供给者
a buying agent	办货代理人/进货经纪人
to create a demand	激发需求
to renew a contract	重订合同

EXERCISES

I. Your company wishes to appoint a sole agent in North America for the sale of Chinese handcrafts. Write a letter to a North America distributor, looking for a reliable firm with good connections, stating your 15 years' experience in the business and having a good knowledge of this market.

II. Write a letter applying for sole agency for Chinese Silk in Europe, stating your many year's experience in the business and how well you know the market.

III. Write an affirmative reply to Letter II.

IV. Write a polite letter rejecting the proposal in Letter II. Remember to give sound reasons.

CHAPTER 12

PUBLIC RELATION LETTERS

BUSINESS INVITATION

How To write an invitation

Here's all the information to include on your next written invitation.

Here's How:
- Names of party hosts or sponsoring organization
- Type of event (birthday party, business networking meeting, etc.)
- Place
- Date
- Time.
- RSVP date and phone number
- Any special dress requirements from black-tie to bathing suits
- Rain date (if any).
- Be specific about who is invited, whether addressee only, with guest, or with spouse and children

Tips:
- Always send written invitations for formal events such as business gatherings, formal dinners, and special occasions like showers, weddings or events honoring someone
- If guests are not from your local area, include a map to location of event
- Send anywhere from 8 – 2 weeks in advance depending on formality of occasion. Weddings require the longest lead time; casual dinners and brunches require the least

Elements of invitations

The 10 elements of an invitation:

Organization's Symbol   1. University Symbol

Mr. and Mrs. Rufus Sean Gallagher

request the pleasure of your company

at a reception and dinner

in honor of
H. E. Ambassador and Signora Robert Car-
acciolo

on Friday, the twenty-second of May

two thousand and two
at eight o'clock

3342 *Sherman Oaks Drive*
Pasadena, California

R. S. V. P.
Black Tie

Office of the Chairman

100 Empire Boulevard

Pasadena, California
Phone number

2. Names of hosts

3. Phrasing the invitation

4. The kind of event

5. Purpose of the event

6. Date

7. Time

8. Place

9. Special instructions

10. Where to R. S. V. P.

1. The university symbol
This is generally a logo or the university seal, and it is often placed at the top of the invitation. Use of the university seal is limited.

2. The names of the hosts
In a formal invitation the full name is spelled out. In an informal one, initials may be used. It is important to remember that people do the inviting, not organizations. There always should be a human being who does the inviting, or at least a group of people, "The Kent State University Board of Trustees cordially invites you to . . . "

When there are several hosts, the senior person's name comes first. If you have a large group of hosts of more or less the same rank, list them alphabetically at the top of the invitation.

3. Phrasing the invitation
"Requests the pleasure of your company at" is the most formal style invitation. Less formal are the

phrases "invite(s) you to" or "cordially invites you to . . . "

4. The kind of event
Is this a reception, buffet, ribbon-cutting ceremony, brunch, etc.?

5. The purpose of the event
Your invitation will be most effective if it includes the purpose of the event. The purpose is best communicated by using a specific action or function: "to meet," "to celebrate," "to commemorate," "to dedicate," "in honor of."

If there is to be a speech or special performance during the event, include that fact on the invitation to ensure the greatest number of guests will be present at that time. For example, in the lower-right hand corner of your reception invitation, you might have: "President Cartwright will address alumni, parents and friends of the university at 6:00 p. m. " "Guided tours of Moulton Hall will depart from the Moulton Hall Lobby at 10:00 a. m. and 10:45 a. m. "

If a special musical group or other live entertainment will be performing after dinner, also give that information on your invitations, so your guests may plan accordingly.

6. The date
The date is always written out in a formal invitation (e. g. a gala, dinner-dance, exhibit opening). Example: Saturday, the twentieth of January. But it is rendered in a simpler manner on the less formal invitation (a social reception, a pre- or post-game event). Example: Saturday, January 20.

Do not use abbreviations for dates on invitations.

7. The time
For more formal invitations, e. g. *six to eight-thirty o'clock in the evening*

The most informal and most commonly used way, e. g. 6:00 to 8:30 p. m.

8. The place
Always include the formal name, the room, the floor, street address and city.

9. Special instructions
To communicate special arrangements for parking:
e. g. *Valet parking*
Parking is available in the Kent Student Center lot.

To assist with transportation to and from the event:

e. g. *Map enclosed.*

To communicate weather arrangements:

e. g. *Rain date: June 26*

      In case of inclement weather, please call 330-672-2727.

      In case of rain, the May 4 Commemoration will be held in the Student Center Ballroom.

To communicate clothing requirements:

e. g. *Black tie or Black tie optional*

      Dress warmly and wear comfortable shoes for the walking tour

10. Where to R. S. V. P.

The letters "R. S. V. P." are in the bottom left-hand corner of the invitation, with the following printed below: the name of the person and his/her telephone number, fax number, e-mail address.

Most commonly used are a printed R. S. V. P card and matching envelope, which are enclosed in the invitation. The invitation, envelope, R. S. V. P. card and return envelope should always be the same paper, font and color. The return address on the envelope should always include the Kent State logo in the upper-left hand corner.

The response card should include a place for the name of the person(s) attending, a space to accept or regret, the telephone number of the respondent and a reply deadline. You may also wish to include a fax number and/or an e-mail address for R. S. V. P. s. The R. S. V. P. card should include a space for the telephone number of the respondent and a listing of event, date, place and time. This assists the person receiving the replies.

The response card envelope should display the return address of the R. S. V. P. contact. Unless you are sending 25 or fewer invitations, you do not need to stamp the response card envelope.

TYPES OF INVITATIONS

Formal invitations

A formal invitation usually implies a large or elaborate function such as an important reception and a formal banquet.

There are no hard and fast rules in laying out an invitation. But it is customary that formal invitations are typed on A5 or A6 good quality paper or decorative card. Often they are specially printed and enclosed in envelopes.

Formal invitations are written in the third person, stating the nature of the event, name of the host, giving the exact time and date, and the venue. If there is any dress requirement for the occasion, it is usually specified on the lower left-hand corner of the invitation.

Formal invitations often require a reply with R. S. V. P. placed at the bottom right. Alternatively some invitations have the following expressions placed immediately before the address of the sender at the bottom left:
- Please reply
- Please answer
- Please send reply to (address)
- Regrets only (It means only those who are unable to attend are required to reply.)

The tone of formal invitations should be made sincere and courteous with words carefully chosen to convey the hospitality and seriousness of the host.

The acceptance or refusal to a formal invitation is prepared in a similar, formal way. It is courteous to give a reason for the refusal of the invitation. The following is an example of reply of acceptance/refusal to the invitation provided above it.

The President of	No salutation needed
✳ **International Airways P. L. C**	Identity of the host
request the pleasure of the company of	
....	Name of invitee hand-written
	on a printed line
at the Banquet celebrating Bluestone's 10th Anniversary	Occasion and place
to be held at	
The Royal Hall	
Hilton Hotel	
2 Aston Road	
East Finchley	
London	
At 6:30 p. m. for 8:00 p. m.	Time and address of sender
On Wednesday 29 June 2005	
Suggested dress code: informal but smart	Dress requirement

Mr. Richard Hamilton

The President

❊International Airways P. L. C

23 Manor Road

London

N3 ED4 AX

Name and address of sender

RSVP

Ask for reply

Mr. Bill Clinton	*Ms. Hilary Clinton*
thanks the President of	*thanks the President of*
❊**International Airways P. L. C**	❊**International Airways P. L. C**
for his kind invitation to	*for his kind invitation to*
the Banquet celebrating the company's 10th Anniversary	*the Banquet celebrating the company's 10th Anniversary*
to be held at	*to be held at*
The Royal Hall	*The Royal Hall*
Hilton Hotel	*Hilton Hotel*
2 Aston Road	*2 Aston Road*
East Finchley	*East Finchley*
London	*London*
at 6:30 p. m. for 8:00 p. m.	*at 6:30 p. m. for 8:00 p. m.*
on Wednesday 29 June 2005	*on Wednesday 29 June 2005*
and has much pleasure in accepting	*but regrets being unable to attend due to a planned business trip to China*
Mr. Bill Clinton	*Ms. Hilary Clinton*
Marketing Manager	*P. R. Manager*
Panton Manufacturing Ltd.	*Universal plc*

Informal Invitations

Informal invitations are usually presented in the form of a letter, known as a letter of invitation. The information given in the invitation should be complete in detail, telling when, where and why.

And, as in formal invitations, the wording should be made sincere and courteous.

Example 1

You are the assistant to Mr. Richard Hamilton, the Managing Director of Blue Stone Ltd. He has received the following invitation, but will be overseas on a business trip so cannot attend the grand opening. Prepare a reply on behalf of the MD.

Sun Medical Supplies Co. Ltd

18 Peace Avenue, Edgewood, Manchester MBW4 6 SQ

Tel 387 – 2398 Fax 387 – 2309

10 May 2005

Dear Mr. Richard Hamilton,

We are pleased to inform you of the Grand Opening of our Sun Medical Supplies Company at 18 Peace Avenue, Edgewood. The ceremony begins at 10:30 on Saturday, 22 May 2005 and a cocktail party and buffet will be held at our restaurant at 12:00 noon. We have pleasure in inviting you to attend.

Your sincerely

C Burns

Chris Burns

General Manager

(**Reply**)

(*Heading*)

15 May 2003

Dear Mr. Burns,

Thank you for inviting me to the Grand Opening of your company on 22 May. I feel much regret to say that I will not be able to be present at this occasion due to a planned business trip to Spain on 21 May.

Please accept my congratulations and best wishes for your future success.

Yours sincerely,
Richard Hamilton
Richard Hamilton

Managing Director

Example 2
Dear Sir/Madam,

I'm delighted you have accepted our invitation to speak at the Conference in Kunming on 18 December 2006.

As we agreed, you'll be speaking on the topic "The Integration of Global Economy and China" from 8:30a. m to 11:30a. m. There will be an additional minutes for questions.

Would you please tell me what kind of audio-visual equipment you'll need? If you could let me know your specific requirements by 15 December, I'll have plenty of time to make sure that the hotel provides you with what you need.

Thank you again for agreeing to speak. I look forward to hearing from you.

Sincerely yours,
Li Wei
Li Wei

P. R. Manager

Example 3
Dear Sir/Madam,

Thank you for your letter of December 12. I'm glad that you are also going to Guangzhou Fair next month. It would be a great pleasure to meet you at the trade fair.

Our company is having a reception at Peace Hotel on the evening of December 20 and I would be very pleased if you could attend.

I look forward to hearing from you soon.

Yours sincerely,
Li Wei
Li Wei

P. R. Manager

Example 4
Dear Sir/Madam,

Panton Manufacturing Ltd. would very much like to have someone from your company speak at our conference on "Public Image". As you may be aware, the mission of our association is to promote.

Many of our members are interested in the achievements your company has made in. Enclosed is our preliminary schedule for the conference which will be reviewed in weeks. I'll call you on November 18 to see who from your company would be willing to speak to us. I can assure you that we'll make everything convenient to the speaker.

Sincerely yours,
Zhang Weibin
Zhang Weibin
President

Example 5
(Invitation)

Dear Sir or Madam,

We should like to invite your Corporation to attend the 2000 International Fair which will be held from August 29 to September 4 at the above address. Full details on the Fair will be sent in a week.

We look forward to hearing from you soon, and hope that you will be able to attend.

Yours faithfully

Wang Dong

Wang Dong
Marketing Manager

(**Acceptance**)

Dear Mr. Wang,

Thank you for your letter of June 28 inviting our corporation to participate in the 2000 International Fair. We are very pleased to accept and will plan to display our electrical appliances as we did in previous years.

Mr. Li Xiaohong, our Sales Manager, will be in your city from July 2 to 7 to make specific arrangements and would appreciate your assistance very much.

Yours sincerely,

Cheng Lin
Cheng Lin

Managing Director

(**Refusal**)

Dear Mr. Wang,

Thank you very much for your invitation to attend the 2000 International Fair. As we are going to open a repair shop in your city at that time, we are sorry that we shall not be able to come.

We hope to see you on some future occasion.

Yours sincerely,

Cheng Lin
Cheng Lin

Managing Director

LETTER OF APPRECIATION

Appreciation letters are among the most important forms of correspondence. An appreciation letter is important because it:

- Can form or strengthen positive business and personal relationships.
- Promotes opportunities for further interpersonal collaboration.
- Praises someone for an outstanding performance or a job well done.
- Encourages or motivates someone to reach even greater accomplishments.
- Thanks someone for their needed assistance or helpful contribution.
- Acknowledges receipt of a resume, invitation, report, or another important document.

Appreciation letter tips to consider:
- Explain why you are writing to express your gratitude.
- Be sincere – most people can sense when you are not being honest.
- Write clearly and concisely; there is no time to be longwinded or flowery.
- Handwrite your personal appreciation letter on a sheet of stationery, but use customized letterhead for business correspondence.
- Avoid thanking the person beforehand—for example: "Thanking you in advance for your help in this matter." To do so is presumptuous and suggests you do not feel the need to write a follow-up letter.
- Write the appreciation letter within a few days of whatever happened to inspire your gratitude.
- Address your appreciation letter to a specific person, if possible, not just to the company or to the organization in general.
- A sincere, well-written appreciation letter can create or strengthen interpersonal rapport and can open doors to other productive opportunities in the future.

Example 1

Dear Minister,

I am writing this letter to thank you for your warm hospitality accorded to me and my delegation during our recent visit to your beautiful country. I would also like to thank you for your interesting discussion with me which I have found very informative and useful.

During the entire visit, my delegation and I were overwhelmed by the enthusiasm expressed by your business representatives on cooperation with China. I sincerely hope we could have more exchanges like this one when we would be able to continue our interesting discussion on possible ways to expand our bilateral economic and trade relations and bring our business people together.

I am looking forward to your early visit to China when I will be able to pay back some of the hospitality I received during my memorable stay in your beautiful country.

With kind personal regards,

Faithfully yours,

Du Bin
Du Bin
Minister of Economic Cooperation

Example 2
Dear Mr. Jones,

Thank you for meeting with me yesterday to talk about the post of Senior Sales Coordinator. I found our discussion informative and interesting and was impressed by the professionalism and enthusiasm of your sales team.

I believe my experience in direct and online sales coordination has prepared me to implement your exciting plans for expansion into e-commerce. I am eager to put my ideas and skills to work for such a dynamic company.

Again, thank you for the interview. I look forward to hearing your decision on the appointment. You may contact me by e-mail at kk2288@yahoo. com. cn or by telephone at 77771234.

Sincerely yours,
Ma Kun
Ma Kun

Example 3
(Letter of Appreciation to Employee)

Dear Mr. Bill Gates,

Your enthusiasm and your ability to motivate your employees has resulted in a significant increase in productivity and profitability.

Example 4
If we had an award to give, you would be the prime candidate.

Please accept my sincerest appreciation for the fine job you are doing in our sales department.

Sincerely yours,

Richard Hamilton
Richard Hamilton

Managing Director

Example 5
Dear Mr. Hunt,

Thanks to you, I'm now assistant to the sales manager of Bluestone Trading Co.

Everything you told me about Mr. Kerry Jackson is true. He wanted to know all about me, such as what subject I liked most at school, what I had done since I left school, etc. Then he read your letter again, and I knew I had satisfied him and I could do the job.

I don't have to tell you that I'm sincerely grateful for all your help in finding a place for me. The mailman will bring you a package tomorrow. That's a small token of appreciation.
Sincerely yours,
Liu Min
Liu Min

SYMPATHY LETTERS

Do you know a friend or relative who has experienced a death, personal loss, or other misfortune? Perhaps this person was recently divorced or has been injured in an accident. Maybe you know an expectant mother who has recently suffered a miscarriage. These are times when you need just the right words to say just the right thing. A store-bought sympathy card is not as personal as a hand – written letter, but you may buy a card and put your letter inside it. Here are some tips to help you write a tactful Sympathy Letter that will be much appreciated:

- Try to be empathetic. Imagine yourself in the other person's place. What would you like to hear? What would make you feel better?
- Be brief. Much is communicated with "I'm so sorry. Please know you're in my thoughts." In times of loss, no one wants to read a lengthy letter (it's hard to read when you're crying). Communicating that you care is enough.
- Don't be dramatic. A Sympathy Letter needs to be written with beautiful prose, but dramatic language may seem insincere. Tell how you learned about the news in simple terms. It is perfectly acceptable to relate your deep shock at hearing about the death or loss. Avoid using graphic terms to refer to a death that was tragic or gruesome.
- Be personal. If your Sympathy Letter concerns a death, be sure to mention the deceased's

name and the circumstances that caused the loss of life. Be honest; don't hesitate to use the word "death" or note the actual cause of death. Share your personal sadness. Remind the bereaved you support them at this difficult time and they are not completely alone in their suffering.

Example
Bill made me feel at home when I first moved here. I am so sorry that cancer took him at such an early age. I will miss him.

- Mention positive memories. If your Sympathy Letter concerns a death, and if you knew the deceased, pay tribute to the person's life by mentioning something positive: a happy memory from your experiences together, a notable achievement, etc. You can even relate a story about how the deceased touched your life. Be sensitive, but it is not necessary to avoid humorous incidents that could help lighten the moment and would be gratefully received. Laughter is a great healer. You could also mention a special characteristic of the deceased—something you will always cherish.

Examples
a contagious sense of humor, a generous nature, love of the arts, courage, leadership, decisiveness.

- Offer encouragement to the bereaved. Assume that the survivor feels overwhelmed by the loss and doesn't know whether or not they have the strength to get through it. State your confidence that they will get through it. Time is also a great healer. A comforting tactic that can have a powerful effect on the survivor is to quote a loving remark that was once made by the deceased about him or her. Remind the person in mourning of their own personal strengths in descriptive terms.

Examples
resilience, patience, competence, religious devotion, faith, optimism, a trusting nature.

- Offer your condolences. How you will craft a condolence statement will depend on your personal relationship with the person to whom you are writing. For example, you may want to avoid being too religious if the person is only an acquaintance or if you do not know if they even have a religious affiliation. Most people would, however, appreciate being told that they are in your prayers and thoughts. You probably know what will bring them comfort. Write something that is congruent with your relationship.
- Offer practical help to the grieving person. Specific offers are better than, "Let me know if there is anything I can do." Then take the initiative—if you don't get immediate acceptance

of an offer, then call back and repeat it. Many people will think your first offer was just to be polite; repeated offers demonstrate your sincerity.

Examples

"Can I help you with the grocery shopping?"
"Can I run any errands for you?"
"Can I help the children?"
"Can I write any letters for you?"

- Show sensitivity. Allow people to grieve in their own way and for as long as is needed. There is a time to mourn! Be careful not to offer advice when none is wanted or needed. Remember, at the moment the bereaved needs a loving friend, not a counselor.

Examples (what not to say)

"You need to go on a long cruise."
"Look on the bright side."
"It's all for the best."

- Close with an expression of comfort. End your Sympathy Letter with an expression of comfort, sympathy, or affection. Let your concluding words reflect the truth of your feelings. You may want to close your letter simply with one word such as "Love," or "Sincerely," or you may want to use a phrase or a complete sentence followed by your name.

Examples

"My love and concern are with you always."
"You are continually in my thoughts and prayers."
"My heart and my tears are with you."
"I share in your grief and send my love."

- Final Note: Use descriptive words when you compose your Sympathy Letter.

Examples

burden, caring, comfort, comforting, compassion, concerned, consolation, difficult, endure, endurance, grief, grieve, heal, healing, heartbreaking, heartfelt, help, hope, hurt, hurtful, loss, love, misfortune, mourn, mourning, overcome, pain, painful, regret, regrettable, sad, shocking, sorrow, sorry, struggle, struggling.

Example 1

Dear David,

I've just the minute heard that you are in hospital. I think you are very wise to find out once and for all what's causing your trouble, and get it over.

I do hope that by the time this note reaches you, you'll be feeling a great deal better. I'm sure that it won't be long before you are entirely and completely yourself again.

Warmest regards!
Nancy

Example 2

Dear Bill,

You will excuse an old friend of yours writing a line to say how grieved she is to hear of the breaking off of your engagement. It's a terrible blow. I know well what you must be feeling and you have indeed my sincere sympathy, but I'm convinced you will hear it like a man. You might feel everything turns against you and time hangs heavy on your hands at the moment. But I'm sure everything will go well soon. When can we fix a date for drinking coffee?

Best wishes!

Jane

Example 3

Dear Ms. Edwards,

I was extremely shocked to hear the sad news. It was only nine months ago I had the opportunity to see Henry Edwards at the American Park. He was delighted and looked quite healthy then.

I know how little words written on a page can possibly mean to you at such a time. But he went as he would have wished – quickly and without suffering. That should be some consolation to you.

Please accept my deepest sympathy.

Very sincerely,

MISCELLANEOUS

In this section we look at some miscellaneous correspondence, much of which one may deal with in daily life.

Poster

Example 1
POSTER

Football Match
All Are Warmly Welcome

Under the auspices of the Student Union of our university, a friendly football match will be held between our team and the team of Chemical Engineering College on our football field on Tuesday, November 29, 2005 at 5:00 p. m.

November 29, 2005

The Student Union

Example 2
GOOD NEWS
Summer Clearance Sales

All the goods on show are sold at twenty percent discount. Please examine and choose them carefully before you pay. There will be no replacement or refunding. You have been warned in advance. You are welcome to make your choice.

Personal Shopping Service

Certificate

Example 1
(Doctor's Certificate)

December 18, 2005

This is to certify that the patient, Mr. Hamilton, male, aged 41, was admitted into our hospital on November 9, 2005, for suffering from acute appendicitis. After immediate operation and ten days of treatment, he has got complete recovery and will be discharged on November 9, 2006. It is suggested that he rest for one week at home before resuming his work.

Jack Hopkins
Surgeon-in-charge

Example 2
(Diploma Certificate)

CERTIFICATE

(90) Lu Zi, No. 1130

This is to certificate that Mr. Zhao Bin holds a diploma issued to him in July, 2004 by Yunnan University (Diploma No. 064) and that we have carefully checked the seal of the University and the signature by President Zhang Min.

Kunming Notary Public Office
Yunnan Province
the People's Republic of China
Notary: Wang Fang
May 2, 2005

Congratulation letter

Example 1
Dear Mr. / Ms,

On the occasion of the 60 anniversary of your National Day, please accept our heartiest congratulations. May the trade connections between our countries continue to develop with each passing day!

Yours faithfully,

Example 2
Dear Mr. Minister,

Allow me to convey my congratulations on your promotion to Minister of Trade. I am delighted that many year service you have given to your country should have been recognized and appreciated.

We wish you success in your new post and look forward to closer cooperation with you in the development of trade between our two countries.

Sincerely,

Example 3
(*Reply to Example 2*)

Dear Mr. / Ms,

Thank you for your letter conveying congratulations on my appointment. I wish also to thank you for the assistance you have given me in my work and look forward to better cooperation in the future.

Sincerely,

IOU

To Mr. Charles Green,

August 18, 2005

I. O. U. three thousand U. S. dollars (U. S. $ 3000) only, within one year from this date with annual interest at four percent (4%).

David Smith

Activity arrangement

Dear Mr. / Ms,

We are very pleased to welcome President William Taylor and Manager James Rogers to Beijing and Shanghai in the second half of April for about a week. As requested, we propose the following itinerary for your consideration.

Monday, April 18

4:00 p. m. Arrive in Beijing by Flt. xx, to be met at the airport by Mr. President of Asia Trading Co.

4:15 Leave for Great Wall Hotel

7:30 Dinner given by President x

Tuesday, April 19

9:30 a. m. Discussion at Asia Trading Co. Building

2:00 p. m. Group discussion

8:00 p. m. Cocktail reception given by the British Commercial Counselor in Beijing

Wednesday, April 20

9:00 a. m. Discussion

12:00 noon Sign the Letter of Intent

1:30 p. m. Peking Duck Dinner

3:30 p. m. visit the Summer palace

6:00 Departure for Shanghai

Would you please confirm by fax so that we can make arrangements accordingly.

Yours faithfully

Notice

Example 1

NOTICE

All professors and associate professors are requested to meet in the college conference room on Saturday, August 20, at 2:00 p. m. to discuss questions of international academic exchanges.

August 16, 2005

Example 2

NOTICE

Dear Examinee,

As you know, due to unfortunate circumstances, ETS was forced to cancel the scores of the October 2004 TOEFL administration in the People's Republic of China. At that time, you were notified that you would be able to take another TOEFL without charge up through the October 2005 administration. You should be aware that the TOEFL program has a long standing policy of not refunding test fees when administrations are cancelled.

We apologize for any inconvenience that this may cause to you.

Russell Webster
Executive Director
TOEFL Program
Educational Testing Service

Request leave of absence

Example 1

Dear Mr. Pike,

I regret very much I was unable to attend school this morning owing to a severe attack of illness. I am enclosing here with certificate from the doctor who is attending me, as he fears it will be several days before I shall be able to resume my study. I trust my enforced absence will not give you any serious inconvenience.

Sincerely yours
Jack

8:30 a. m.

Example 2

Dear Peter:

I have done all my things here. I sincerely thank you for the trouble you have taken for my sake. I am leaving for home by train at two this afternoon. This is to say good-bye to you. Please kindly remember me to your wife.

Yours ever,
Paul

Example 3

To John Smith, Supervisor
From: George Chen, Accounting Department
Date: March 11, 2005

Subject: *Casual Leave of Absence*

John, I would like to know if I could ask for a casual leave of absence from March 23 to 27. Yesterday I received a letter from my parents, who are both over 70, telling me that a big flood took place at my home village, causing serious damage to my house. As the only son of my parents, I should be back to assess the situation, and help them to get over these difficulties. Though I cannot stay at home for too long a time, I should at least make arrangements for repair work. I believe my relatives in the village and my neighbors will also come to help. Financially I have no difficulties.

I will call you at 1:30 p. m. or you can call me at any time.

Sincerely yours
Li Hua

USEFUL WORDS & EXPRSSIONS

Host a dinner/banquet/luncheon in honor of...	为……举行宴会/宴请
Welcome dinner	欢迎宴会
Informal dinner	便宴
Light meal	便餐
Working luncheon	工作午餐
Buffet dinner/luncheon	自助餐
Return dinner	答谢宴会
Farewell dinner	告别宴会
Hold seminar/forum/symposium	举行研讨会/座谈会/学术报告会
Patron/sponsor/organizer/co-organizer	赞助人/主办人/承办人/协办人
Enter into negotiation	举行谈判
Talks at working level	事物性会谈
Counterpart talks	对口会谈
Items on the agenda	议程项目
14 February Valentine's Day	情人节

16 February President's Day	总统日
1 April Fools Day	愚人节
10 April Good Friday	耶稣受难节
12 April Easter	复活节
6 May Nurses'Day	护士节
10 May Mother's Day	母亲节
21 June Father's Day	父亲节
4 July Independence Day	美国独立日
31 October Halloween	万圣节前夜
11 November Veterans Day	退伍军人节
26 November Thanksgiving	感恩节

EXERCISES

I. You work at the Publicity Department of H & D Co. Ltd. Your company will be opening its new branch in a nearby town next month and is now arranging a cocktail reception to mark the occasion. Prepare a formal invitation which can be printed to send to a large number of business associates and special guests. You should make up any necessary details.

II. You are the assistant to Mr. Russell Webster, the President of New York State University. He has received the following invitation, but will be overseas on a business trip so cannot attend the grand opening. Prepare a reply on behalf of the MD.

Dear Mr. Webster,

We would like to invite you to attend our award ceremony at New York University which is being held 18 December this year. The proceedings will begin about 9.00a. m. and end around 11:30 am in the morning, after which a dinner will be given at 12:30 for our prominent visitors.

As one of our distinguished ex-students, we would like you to address the parents and students with a short speech of your choice before handing out the awards.

Although we realize you are busy we hope you can find time to accept the invitation and look forward to seeing you.

Yours sincerely,

Charles Green

Charles Green
President

III. Situation: You have obtained a good job you applied for, because your friend Susan has recommended you for the job.

Task:

- Write a short letter to Susan.
- Inform her that you have already obtained the job.
- Express your thanks for the recommendation and your determination to be worthy of their assistance.
- Your part of writing should be around 30 – 40 words.

Chapter 13

Employment Related Letters

Writing Letter of Application

Your application letter is one of your most important job-search documents. An effective letter can get you a phone call for an interview, but a poorly written application letter usually spells continued unemployment. The difference can be a matter of how you handle a few key points. The following are some tips to help you develop effective application letters.

Some useful tips concerning the effective writing of application letters

Individualizing your letter

Give your readers some insight into you as an individual. In the example below the writer chose to describe particular experiences and skills that could not be generalized to most other recent graduates. Draft your letter to show how your individual qualities can contribute to the organization. This is your letter, so avoid simply copying the form and style of other letters you've seen. Instead, strive to make your letter represent your individuality and your capabilities.

Addressing a specific person

Preferably, the person you write to should be the individual doing the hiring for the position you're seeking. Look for this person's name in company publications found at the University Placement Service, the Krannert Business Library, or the Reserve Desk in the Undergraduate Library. If the name is unavailable in these places, phone the organization and ask for the person's name or at least the name of the personnel manager.

Catching your reader's attention

Your introduction should get your reader's attention, stimulate interest, and be appropriate to the job you are seeking. For example, you may want to begin with a reference to an advertisement that prompted your application. Such a reference makes your reason for contacting the company clear and indicates to them that their advertising has been effective. Or you may want to open by referring to the company's product, which you want to promote. Such a reference shows your knowledge of the company. Whatever opening strategy you use, try to begin where your reader is and lead quickly to your purpose in writing.

Effective writing of application letters

1. First paragraph tips: make your goal clear

If you're answering an advertisement, name the position stated in the ad and identify the source, for example: "your advertisement for a graphic artist, which appeared in the *Chicago Sun Times*, May 15, 1998..."

If you're prospecting for a job, try to identify the job title used by the organization.

If a specific position title isn't available or if you wish to apply for a line of work that may come under several titles, you may decide to adapt the professional objective stated in your resume.

Additionally, in your first paragraph you should provide a preview of the rest of your letter. This tells your reader what to look for and lets him or her know immediately how your qualifications fit the requirements of the job. In the example letter, the last sentence of the first paragraph refers to specific work experience that is detailed in the following paragraph.

2. Highlighting your qualifications

Organize the middle paragraphs in terms of the qualifications that best suit you for the job and the organization. That is, if your on-the-job experience is your strongest qualification, discuss it in detail and show how you can apply it to the needs of the company. Or if you were president of the Marketing Club and you are applying for a position in marketing or sales, elaborate on (详细说明) the valuable experience you gained and how you can put it to work for them. If special projects you've done apply directly to the job you are seeking, explain them in detail. Be specific. Use numbers, names of equipment you've used, or features of the project that may apply to the job you want.

One strong qualification, described so that the reader can picture you actively involved on the job, can be enough. You can then refer your reader to your resume for a summary of your other qualifications. If you have two or three areas that you think are strong, you can develop additional paragraphs. Make your letter strong enough to convince readers that your distinctive background qualifies you for the job but not so long that length will turn readers off. Some employers recommend a maximum of four paragraphs.

3. Other tips

Refer to your resume: Be sure to refer to your enclosed resume at the most appropriate point in your letter, for example, in the discussion of your qualifications or in the closing paragraph. Conclude with a clear, courteous request to set up an interview, and suggest a procedure for doing so: The date and place for the interview should be convenient for the interviewer. However, you're welcome to suggest a range of dates and places convenient to you, especially if you travel at your own expense or have a restricted schedule. Be specific about how your reader should contact you. If you ask for a phone call, give your phone number and the days and times of the week when you can be reached.

- **Be professional**: Make sure your letter is professional in format, organization, style, grammar, and mechanics. Maintain a courteous tone throughout the letter and eliminate all errors. Remember that readers often "deselect" applicants because of the appearance of the letter.
- **Seek advice**: It's always good idea to prepare at least one draft to show to a critical reader for comments and suggestions before revising and sending the letter.
- **Emphasize reader benefits**: Stress the contribution you are able to make to the company. Having researched the company beforehand, you should have an understanding of the particular skills and experience that are most valued.
- **Display courteous tone**: You can sell yourself without biasing. Avoid lengthy discourse on your superior talents and skills; your skills and qualifications will speak for themselves.
- **Be concise**: It is not necessary to reiterate all of the points in your resume. After all , you are sending the letter as an accompaniment to the resume. Highlighting your most marketable skills and experience in the second and third paragraphs of the letter is certainly acceptable. You might explain your experience in terms of company benefit.
- **Request action on the part of the employer**: Since your goal is to secure an interview, use the final paragraph to explicitly request an agreeable interview date and time. Of course, you will want to leave the exact date and time to the discretion of the employer; however, it is acceptable to state weeks or days when you will be available to discuss job possibilities.
- **Be Neat and correct any Errors in Punctuation, Grammar, or Spelling.**
- **Provide Your Phone Number and Address.**

Sample Letter 1

311 Nestor Street
West Lafayette, IN 47902

June 6, 2004

Ms. Christine Rennick
Engineer
Aerosol Monitoring and Analysis, Inc.
P. O. Box 233
Gulltown, MD 21038

Dear Ms. Rennick,

Dr. Saul Wilder, a consultant to your firm and my Organizational Management professor, has informed me that Aerosol Monitoring and Analysis is looking for someone with excellent communications skills, organizational experience, and leadership background to train for a management position. I believe that my enclosed resume will demonstrate that I have the characteristics and experience you seek. In addition, I'd like to mention how my work experience last summer makes me a particularly strong candidate for the position.

As a promoter for Kentech Training at the 1997 Paris Air Show, I discussed Kentech's products with marketers and sales personnel from around the world. I also researched and wrote reports on new product development and compiled information on aircraft industry trends. The knowledge of the aircraft industry I gained from this position would help me analyze how Aerosol products can meet the needs of regular and prospective clients, and the valuable experience I gained in promotion, sales, and marketing would help me use that information effectively.

I would welcome the opportunity to discuss these and other qualifications with you. If you are interested, please contact me at (317) 555 – 0118 any morning before 11 : 00 a. m. , or feel free to leave a message. I look forward to meeting with you to discuss the ways my skills may best serve Aerosol Monitoring and Analysis.

Sincerely yours,

Enclosure: resume

Sample Letter 2

321 Linden Avenue, #2A
Ithaca, New York 14850

January 10, 2003

Betsy Lydon
Outreach Director
Mothers & Others for a Livable Planet
40 West 20th Street, 9th Floor
New York, New York 10011

Dear Ms. Lydon,

The connections between agricultural, environmental, and economic sustainability have been a focus of my studies as a natural resources major at Cornell University. I am eager to apply my knowledge and experience to an environmental advocacy organization when I graduate from Cornell in May, and would like to be considered for the consumer outreach and marketing specialist position advertised in Nonprofit Times. I enclose my resume for your consideration.

Through volunteer activities, I have actively promoted sustainable agriculture and environmental issues. As president of the Cornell Greens, I organized meetings, workshops, rallies, and Earth Day activities for the Cornell campus, and also established an environmental educational curriculum for an after – school program. Last year, I helped found the Student Garden Group to introduce organic gardening to Cornell students and promote local agriculture to the Ithaca community. The Group's accomplishments included running produce stands at apartment complexes for economically disadvantaged families and senior citizens, and working with Cornell Cooperative Extension to expand outreach programs.

To develop my public speaking, communication, and teaching skills while an undergraduate, I have participated in a training course for peer counselors, completed a course in oral communication, spoken at rallies and festivals, and worked as an educator in a variety of teaching situations.

I will call you next week to schedule a time to discuss my interest in increasing public awareness about ecological agriculture and environmental conservation. Thank you for your consideration.

Sincerely,
Betsy Crawford
Betsy Crawford
Enclosure

Sample Letter 3
(*Heading*)

18 August 2000

Suzanne P. Greene
Director
Public Relations
American Chemical Company
Nova Green, WI 40000

Dear Ms. Greene,

As a graduating senior from Western Michigan University with a major emphasis in public Relations, I am interested in working for your organization. I believe that my academic and work experience are appropriate to the entry-level position you have advertised in the August 17 Wall Street Journal.

Because the position requires extensive contact with the media, my training in journalism and experience as a staff newswriter may be particularly suited to your needs. The enclosed resume details my involvement in the field of public relations and written communication.

In addition to maintaining a 3. 32 grade-point average, and participating in university extracurricular activities (课外活动), I devoted time and energy to enhancing my leadership skills. As a participant in two leadership conferences and Public Relations Director for the Inter – Fraternity Council (兄弟会) at Western, I was able to develop the leadership skills vital to effective public relations work.

An opportunity to discuss the nature of the position more specifically with you would be most appreciated, I am available on short notice for an interview at (616)349-0000.

Sincerely,

Daniel E. Bourcier

Daniel E. Bourcier

1925 Elkerton

Kalamazoo, MI 49001

Sample Letter 4

Dear Mr. Stark,

This is to apply for a position in labor relations with your company.

Presently I am completing my studies in labor at Olympia University, and I will graduate with a Bachelor of Business administration degree with a major in labor relations this May. I have taken all the courses in labor relations available to me, as well as other helpful courses, such as statistics, law, and report writing.

I have had good working experience as a shipping and receiving clerk, truck driver, and repairperson. Please see details on the resume that is attached. I feel that I am well qualified for a position in labor relations and am considering working for a company of your size and description.

As I must make a decision on my career soon, I request that you write me soon. For your information, I will be available for an interview on March 17 and 18.

Sincerely,

Sample Letter 5

Dear Ms. Alderson,

Sound background in advertising... well-trained... work well with others....

These key words in your July 7 advertisement in the Times describe the person you want, and I believe I am that person.

For the past four years, I have gained experience in every phase of retail advertising working for the Lancer, my college newspaper. I sold advertising, planned layouts, and wrote copy. During the last two summers, I got more firsthand experience working in the advertising department of Wunder & Son. I wrote a lot of copy for Wunder, some of which I am enclosing for your inspection; but I also did just about everything else there is to do in advertising work. I enjoyed it, and I learned from it. I am confident that this experience will help me to fit in and contribute to the work in your office.

In my concentrated curriculum at the University, I studied marketing with a specialization in advertising. As you will see from the attached resume, I studied every subject offered in advertising and related fields, and I believe that my honor grades give some evidence that I worked hard and with sincerity. I am confident that upon my graduation in June I can bring to your organization the firm foundation of knowledge and imagination your work demands.

Understanding the importance of being able to get along well with people, I actively participated in Sigma Chi (social fraternity), the First Methodist Church, and Pi Tau Pi (honorary business fraternity). From the experience I gained in these associations, I am confident that I can fit in harmoniously with your close-knit advertising department.

The preceding review of my qualifications summarizes my case for a career in advertising. May I now meet with you to discuss the matter further? I could visit your office at any time convenient to you to talk about doing your advertising work.

Sincerely,

Sample Letter 6

I learn from your ad in the Commercial Journal that you are looking for an experienced sales represent-ative for your food products.

I should like to offer myself for the post. I am thirty years old and had six years' experience in the sales department of the largest food producer in this area— GENERAL FOOD CORP. I left the Corporation a month ago to open an agency.

Mr. James Wellington, Managing Director, and Mr. Edward Cook, Sales Manager of my former corporation, have both consented to my naming them as references.

I shall be pleased to provide you any information you may need and hope I may be given the opportuni-ty of an interview.

Yours faithfully,

Enc. Resume

Sample Letter 7
(A solicited Application Letter)

166 Eas Taylor drive
Mayflair, OH 45333

December 12, 2002

Mr. Hardy Samuels
Personnel Director
Merchants Department Store
222 Medium Road
Columbus, OH 43215

Dear Mr. Samuels,

Please consider my application for administrative assistant that you advertised in the December 1 edi-tion of the Columbus Herald (《哥伦布先驱报》). The requirements you describe match my qualifi-cations.

I will be graduating from the business program at Pace County Community College (PCCC) at the end of the month. I'm planning to enroll part time at the Ohio State University in the fall to complete a bachelor's degree in business administration. However, I would like to begin working full time to apply what I've learned at PCCC.

Please note on my enclosed resume the part-time and temporary positions I've held over the past three years. As a result, you could hire an administrative assistant with experience in office management and customer relations with strong word processing skills.

After you have read my credentials(证明身份、学历等的信件或文件), I would like to meet you to discuss how I can contribute to Merchants's operations in the Columbus area. I will call next week to see if we can arrange a convenient time. If you wish to reach me before then, please leave a message at (614) 235-6677.

Sincerely,
Charles Jacobs
Charles Jacobs

Enclosure

Sample Letter 8
(An Unsolicited application Letter)

Dear Mr. Masters,

Do you recall our conversation early this year when we discussed marketing research? At the time, I expressed interest in the details you had gathered about the impact of various media. I am now completing my program in general business at Southern Indiana University, and I want to apply my knowledge of marketing to your organization's needs.

My academic preparation has focused on marketing. Although I have completed the program in general business, my personal interest has been on the relationship between the consumer and the seller through advertising.

I completed a senior project where I reached and outlined a campaign for a new hair spray. I also worked with an advertising agency on a part-time basis last summer. Please note the additional details about my background and experience in my attached resume and how they can benefit your company.

I would like an opportunity to discuss how I can apply my skills developed in college to Pierson's enter-tainment projects. I will call your office next week to arrange a convenient time for an interview. If you want to meet before then, you can reach me at 555 – 7788.

I am looking forward to our meeting.

Sincerely,
Susan Runnels
Susan Runnels

Sample Letter 9

Dear Sir,
I wish to apply for admission to your Graduate School to pursue a Master's degree in Economics. I in-tend to enter in the Fall of 2003.

I graduated from Yunnan University and got my B. A. degree in 2000. Upon my graduation, I was employed in Bank of Communications, Kunming Branch. I have a strong interest in my career, so I wish to further my study at your University.

I have taken the TOEFL and got a score of 607. I'll take the GRE General Test in the coming April.

I really appreciate it if you send me the application form for graduate admission.

Sincerely yours,
Li Mei
Li Mei

Sample Letter 10

Dear Director,
I completed my undergraduate study in the Department of International Trade of Yunnan University and obtained my B. A. degree in July 1992. After graduation I was assigned to work in Yunnan Inter-national Trade Development Company.

I have taken TOEFL, GRE General, and GRE Advanced with scores of 625, 2100, and 920 respec-tively.

I would like to request application materials for graduate admission and financial support. I plan to pursue a Master's degree and then a Doctor's Degree in International Economics and begin my study in the Fall of 2001.

I am looking forward to your response at your early convenience.

Sincerely yours,
Wang Dan
Wang Dan

WRITING THE RESUME

The following steps are recommended while drafting a resume:

Step 1

1. Choose your most marketable skills

Select those skills from your list which can be translated into marketable abilities. It is best to provide an example of your skills put to use.

2. Use action verbs in describing your skills and experience

For each job experience that you have listed, begin sentences with action verbs and delete the personal pronoun "I". Here are some useful verbs:

ORGANIZED	DESIGNED	INVESTIGATED
MANAGED	TRAINED	EVALUATED
SUPERVISED	ASSISTED	COORDINATED
RESPONSIBLE FOR	ANALYZED	PERFORMED
DEVELOPED	CREATED	INSTRUCTED

Step 2 Outline a rough draft

- Write out your name, address, and phone number. Be sure to include your telephone area code.
- State your career objective in one or two concise sentences.
- List the job experiences you plan to include, the skills you employed while working, and the title or position you held.
- List the organizations you belong to, special activities you have participated in, and any miscellaneous information that you wish to include.

Step 3 Prepare an effective format

- **Resumes should be limited to one page unless otherwise specified by a prospective employer.** Employers do not have time to read long, embellished resumes. One page is sufficient to make a good impression.

- **Organize the sections of your resume in the order listed in step two.** End your resume with the statement "References available upon request" or "References available at the time of interview" rather than a list of references.

Resumes should be sent with a cover letter of application.

Example 1

ROGER DALE MAGOON

1108 Oak Street Kalamazoo, Michigan 49007 (616) 388 – 0000

PROFESSIONAL OBJECTIVE: *To apply communication, data processing, and marketing skills in a sales-related position which offers the opportunity for professional growth and advancement.*

QUALIFIED BY:

Education

Bachelor of Business Administration, Western Michigan University, June 1983.
Double Major: General Marketing and Electronic Data Processing
Minor: General Business
Organizations: *Marketing Club; Data Processing Management Association. Responsible for fund – raising activity planning; wrote programs for general university use.*
Awards: *Recipient of American College Testing Academic Scholarship; met qualifying criteria for Basic Educational Opportunity Grant.*

Work Experience

Funded 100% of my education by working for:
- *Pepsi-Cola Bottling Group, Kalamazoo, MI. Merchandise and deliveryman responsible for warehouse schedules; operated heavy machinery, Summer 1980.*

- *Acorn Building Components, Quincy, MI. Assembled sliding glass doors and windows. Summer 1979.*

Special Interests

Avocational interest include participation in sports, musical events, and travel. Avid reader of nonfiction, particularly autobiographies.

References are available from Western Michigan University Placement Services, Ellsworth Hall, Kalamazoo, MI 49007, or at time of interview.

Example 2

DON R. ANDERSON'S PREPARATION FOR WORK AS A LEGAL SECRETARY

Permanent address: 1366 Hyacinth Street
Baton Rouge, LA 70803
Telephone: AC 512, 433 – 6605

Job objective: To work as a legal assistant and secretary while completing law school

Versatile Experience

1979-80 Part-time work while in high school as office clerk for Nowotny Construction Company, Houston, TX. Work involved typing, filing, and preparing reports.

1980-82 Manuscript typist and editor for Kenyon Publishing Company, Houston, TX. Responsible for editing, typing, and proofreading manuscripts.

1982-86 Active duty with United States Navy, two years of which were in rating of yeoman, first class. Navy work was primarily clerical and administrative. As senior petty officer, assumed responsibility for offices assigned to, both ashore and afloat.

Specialized Education

1980 Developed skills in word processing and office procedures through six months intensified study and practice at BARKER BUSINESS COLLEGE, Houston, TX.

1984-86 While on active duty with Navy, commenced part-time prelaw study at Iowa State University, Ames, IA.

1986 – 88 Completed prelaw curriculum in General Business at Louisiana State University with grade-point average of 3.53 (4.0 basis).

Personal Information

Family status: married, one daughter, age three
Date of birth: June 17, 1962
Interests: golf, fishing, hunting, reading, bridge
Memberships: Delta Sigma Pi (professional business), Beta Gamma Sigma (honorary business), Baton Rouge Forensic Society

WRITING PERSONAL STATEMENT

The personal statement, your opportunity to sell yourself in the application process, generally falls into one of two categories:

1. The general, comprehensive personal statement

This allows you maximum freedom in terms of what you write and is the type of statement often prepared for standard medical or law school application forms.

2. The response to very specific questions

Often, business and graduate school applications ask specific questions, and your statement should respond specifically to the question being asked. Some business school applications favor multiple essays, typically asking for responses to three or more questions.

Questions to ask yourself before you write

What's special, unique, distinctive, and/or impressive about you or your life story? What details of your life (personal or family problems, history, people or events that have shaped you or influenced your goals) might help the committee better understand you or help set you apart from other applicants?

When did you become interested in this field and what have you learned about it (and about yourself) that has further stimulated your interest and reinforced your conviction that you are well suited to this field? What insights have you gained?

How have you learned about this field—through classes, readings, seminars, work or other experiences, or conversations with people already in the field?

If you have worked a lot during your college years, what have you learned (leadership or managerial skills, for example), and how has that work contributed to your growth?

What are your career goals?

Are there any gaps or discrepancies in your academic record that you should explain (great grades but mediocre LSAT or GRE scores, for example, or a distinct upward pattern to your GPA if it was only average in the beginning)?

Have you had to overcome any unusual obstacles or hardships (for example, economic, familial, or physical) in your life?

What personal characteristics (for example, integrity, compassion, persistence) do you possess that would improve your prospects for success in the field or profession? Is there a way to demonstrate or document that you have these characteristics?

What skills (for example, leadership, communicative, analytical) do you possess? Why might you be a stronger candidate for graduate school—and more successful and effective in the profession or field than other applicants?

What are the most compelling reasons you can give for the admissions committee to be interested in you?

General advice

1. Answer the questions that are asked
If you are applying to several schools, you may find questions in each application that are somewhat similar.

Don't be tempted to use the same statement for all applications. It is important to answer each question being asked, and if slightly different answers are needed, you should write separate statements. In every case, be sure your answer fits the question being asked.

2. Tell a story
Think in terms of showing or demonstrating through concrete experience. One of the worst things you can do is to bore the admissions committee. If your statement is fresh, lively, and different, you'll be putting yourself ahead of the pack. If you distinguish yourself through your story, you will make yourself memorable.

3. Be specific
Don't, for example, state that you would make an excellent doctor unless you can back it up with specific reasons. Your desire to become a lawyer, engineer, or whatever should be logical, the result of specific experience that is described in your statement. Your application should emerge as the logical conclusion to your story.

4. Find an angle

If you're like most people, your life story lacks drama, so figuring out a way to make it interesting becomes the big challenge. Finding an angle or a "hook" is vital.

5. Concentrate on your opening paragraph

The lead or opening paragraph is generally the most important. It is here that you grab the reader's attention or lose it. This paragraph becomes the framework for the rest of the statement.

6. Tell what you know

The middle section of your essay might detail your interest and experience in your particular field, as well as some of your knowledge of the field. Too many people graduate with little or no knowledge of the nuts and bolts of the profession or field they hope to enter. Be as specific as you can in relating what you know about the field and use the language professionals use in conveying this information. Refer to experiences (work, research, etc.), classes, conversations with people in the field, books you've read, seminars you've attended, or any other source of specific information about the career you want and why you're suited to it. Since you will have to select what you include in your statement, the choices you make are often an indication of your judgment.

7. Don't include some subjects

There are certain things best left out of personal statements. For example, references to experiences or accomplishments in high school or earlier are generally not a good idea. Don't mention potentially controversial subjects (for example, controversial religious or political issues).

8. Do some research, if needed

If a school wants to know why you're applying to it rather than another school, do some research to find out what sets your choice apart from other universities or programs. If the school setting would provide an important geographical or cultural change for you, this might be a factor to mention.

Write well and correctly

Be meticulous (小心翼翼的). Type and proofread your essay very carefully. Many admission officers say that good written skills and command of correct use of language are important to them as they read these statements. Express yourself clearly and concisely. Adhere to stated word limits.

Avoid clichés (陈词滥调). A medical school applicant who writes that he is good at science and wants to help other people is not exactly expressing an original thought. Stay away from often-repeated or tired statements.

Some examples of successful statements

Sample 1

My interest in science dates back to my years in high school, where I excelled in physics, chemistry, and math. When I was a senior, I took a first-year calculus course at a local college (such an advanced-level class was not available in high school) and earned an A. It seemed only logical that I pursue a career in electrical engineering.

When I began my undergraduate career, I had the opportunity to be exposed to the full range of engineering courses, all of which tended to reinforce and solidify my intense interest in engineering. I've also had the opportunity to study a number of subjects in the humanities and they have been both enjoyable and enlightening, providing me with a new and different perspective on the world in which we live.

In the realm of engineering, I have developed a special interest in the field of laser technology and have even been taking a graduate course in quantum electronics. Among the 25 or so students in the course, I am the sole undergraduate. Another particular interest of mine is electromagnetics（电磁学）, and last summer, when I was a technical assistant at a world-famous local lab, I learned about its many practical applications, especially in relation to microstrip（微波传输带）and antenna design. Management at this lab was sufficiently impressed with my work to ask that I return when I graduate. Of course, my plans following completion of my current studies are to move directly into graduate work toward my master's in science. After I earn my master's degree, I intend to start work on my Ph. D. in electrical engineering. Later I would like to work in the area of research and development for private industry. It is in R & D that I believe I can make the greatest contribution, utilizing my theoretical background and creativity as a scientist.

I am highly aware of the superb reputation of your school, and my conversations with several of your alumni have served to deepen my interest in attending. I know that, in addition to your excellent faculty, your computer facilities are among the best in the state. I hope you will give me the privilege of continuing my studies at your fine institution.

Sample 2

Having majored in literary studies (world literature) as an undergraduate, I would now like to concentrate on English and American literature.

I am especially interested in nineteenth-century literature, women's literature, Anglo-Saxon poetry, and folklore and folk literature. My personal literary projects have involved some combination of these subjects. For the oral section of my comprehensive exams, I specialized in nineteenth century novels by and about women. The relationship between "high" and folk literature became the subject for my honors essay, which examined Toni Morrison's use of classical, biblical, African, and Afro-American folk tradition in her novel. I plan to work further on this essay, treating Morrison's other novels and perhaps preparing a paper suitable for publication.

In my studies toward a doctoral degree, I hope to examine more closely the relationship between high and folk literature. My junior year and private studies of Anglo-Saxon language and literature have caused me to consider the question of where the divisions between folklore, folk literature, and high literature lie. Should I attend your school, I would like to resume my studies of Anglo-Saxon poetry, with special attention to its folk elements.

Writing poetry also figures prominently in my academic and professional goals. I have just begun submitting to the smaller journals with some success and am gradually building a working manuscript for a collection. The dominant theme of this collection relies on poems that draw from classical, biblical, and folk traditions, as well as everyday experience, in order to celebrate the process of giving and taking life, whether literal or figurative. My poetry draws from and influences my academic studies. Much of what I read and study finds a place in my creative work as subject. At the same time, I study the art of literature by taking part in the creative process, experimenting with the tools used by other authors in the past.

In terms of a career, I see myself teaching literature, writing criticism, and going into editing or publishing poetry. Doctoral studies would be valuable to me in several ways. First, your teaching assistant ship program would provide me with the practical teaching experience I am eager to acquire. Further, earning a Ph. D. in English and American literature would advance my other two career goals by adding to my skills, both critical and creative, in working with language. Ultimately, however, I see the Ph. D. as an end in itself, as well as a professional stepping stone; I enjoy studying literature for its own sake and would like to continue my studies on the level demanded by the Ph. D. program.

WRITING LETTERS OF RECOMMENDATION

As an employer, coworker or friend, you may at some point in your career be called upon to write a letter of recommendation. If you are unsure about how to go about it or simply don't know what to say, here are some tips about what to include and how to structure a typical letter of recommendation. This advice may also be useful if you request a letter of recommendation from someone who is not familiar with how to write one.

- **First Paragraph—Start out by specifying in what capacity and for how long you have known the person whom you are recommending.** If the person is an employee or coworker, indicate the term of employment, the responsibilities of the position, and any significant projects undertaken by the individual. You may wish to include a sentence about the nature of your company and its activities. Here, you can also give a one-sentence summary or overview of your opinion of the recommended individual.

- **Second Paragraph—In the next paragraph provide a more detailed evaluation of the person as an employee.** Describe his or her performance on specific assignments and list any important accomplishments. What are the individual's strengths or shortcomings in the workplace? What was it like to interact with him or her?

- **Third Paragraph—To sum things up you can make a more broad characterization of the individual and his or her demeanor.** Overall, was the person responsible, polite, warm, disagreeable, lazy, spiteful? Finally, indicate the degree to which you recommend the individual for the position she or he is seeking: without reservation, strongly, with some reservation, or not at all.

Before writing the letter, you may want to ask the person for a list of his or her projects, since you probably will not be aware of all the work they've done. Finally, if you have not had much contact with the person, you may be better off declining to write the letter of recommendation, rather than putting together something vague and dispassionate.

Sample 1
(Positive Recommendation Letter)

Hart Publications, Inc.
1400 Fifth Avenue,
New York, NY 10012
(212) 555-6239

April 10, 2005

Subject: Letter of Recommendation for Mr. James Miller

To Whom It May Concern:

James worked under my supervision as an editorial assistant from September 10, 1997, until April 5, 1998. His responsibilities included conducting research and interviews, fact checking, and writing brief front-of-the-book pieces, in addition to some clerical duties. During the course of his employ-

ment, James proved himself to be an able employee, a hard worker, and a talented writer.

I was quite impressed by James' ability to complete all work assigned to him on time, if not before it was due. His research was always thorough and comprehensive, and his fact checking always accurate. We sometimes allow our editorial assistants to do some writing, but James' talents prompted us to assign him more pieces than the norm. His writing is clear, concise, and evocative.

Overall, James is a very conscientious and able employee. I certainly believe he has what it takes to make a wonderful editor someday, and I am sad to see him leave. I strongly recommend James for any mid-level editorial position in publishing.

Sincerely,
Edward P. Larkin
Edward P. Larkin
Executive Editor

Sample 2
(Peer Recommendation Letter)

Peter S. Simpson
72 East 83rd Street
New York, NY 10019
(212) 555-4635

Letter of Recommendation for Ralph Morris

June 2, 2004

To Whom It May Concern:

I had the pleasant opportunity to work closely with Ralph for six months during his employment at Q & R Services International. He occupied the desk next to mine, and we collaborated on several projects together. I am pleased to say that Ralph is a team player, a kind and sincere individual, and an ideal coworker.

Ralph always did more than his share of the work on the projects we shared. He often took the initiative to get things started and picked up the slack when things were going slowly. I was glad to work with him, since the higher-ups always praised the assignments we completed together. Ralph was nice to everybody at the office, and just about everyone seemed to like him.

I highly recommend Ralph for whatever position he may decide to take up next. He is the type of employee that anyone would be happy to work with.

Sincerely,
Peter S. Simpson
Peter S. Simpson

Sample 3

To whom it may concern:

This is to certify that Mr. Yang Ming, 26, graduated from International Department of Yunnan University with excellent records in 2000 and is now in the service of Kunming Trading Company. He is going to major in International Economics in the Graduate School of your university.

I can assure you of his sincerity and industry. As to his character, talent, and health, I can commend him in the highest terms. I should be highly gratified if you would be kind enough to provide him with guidance and convenience while he is in your institution.

Yours sincerely,
Zhang Hua
Zhang Hua
Professor of Economics

Sample 4

To whom it may concern:

I have the pleasure of recommending Mr. Hao Yangchun for admission to your university to pursue Master's degree in Computer science. He is now a department manager in our company and has displayed a great deal of efficiency. He proves himself to be firmly grounded in basal computer science.

Owing to his intelligence and diligence, he advances swiftly in our company and has got admiration from both his staff and colleagues. He always pays great attention to his work and under any circumstances he shows his perseverance and honesty. His strong sense of responsibility impresses us deeply. He is so reliable that I often trust him with heavy and important responsibilities.

I thus believe he has the ability to carry on successfully his advanced studies at your university. I strongly recommend this promising young man and your favorable consideration and assistance to him will be very much appreciated. If there is any more information concerning his background or work experience, I would like to help you to acquire it. Please contact me without hesitation.

Sincerely yours,
Li Chang
Li Chang
Manager of Kunming Trading Company

RESIGNATION LETTERS

Before resigning:

- **Gather your friends'contact information.** You will probably network with your associates for future jobs.
- **Secure a new job before quitting.** Employers find it difficult to hire people who are unemployed.

Resignation letter tips that may impact your job prospects:

1. Your resignation letter may be read by future employers.

Since your resignation letter will be the final document in your company's personnel file, it will be the first document seen when a future employer calls for a reference or if you reapply at your company.

- Maintain a good relationship with your employer and associates
- Show enthusiasm and appreciation for the work have done
- Emphasize what you have contributed
- Highlight your skills
- Fix all spelling errors and types in your resignation letter

2. Can the tone of the resignation letter hurt the writer later?

Yes! Are you considering writing a resignation letter to vent(发泄)your feelings or get even(平静的)? That is the wrong approach.

If you are angry or see your resignation letter as an opportunity to get revenge, follow this rule: write your letter and set it aside for a day or so. Once you are calm, rewrite it in a way that will help you get future jobs because:

- You may want to reapply for another job with your current employer. Many people do.

- Future employers may call your old boss.
- Your colleagues are watching you as you transition away from your present job. You'll probably want to network with them for your next job.
- Your letter of resignation is the last reflection of your character. Now is the time for grace and class, not revenge.

3. What should my resignation letter accomplish?
- Maintain professional relationships
- Maintain your dignity
- Keep doors open (don't burn bridges)

Write a well-worded resignation letter that highlights your accomplishments. Read a variety of sample resignation and cover letters before writing your own.

Example 1

To: Robert Smith, Sales Manager
From: Bob Fu, Sales Development
Date: May 6, 2001
Subject: Terminating Engagement

Mr. Smith, I have worked in the Sales Development as a salesman for six years, and I have been satisfied with this position. However, a friend of mine introduced me to Goldlion Company, and I have decided to accept a post that will give me greater possibilities for promotion and an increase in my salary. I therefore write this memo as formal notice to terminate my engagement with you one month from today's date.

Example 2

To: Francis Wu, General Office
From: Marc Morgan, Director of Personnel
Date: June 5, 2001
Subject: Terminating Engagement

Mr. Wu, you may already know that the Directors of the company will soon have finished the reorganization of the business and that this will result in a decrease in staff. I am very sorry to inform you that your position is one that will shortly become redundant, and that your services will not continue after the end of this month. We have no cause of complaint against you, on the contrary, we are quite satisfied with your services during the three years. The reduction of staff is entirely due to business dol-

drums. You will of course be entitled to a redundancy payment. In your case you will be given one month's salary for every year of service with the company. Besides, we shall be pleased to provide any prospective employer with a testimonial of your character and ability.

Please contact me if you have any questions.

USEFUL WORDS & EXPRESSIONS

个人品质

able	有才干的，能干的
adaptable	适应性强的
active	主动的，活跃的
aggressive	有进取心的
ambitious	有雄心壮志的
amiable	和蔼可亲的
amicable	友好的
analytical	善于分析的
apprehensive	有理解力的
aspiring	有志气的，有抱负的
audacious	大胆的，有冒险精神的
capable	有能力的，有才能的
careful	（办理）仔细的
candid	正直的
competent	能胜任的
constructive	建设性的
cooperative	有合作精神的
creative	富创造力的
dedicated	有奉献精神的
dependable	可靠的
diplomatic	老练的，有策略的

disciplined	守纪律的
dutiful	尽职的
well-educated	受过良好教育的
efficient	有效率的
energetic	精力充沛的
expressivity	善于表达
faithful	守信的，忠诚的
frank	直率的，真诚的
generous	宽宏大量的
genteel	有教养的
gentle	有礼貌的
humorous	幽默的
impartial	公正的
independent	有主见的
industrious	勤奋的
ingenious	有独创性的
motivated	目的明确的
intelligent	理解力强的
learned	精通某门学问的
logical	条理分明的
methodical	有方法的
modest	谦虚的
objective	客观的
precise	一丝不苟的
punctual	严守时刻的
realistic	实事求是的
responsible	负责的
sensible	明白事理的
sporting	光明正大的

steady	踏实的
systematic	有系统的
purposeful	意志坚强的
sweet-tempered	性情温和的
temperate	稳健的
tireless	孜孜不倦的

教育程度

education	学历
educational history	学历
educational background	教育程度
curriculum	课程
major	主修
minor	副修
educational highlights	课程重点部分
curriculum included	课程包括
specialized courses	专门课程
courses taken	所学课程
special training	特别训练
social practice	社会实践
part-time jobs	业余工作
summer jobs	暑期工作
vacation jobs	假期工作
refresher course	进修课程
extracurricular activities	课外活动
physical activities	体育活动
recreational activities	娱乐活动
academic activities	学术活动
social activities	社会活动

rewards	奖励
scholarship	奖学金
excellent League member	优秀团员
excellent leader	优秀干部
working model	劳动模范
advanced worker	先进工作者
student council	学生会
off-job training	脱产培训
in-job training	在职培训
educational system	学制
academic year	学年
semester	〈美〉学期
term	〈英〉学期
supervisor	论文导师
pass	及格
fail	不及格
marks	分数
examination	考试
degree	学位
post doctorate	博士后
doctor（Ph. D）	博士
master	硕士
bachelor	学士
graduate student	研究生
abroad student	留学生
undergraduate	大学肄业生
government-supported student	公费生
commoner	自费生
extern	走读生

intern	实习生
prize fellow	奖学金生
boarder	寄宿生
graduate	毕业生
guest student	〈英〉旁听生
auditor	〈美〉旁听生
day-student	走读生

工作经历

work experience	工作经历
occupational history	工作经历
professional history	职业经历
specific experience	具体经历
responsibilities	职责
second job	第二职业
achievements	工作成就，业绩
administer	管理
assist	辅助
adapted to	适应于
accomplish	完成(任务等)
appointed	被认命的
adept in	善于
analyze	分析
authorized	委任的；核准的
behave	表现
break the record	打破纪录
breakthrough	关键问题的解决
control	控制
conduct	经营，处理

create	创造
demonstrate	证明，示范
decrease	减少
design	设计
develop	开发，发挥
devise	设计，发明
direct	指导
double	加倍，翻一番
earn	获得，赚取
effect	效果，作用
eliminate	消除
enlarge	扩大
enrich	使丰富
exploit	开发(资源,产品)
enliven	搞活
evaluation	估价，评价
execute	实行，实施
expedite	加快促进
generate	产生
guide	指导；操纵
initiate	创始，开创
innovate	改革，革新
invest	投资
integrate	使结合；使一体化
justified	经证明的；合法化的
launch	开办(新企业)
maintain	保持；维修
modernize	使现代化
nominated	被提名；被认命的

perfect	使完善；改善
perform	执行，履行
be promoted to	被提升为
be proposed as	被提名（推荐）为
recorded	记载的
refine	精练，精制
registered	已注册的
regenerate	更新，使再生
retrieve	挽回
revenue	收益，收入
self-dependence	自力更生
serve	服务，供职
shorten	减低……效能
simplify	简化，精简
standard	标准，规格
supervises	监督，管理
systematize	使系统化
well-trained	训练有素的
target	目标，指标

个人资料

in.	英寸
pen name	笔名
ft.	英尺
alias	别名
district	区
house number	门牌
lane	胡同，巷
height	身高

weight	体重
blood type	血型
permanent address	永久住址
home phone	住宅电话
prefecture	专区
office phone	办公电话
autonomous region	自治区
business phone	办公电话
nationality	民族；国籍
current address	目前住址
citizenship	国籍
native place	籍贯
postal code	邮政编码
dual citizenship	双重国籍
marital status	婚姻状况
family status	家庭状况
married	已婚
single	未婚
divorced	离异
separated	分居
number of children	子女人数
health condition	健康状况
health	健康状况
excellent	（身体）极佳
short-sighted	近视
far-sighted	远视
ID card	身份证
date of availability	可到职时间
membership	会员、资格

president	会长
vice-president	副会长
director	理事
standing director	常务理事
society	学会
association	协会
secretary-general	秘书长
research society	研究会

其他内容：应聘职位

objective	目标
position desired	希望职位
job objective	工作目标
employment objective	工作目标
career objective	职业目标
position sought	谋求职位
position wanted	希望职位
position applied for	申请职位

离职原因

for more specialized work	为更专门的工作
for prospects of promotion	为晋升的前途
for higher responsibility	为更高层次的工作责任
for wider experience	为扩大工作经验
due to close-down of company	由于公司倒闭
due to expiry of employment	由于雇用期满
sought a better job	找到了更好的工作
to seek a better job	找一份更好的工作

业余爱好

hobbies	业余爱好
play the guitar	弹吉他
reading	阅读
play chess	下棋
play	话剧
long distance running	长跑
play bridge	打桥牌
collecting stamps	集邮
play tennis	打网球
jogging	慢跑

EXERCISES

Ⅰ. Prepare your own C. V.

Ⅱ. Assume you're applying for the job position advertised in a local newspaper. Prepare your resume and letter, following the format of the Application Letter and Resume you've learnt.

Ⅲ. Assume you are the dean of School of Economics, Yunnan University. One of your students is applying for admission to a foreign university to pursue Master's degree in economics. He/She asks you to write a letter of recommendation for him/her in support of his/her application.

CHAPTER 14

MEMOS

THE NATURE OF MEMORANDUMS

Memorandums or memos are letters sent within the company, although a few companies use them in outside communication. Primarily memorandums are the written messages exchanged by employees in the daily conduct of their work.

MEMO FORMATS

Memos have different layouts, and different companies have their own styles and sometimes specific form. Most memos include the following elements:

- Title. The word MEMORANDUM or MEMO is usually centered at the top of the page of place at the left margin.
- "To" and "From" Lines. The memo always includes lines using the words "To" and "From" to quickly show who the addressee and sender are. Titles are usually not used, as the parties usually know one another and because this in-house communication is not formal. However, some companies choose to have their employees include titles on memos.
- Date. Dates are important for filing and tracking chronology.
- Subject Line. This concisely summarizes the contents of the memo.

The components can be arranged in different formats in different organizations. Here are four ways you may see them:

TO: TO:

FROM: or   FROM:

SUJECT: SUJECT:

DATE: DATE:

or

TO:

FROM:

DATE:

SUJECT:

or

TO: FROM:

RE: DATE:

Sample Memos

Sample 1

Situation: A general manager Sue Button wants to hold a meeting on quality control. The meeting will be on 18th November, 2003. It will start at 2 o'clock in the afternoon. He wants every department manager to come to the meeting, so he writes a business memo to inform everybody. The memo is as follows:

1.   *MEMO*

2.   *TO:*   *All department managers*

3.   *FROM:*   *Sue Button, General Manager*

4.   *DATE:*   *18 November, 2003*

5.   *SUBJECT:* *A meeting on quality control*

6.   *All department managers should attend a meeting on quality control at 2. 00p. m. on Thursday. Before the meeting, please prepare a list of actions which your department can take to improve our product quality. Unless there is some urgent event, everyone should be present.*

Sample 2

Situation: Tom Brown is the marketing manager of a foreign mobile phone producing company. In order to compete with the Chinese home-made mobile phones, the company wants to lower its prices. The price cut will take effect on 2004 – 1 – 1. In order to inform the wholesalers, Tom writes a business memo as follows.

1. *MEMO*

2. *TO*:   *All sales representatives*

3. *FROM*:   *Tom Brown, Manager of the Marketing Department*

4. *DATE*:   *December 20, 2003*

5. *SUBJECT*:   *Price adjustment*

6. *In 2003, we saw more intensive competition between low price home-made mobile phones and imported mobile phones.*

7. *In order to compete with the low price home-made mobile phones, the company decides to reduce the price of all models of Nokia handsets by 10%. This price reduction will take effect on January 1st, 2004.*

8. *Please inform the wholesalers about this decision as soon as possible.*

Sample 3

MEMO
TO: *All*
FROM: *Martha Cooper, Secretary to Mr. Kellor*
DATE: *March 18, 2003*
SUBJECT: *Long-Distance Telephone Logs*

Please Remember to fill out your long-distance telephone logs each time you place a long distance call. Note the date, time, number called, person called, and the purpose of the call.

Carole or Joan in the print room can give you blank log books when you need them.

Sample 4

> MEMO
> TO: *Sales Staff*
> FROM: *Helen Conroy*
> DATE: *February 26, 2004*
> SUBJECT: *Sales Contest*
>
> *We're ready to go with our March sales contest. Here's how it will work. Gross dollar volume will be tallied at the end of the month. The top three sales people will receive a bonus. Number one will receive $ 150.00; Number two, $ 100; and Number three, $ 76.00. The prizes will be awarded at the April 15 sales meeting.*
>
> *Good luck!*

Sample 5

> MEMO
> TO: *All Agency Staff*
> FROM: *Veroneca Presnell, Office Manager*
> DATE: *June 5, 2004*
> SUBJECT: *NEW CARPET FOR AGENCY OFFICE*
>
> *Next weekend, June 13 – 14, we will be recarpeting the entire agency office. There-fore, before you leave work on Friday, please make sure all wastebaskets, chairs, boxes and other items on the floors are moved into the hallway.*
>
> *Also, clear your desk tops and either put your belongings in your desk drawers (which should be locked) or in boxes. Please label your boxes so that you can find your belongings easily Monday morning. I'm sure we all appreciate getting the new carpeting. Our old carpet has definitely seen better days!*

PLAN FOR WRITING EFFECTIVE MEMOS

Good planning is essential for all business documents you write. Remember, memos and letters are effective to the extent that you carefully plan, organize, and present yours ideas in a concise and clear way. The following six stages are commonly used in practicing writing memos.

Stage 1　Identify the task

Lay your answer out as a memo (or: Set out the memo)

Stage 2　Layout

A memo should include the following information:

- Who is the memo to ?
- Who is the memo from?
- What is the subject of the memo?
- What is the date?

These should be positioned as opposite:

MEMO

To:

From

Subject:

Date:

Stage 3　Identify relevant information

A memo is usually fairly short. It should include enough so that the correct information is communicated, but should not include anything extra to this.

Stage 4　Group/Order relevant information

Often the information in the question is presented in a suitable order. Sometimes, however, the different information may be mixed up. In this case it is useful to group information according to themes.

Stage 5　Write the memo

Language in memos is shorter and more direct than in a letter. Stay to the point, but be polite. Be careful for extra instructions, e. g. questions which say "make up any necessary details".

Stage 6　Check your work

Checklist: Memo

- Have you completed the task? (Will the person who receives the memo be able to understand the message?)
- Is it to the correct person? Is it from the correct person? (Are you writing it under your name?)
- Does the subject line describe the main content in a few words?
- Is the date correct? (The day of writing).

- Have you included all relevant information? [Is any information missing which will hinder (妨碍) understanding of the message?]
- Have you left out all irrelevant information?
- Have you grouped/ordered information in the best way?
- Is the language appropriate for a memo? (Not too polite, but not too short.)
- Have you checked spelling, grammar and punctuation?

Example 1

Situation: At a staff meeting last week it was decided for environmental reasons to save waste paper for recycling.

Task: As Office Manager you are to send a memo to the Managing Director Frank Chadburn, explaining what was decided and why. You should also give brief details of where containers are to be placed in your three-storey office block, and when and by whom they are to be collected.

Note: Lay out your answer as a memo. Make up any necessary details.

Stage 1   Identify the task
Write the memo.

Stage 2   Layout
To: Frank Chadburn , Managing Director
From: (your name), Office Manager
Subject: Recycling waste paper
Date: (today's date)

Stage 3   Identify relevant information
- Introduce new scheme
- Save waste paper for recycling
- Value of waste paper
- Environmental reasons
- Saving trees
- Containers on all floors
- Emptied weekly
- Can sell to recycling firm
- Containers to be placed next to lifts

Stage 4　Group/Order relevant information

- Introduce new scheme
- Save waste paper for recycling
- Environmental reasons
- Saving trees
- Value of waste paper
- Sell to recycling firms
- Containers on all floors
- Next to the lifts
- Emptied weekly

Stage 5　Write the memo

MEMO

To: *Frank Chadburn* , *Managing Director*

From: (*your name*) , *Office Manager*

Subject: *Recycling waste paper*

Date: (*today's date*)

Last week's staff meeting decided to introduce a scheme to save waste paper for recycling , as a way of helping environment.

There are many environmental reasons for this , not least , saving trees. The paper we save is also worth a lot to the company as we can sell it to a recycling firm who will place containers on all floors next to the lifts and will empty them once a week.

Example 2

Situation: You work for a large manufacturing company in the capital of your country. Mr. J Ruru , an executive of your company's branch in Indonesia , is visiting Head Office in your country. You have to arrange the details of his program for tomorrow. He has asked to visit one of the company's main suppliers. Their factory is about 100 kilometers (60 miles) from the capital.

Task: Write a memo to Mr. Ruru , giving the following information:

a. Details of the company he is visiting—name, brief information of its value to your company, time of meeting, the people he is meeting, etc.

b. Details of the transport you have arranged for him—how he is to travel, time he must leave his hotel, expected time of return etc.

c. Suggestions for an evening out in the capital for him—such as restaurant or theater visit with appropriate directions and transport advice.

Note: Set out the memo appropriately, using tomorrow's date. You should make up other appropriate information (names of companies, your position, etc.).

Stage 1　Identify the task

Write a memo.

Stage 2　Layout

To: Mr. Ruru

From: (your name) , Office Manager

Subject: Visit to Glenisia Electronics

Date: (today's date)

Stage 3　Identify relevant information

- Glenisia Electronics
- Supplies electrical systems to our company
- Arrange 11. 30am meeting, Mr. Robert, Development Manager
- Leave Mr. R's hotel 9. 00am by car
- Chauffeur to be back at 6. 00pm
- Unfortunately unable to dine with him tomorrow evening
- Recommend Manuel's Restaurant or Taj Mahal
- Both near main station
- 200m walking distance from hotel

Stage 4　Group/Order relevant information

- Arranged 11. 30a. m. meeting with Mr. Robert Development Manager
- Glenisia Electronics
- Supplies electrical systems to our company
- Chauffeur will collect you 9. 00a. m. at your hotel
- Expect to be back at 6. 00p. m
- Unfortunately unable to dine with you tomorrow evening
- Recommend Manuel's Restaurant or Taj Mahal
- Both near main station

- 200m walking distance from hotel

Stage 5   Write the memo

MEMO

To: *Mr. Ruru*

From: (*your name*), *Office Manager*

Subject: *Visit to Glenisia Electronics*

Date: (*today's date*)

I have arranged a meeting at 11. 30a. m. tomorrow for you with Mr. Roberts, Development Manager at Glenisia Electronics. They are our main supplier of electrical systems. Our chauffeur will collect you at your hotel at 9. 00a. m. and he will return you at 6. 00p. m. .

Unfortunately, I am unable to dine with you tomorrow evening, but I recommend Manuel's Restaurant for Spanish food or the Taj Mahal if you like Indian food. Both are near to the main station and within 200 metres of your hotel.

USEFUL WORDS & EXPRESSIONS

memo /memorandum	备忘录
subject	主题，事由
issue	事由，事件
topic	题目，主题
department	部门
division	部分;部门;(机关的)科,处
section	部门/处/司
office	办公室，办事处，办公厅
gathering	集会，聚会
briefing	发布会，介绍会，吹风会

manager	经理
general manager	总经理
marketing manager	营销经理
human resource manager	人力资源经理，人事部经理
production manager	生产经理，运营经理
accounting manager/ finance manager	财务经理
CEO（Chief Executive Officer）	首席执行官，总经理
CFO（Chief Finance Officer）	首席财务官，财务总监
COO（Chief Operation Officer）	首席运营官，生产总经理
sales representative	营销经理/销售经理/销售代表
head	主任，首长，长
secretary general	秘书长
senior manager	高级经理，高层经理
to improve quality	提高质量，改进质量
to ensure quality	保证质量，提高质量
to enhance quality	提高质量，改善质量
to control quality	控制质量
to attend a meeting	参加会议，出席会议
to take part in a meeting	参加会议，出席会议
to participate a meeting	参加会议，出席会议
to be present at a meeting	参加会议，出席会议
to host a meeting	主办会议，主持会议
to preside over a meeting	主持会议
to chair a meeting	主持会议
price adjustment	价格调整，调价
price cut, price reduction/ price drops	降价
price raising/price increase	提价
to cut price/to reduce the price/price drops/to lower the price	降价

to raise price/to push up price/to increase price/price rises	提价
to adjust the price	调价
competition	竞争
to compete	竞争
competitive	竞争的，有竞争力的
intensive	激烈的
cut throat	白热化的/你死我活的
home-made	国产的
imported	进口的
exported	出口的
foreign	外国的
mobile phone	移动电话，手机
cell phone	移动电话，手机
handset	手机
fixed line phone	固定电话，固话
long distance service	长途电话，长话
PHS (personal handset service)	小灵通
SMS (short message service)	手机短信
WAP	无线上网
wireless service	无线业务
model	款式，型号
brand	品牌
to take effect	生效
to be in effect/ to come into effect/to go into effect	生效
to inform	通知，告知，知会
to tell, to notify	通知，告知
wholesaler	批发商

retailer	零售商
chief sales representative	销售总代表
in order to	为了
for the purpose of	为了
to strengthen/ to enhance	加强
to increase/ to enlarge	扩大
market share	市场份额
incorporate group	集团
stay to the point	紧扣主题

EXERCISES

I. Complete the Stage 4 and Stage 5 of the following memo:

Situation: The staff restaurant on the fourth floor of your office block is to be closed for one week for re-decoration.

Task: As Catering Manager(餐厅经理)you are to send a memo to the Office Manager, Peter MacParland, explaining why the restaurant is to close and for how long. Specify what alternative(另一个可选择的)arrangements will be made for providing drinks and snacks（快餐）during the morning and afternoon breaks, and providing meals at lunch time.

Note: Lay out your answer as a memo. Make up any necessary details.

Stage 1   Identify the task
Write the memo.

Stage 2   Layout
To: Peter MacParland, Office Manager
From: (your name), Catering Manager
Subject: Closure of staff restaurant
Date: (today's date)

Stage 3   Identify relevant information
   • restaurant closed for one week, from next Monday

- re-decoration
- catering firm will sell drinks and sandwiches during morning and afternoon breaks
- near reception, first floor
- lunches provided at Rafters Restaurant in the High Street
- open 12p. m. – 1p. m.
- special menu for employees at usual prices

Now complete the following stages.

Stage 4　Group/Order relevant information
....

Stage 5　Write the memo
....

II. Use the word list to help replace the Chinese words with suitable English words

1	备忘录	
2	致:	All sales representatives
3	自:	Tom Brown, Manager of the Marketing Department
4	日期:	December 20, 2003
5	事由:	Price adjustment
6	In 2003, we saw 激烈竞争 between 低价国产手机 and imported mobile phone.	
7	为了 compete with the low price homemade mobile phones, 公司决定 to reduce the price of 诺基亚各款手机 by 10%. 这次降价 will take effect in January 1st, 2004.	
8	请通知各批发商 about this decision as soon as possible.	

III. Replace the Chinese words with suitable English words

1	备忘录	
2	致：	All department managers
3	自：	Sue Button, General Manager
4	日期：	18 November, 2003
5	事项：	A meeting on quality control
6	各部门经理 should attend a meeting 关于质量控制 on Thursday afternoon, at 2:00 p. m. Before the meeting, please 列举各种行动 which your department can take to improve our product quality. Unless there is some urgent event, 不得缺席	

IV. Correct the following memo according to what you've learnt in this chapter.

Memo
FROM: Helen Conroy
TO: Sales Staff
ABOUT: Sales Contest
TIME: February 25, 2004

We're ready to go with our March sales contest. Here's how it will work. Gross dollar volume will be tallied at the end of the month. The top three sales people will receive a bonus. Number one will receive $ 150.00; Number two, $ 100, and Number three, $ 76.00. The prizes will be awarded at the April 15 sales meeting.

Good luck!

V. Reorder the following pieces of information and make them into a memo according to the structure analysis.

1. SUBJECT: NEW CARPET FOR AGENCY OFFICE
2. Also, clear your desk tops and either put your belongings in your desk drawers (which should be locked) or in boxes.
3. TO: All Agency Staff
4. I'm sure we all appreciate getting the new carpeting.
5. Next weekend, June 13 – 14, we will be recarpeting the entire agency office.
6. DATE: June 5, 2004
7. Therefore, before you leave work on Friday, please make sure all wastebaskets, chairs, boxes and other items on the floors are moved into the hallway.
8. Please label your boxes so that you can find your belongings easily Monday morning.
9. MEMO
10. Our old carpet has definitely seen better days!
11. FROM: Veroneca Presnell, Office Manager

CHAPTER 15

BUSINESS REPORT WRITING

There are many different types of reports—scientific lab reports, business reports, systems analysis reports, management case study reports, feasibility studies, client case work reports. All of these different reports have their own formats and conventions. In your field of study, you will need to find out exactly what the accepted report conventions are. Note that these conventions may vary from one subject to another.

All students who choose Business Studies must learn to write business reports. It is undeniable that writing a business report is not an easy job. With practice, however, business report writing can be an easy skill to master.

Business reports are a means of communication to gain and give information on which business decision making is based on. In general, business reports fall into 4 major categories: feasibility reports, comparative reports, evaluation reports and project reports. They can be submitted as routine reports at regular intervals, for example, representative's report on regional sales, or produced as non-routine reports as requested, say a detailed report on a major complaint concerning product quality.

LAYOUT OF BUSINESS REPORT

Both routine or non-routine business reports have the same structural parts – head, introduction, middle, end and bottom.

Formal reports

Formal reports are usually produced by a management executive in charge, a committee or a group of people after fairly detailed investigation or research. They are often presented under the following fixed headings:

| **Head** | **Title of Report** | Name of the company |

		Heading of the report
		Why is the report needed?
	Terms of reference	What is requested?
		Who requested it?
Introduction		
	Procedure	How the information is collected.
		Central part of the report
Middle	**Findings**	Information presented logically in sections
		Sub-headings and enumeration used
End	**Conclusions**	Based on the information in findings
		Statement of logical implication of findings
	Recommendations	Based on finding and conclusions
		Suggestions and actions to be taken
Bottom	**Signature**	Name of the report writer
	Date	Date of completion of report

Formal business reports can also be presented with headings specific to the subject matter, or with findings divided into pro and cons, for and against etc. , as often seen in reports requiring an argument. The following format is suggested:

XXXXXXXXXXXXXXXXXXXXXXXXXXX   Report title (Initial capitals)

– – – – – – – – – – – –   Introduction connecting terms of ref-
– – – – – – – – – – – –   erence and procedure (who? what?
– – – – – – – – – – – –   why? and how?)

1. nnnnnnnnnnnnnnnnnnnnnnn   Findings

– – – – – – – – – – – –   Use sub-headings to classify the in-
– – – – – – – – – – – –   formation logically with consistent use
– – – – – – – – – – – –   of enumeration.

2. nnnnnnnnnnnnnnnnnnnnnnn

2. 1 – – – – – – – – – –   Break up information into two sec-
2. 2 – – – – – – – – – –   tions: The case for/pros/benefits and
2. 3 – – – – – – – – – –   the case against/cons/drawbacks.

XXXXXXXXXXXXXXXXX   Conclusions

– – – – – – – – – –   State the logical implications of the
– – – – – – – – – –   findings.

XXXXXXXXXXXXXXXXX

1. – – – – – – – – – –   Recommendations
2. – – – – – – – – – –   Suggest actions and give reasons
3. – – – – – – – – – –   if necessary

– – – – – – – – – – – –   Name
– – – – – – – – – – –   Date

Informal reports

Informal reports are often produced as accounts of daily business matters, or anything requiring quick decisions. These reports often take the form of a memorandum, with simplified layout.

To   the name and position of the person requesting the report

From	the name and position of the person submitting the report
Date	day/month/year of writing the report
Subject	a brief and specific title for the report

Introduction

Findings

Recommendations

or:

To	the name and position of the person requesting the report
From	the name and position of the person submitting the report
Date	day/month/year of writing the report
Subject	a brief and specific title for the report

Introduction

The case for/Pros/advantages

The case against/Cons/disadvantages

Recommendations

Reasons

Sections and contents of business report

A typical business report usually consists of the following parts:

Title page
Abstract
Table of Contents
Introduction
Purpose
Methodology
Limitations etc.
Findings

Discussion

Conclusions

Recommendations

References

Appendices

Title page

The title page should show the title of the report, the course, the author(s), and the date the report was submitted. This is very useful information; do not omit it.

Abstract

The abstract is a brief (one or two paragraph) description of what you did and what you found. You may also include a sentence or two about why you did whatever you did as well, if you feel it's important. The abstract must not be a summary of your thought processes for writing the report. Do not write the experiment was completed, the data was analyzed, and conclusions were drawn. Remember, the higher a person is in an organization, the less likely he/she is to read the entire report. The top managers will often read only the abstract (and if this is interesting, they may read the conclusions) and decide whether or not your project was worthwhile. Also, abstracts of engineering reports and scientific papers are made available to other researchers through computer data bases. Since a potential reader may have to sift (审查; 仔细检查和挑选) through a lot of abstracts, the relevance and quality of your work may be judged on the basis of your abstract alone. Therefore, the abstract must stand on its own.

Table of contents

The table of contents (or contents) is a very important part of any report, yet it is often neglected by students. It is important because it tells the reader, who doesn't want to spend a lot of time turning pages, where to find the information he/she is looking for. You should include a table of contents in every report you prepare. The longer the report, the more important the table of contents becomes. If the document is too short (only a few pages) to warrant a table of contents, you should consider writing a memorandum instead of a report. (A memorandum does not require a table of contents) Look in any text book and you will find a good example of a table of contents. Basically, the Contents list the sections and subsections of the report and show the number of the page on which each section and subsection begins. Some word processing programs (including WordPerfect) can generate a table of contents based on your section and sub-section headings.

In some reports, a list of figures and a list of tables are also included immediately following the Contents. If used, each of these begins on a new page and lists the figure/table numbers, titles, and the corresponding page numbers.

The page on which the Introduction begins is page one (1). Any pages that appear before page 1 are preliminary pages and are usually given lower case Roman numerals beginning with the title page as page i, the abstract as page ii, and so on. The page number is not printed on the title page, but should appear on all subsequent pages.

Introduction

The introduction to your report should provide background information about the subject and a clear statement of the objectives of the project. This means that you have to do some research on the subject, recall what you actually did, and then get it down on paper in a clear and logical fashion. Ideally two sub-sections are to be included in Introduction: Background and Objectives (Purpose).

Other sections that may be included in your Introduction are Limitations, Methodology, and Assumptions.

Findings

This section involves problem identification and analysis. It is often divided into sub – sections, one for each problem. Each problem identified should be related to theory, and to evidence from the case.

Discussion

This section involves summarising major problems and evaluating alternative solutions. There is likely be more than one solution per problem. Strengths and weaknesses should be examined.

Conclusion

The Conclusion sums up the main points which have emerged from the Findings and the Discussion. In some reports, it may be combined with Recommendations.

Recommendations

This section should put forward which of the proposed solutions should be adopted. It is intended to persuade, and so should be written in a forceful style. You can use the theory (again) to justify your proposals.

Implementation (执行, 落实)

This section is a practice and should explain what should be done, by whom, and in what time frame. Cost details should be included if appropriate. In some reports, this section may be combined with Recommendations.

References

Be careful to cite your sources correctly, using either the in-text (Harvard) or the Endnote system.

Appendices (if any)

Appendices contain original data relevant to the study, but which would interrupt the flow of the main body.

REPORT WRITING STYLE

There are at least 3 distinct report writing styles that can be applied by students of Business Studies. They are called:

- Conservative
- Key points
- Holistic(整体的,全盘的)

These styles are sequential. This means, the report is structured around the format of the question. Thus the question provides the framework for the answer.

Conservative style

This suits students who are good essay writers and who feel a bit uncomfortable with the idea of utilizing the report writing tools. They may feel that application of margins or using a colored highlighter might make their report look less 'serious'.

In such cases a conservative style should be applied. Essentially, the conservative approach takes the best structural elements from essay writing and integrates these with appropriate report writing tools. Thus headings would be used to deliberate different sections of the answer. In addition, space would be well utilised by ensuring that each paragraph is distinct (perhaps separated from other paragraphs by leaving two blank lines in between).

Key point style

This style utilizes all of the report writing tools and is thus more overtly "report-looking".

Use of headings, underlining, margins, diagrams and tables are common. Occasionally students might even use indentation and dot points.

The important thing for students to remember is that the tools should be applied in a way that adds to the report. The question must be addressed and the tools applied should assist in doing that.

An advantage of this style is the enormous amount of information that can be delivered relatively quickly.

Holistic style

The most complex and unusual of the styles, holistic report writing aims to answer the question from a thematic(主题的,论题的) and integrative(综合的,一体化的) perspective. This style of report writing requires that students have a strong understanding of the course and are able to see which outcomes are being targeted by the question.

In conclusion, students should practice writing business reports that integrate the Topic areas. This should help them feel confidence prior to attempting their major exams. Well structured reports enable students to demonstrate their knowledge and understanding of the Business Studies course. Good reports convey a huge amount of relevant information and can be written in about 40 minutes. Students need to settle on a preferred style and need to ensure that they utilize appropriate business terminology and link their response to the stimulus.

THE EFFECTIVE WRITING OF BUSINESS REPORT

A three-stage approach of writing business report

A three-stage approach is recommended when writing your report:

Stage 1　Case analysis

Stage 2　Report planning
Develop a report outline (i. e. , the overall structure of your report) by identifying particular headings and subheadings. The framework structure may be helpful, but you may use another structure if it presents your analysis in a better fashion.

- List the ideas associated with each heading and subheading. Group related ideas where possible and then arrange them in a logical order.
- Plan exhibits
- Plan the introduction and the conclusion (but do not use phrases such as "The Introduction," "The Conclusion," or "The Main Body" as the headings).

Stage 3　Report writing
- Use the outline you developed in stage 2. Write the first draft.
- Develop one paragraph for each idea or topic. Write a strong opening sentence for each paragraph, which will indicate the conclusions you made at the case analysis stage.

- When presenting more than three facts or numbers at one time, consider whether a table or chart might communicate the information better in fewer words.
- Avoid redundant or overblown words.
- Be concise. When 6 words will replace 14 words, let them do so!
- Check grammar, spelling, and punctuation.
- Number the pages.
- Write draft 2, correcting for errors, wordiness and unnecessarily pretentious words.
- Proofread draft 2. It's a good idea to have another person do this. Correct/improve as necessary.
- Are exhibits labeled and numbered, and in the order they are mentioned in the report?

The four-step process of compiling business reports recommended by LCCI

The following four steps have proved effective in business report writing:

Step 1   Thinking and planning

The compiling of business reports should begin with careful thinking. And in the course of thinking the following four questions must be answered:
- Why does this report have to be produced?
- Who is going to read the report?
- What information is required?
- How is the data to be collected?

While answering the above four questions you can plan how to proceed to the next step of the report writing.

Step 2   Collecting/Selecting and grouping data

Data are vital to business report writing. Data can be collected verbally or in writing. Verbal data collection usually means formal or informal conversations with people (e. g. an opinion survey), attending presentations, meetings and so on. Written data collection means collecting relevant written information which you can use in your report. It is quite common to write to people either outside your company (by letter) or inside your company (by memos) asking for information.

The information collected need to be selected and grouped into different sections – introduction, findings, conclusions and recommendations. Subheadings are very helpful in grouping the information, especially the findings.

Step 3 Presenting information

• Presentation of findings

Findings are simple descriptions of what you have found out, they should be written clearly and briefly, in short, logically connected paragraphs.

In writing business report, topic sentences are very important in helping you organize your paragraphs logically and clearly. In terms of writing business report, topic sentences are very simple, and they do not contain complex ideas or detail. They contain global ideas that act as an introduction to details later, or as a summary of details presented earlier.

• Presentation of conclusions

While writing business report, you will often have to compare and contrast two or more things in order to come to conclusions. Comparisons involve looking at the similarities between two or more things while contrasts mean looking at the differences between two or more things.

• Making Recommendations

Recommendations should be specific and constructive. And it is normal to describe what will happen if your recommendation is followed (and what might happen if it is not). For example, if you recommend a change of policy, what will the result be in terms of costs, procedures, etc?

e. g. *These measures will result in an improvement in working and living conditions.*

The policy may lead to an economic recession in the long run.

The changes might allow for a shortage of experienced technicians.

Step 4 Revising

It is necessary to make revisions while writing a business report. If you adopt a continuous revision policy then the report should be effective.

Two checklists for writing business report

The following two checklists are suggested by the LCCI: one to check the language, the other to evaluate the effectiveness of the report.

Ten linguistic guidelines

• Limit a sentence to a single statement of fact or one idea. This will produce simple or compound sentences rather than complex ones, in which there are the problems of handling support clauses.

• The optimum sentence length is approximately 20 words. However, in order to prevent your report from becoming monotonous, occasionally introduce shorter and longer sentences.

- Ensure that your sentences are properly linked.
- Check your pronouns. Make sure that the identity of the noun to which the pronoun relates is immediately clear.
- Make a conscious choice between using active or passive sentences.
- If you are not fully satisfied with a sentence, it may be better to rewrite it completely rather than try to alter parts of the original.
- Reread everything you write, with the aim of removing ambiguities(含糊,不明确). Make sure that your words and sentences can only have one possible meaning—the meaning which you intend.
- Learn to identify and avoid verbiage(空话), jargon, circumlocution(婉转曲折的陈述), clichés(陈词滥调) and slang(俚语,行话).
- Check the word order of your sentences.
- Check all tenses, prepositions and subject/verb agreements(一致), spelling and punctuation.

Ten evaluation questions

- Does the report relate to the aim?
- Does the reader get sufficient information?
- Is the information necessary for the reader?
- Is the subject heading appropriate?
- Can the reader get the important details quickly and easily?
- Can your reader follow the development of your ideas?
- Is your tone suitable to your reader and your aim?
- Is your layout correct and consistent?
- Are any of the words or expressions superfluous?
- Is your style suitable? (formal/informal, personal/impersonal, vocabulary, grammar)

SAMPLE BUSINESS REPORT

Report on campus canteen improvement

Terms of reference
Faculties as well as students have put ideas forward to improve the auditorium. The President has asked for a report to be drawn up with suggestions on the subject.

Proceedings

I have questioned a large number of students and faculty members.

Findings

- *Most think that auditorium should be enlarged to hold more audience.*
- *Many believe that the auditorium could be refurnished to save space.*
- *Some think that staggering the business hour is a good idea.*
- *Others propose that effective measures be taken to improve the management.*
- *Few recommend the auditorium setting be beautified.*

Conclusions

Most people agree that the auditorium cannot function efficiently under the present system.

Recommendations

I recommend that staggered business hour be introduced to alleviate(减轻) the overcrowding and save the cost of enlarging the auditorium.

Hamilton

25 November 2005

Report on petty pilfering and vandalism in the company

Introduction

There has been increasing evidence recently of petty pilfering(偷,窃) and vandalism(恶意破坏的行为) in the company. Following the request of Mr. Smith to prepare a report for him to submit to the next Directors'meeting, I have collected relevant information and analyzed it.

Findings

Lost Items

Some items which have been reported missing are staplers, whole reams of stationery, filing wallets, 2 pocket walkmans, a leather coat, several purses, and many small items taken from the cloakroom(衣帽间).

Vandalism

Although no major damage has been reported, graffiti(在墙壁等上的乱涂乱抹) in cloakrooms and lifts is annoying. There has been an increasing number of reports of machinery and equipment suddenly being discovered to be faulty, for which there is no apparent reason. However, they are happening too often to be accidental.

Problems of Access

A lot of new, mainly young staff on work experience programmes have easy access to and from production and office areas. This makes it difficult for security to check and recognize new faces. This is not thought to be a case of intruders breaking into the buildings. There has been no evidence of such incidents.

Staff Morale

The recent compulsory redeployment of some of our factory operators has upset many staff members, and the lack of union opposition has left them feeling "betrayed". Although it is difficult to assess the mood of all staff, it is clear that they are more tense than last year. Supervisors have also reported increasing absenteeism(旷课,旷工) and grievances about working conditions.

G. Wells
Personnel Director
15 December, 2005

Conclusions

It must be stressed that the present situation does not warrant over-reaction. Ther are clearly signs of dissatisfaction among staff, however, possibly over the redeployment (调遣，调换) issue.

Recommendations

- *Senior staff should be more alert in noting misbehavior or anything suspicious, and look carefully into grievances.*
- *Tighter checks should be made on locking away removable, again by senior staff and supervisors.*
- *Notices should be displayed in all working areas warning staff of the risk of personal accidents from damaged equipment, and asking for such equipment to be reported immediately.*
- *The situation should be closely monitored. Advice and information must be gathered at senior and supervisory levels.*

Report highlights

Optimism grows ...

Those who are bearish about North America are an endangered species. Almost nobody thinks business will get worse next year and three quarters think it will improve, compared with a half last time.

... even in Europe

Nearly 60% think business will improve in Europe and very few think it will deteriorate —but this re-

sult is heavily driven by optimists, so beware.

Fear of recession a fading memory
Today's major concerns are about the threat to business of a falling dollar and acts of terrorism.

... but ...
Only one in three companies have tried and tested plans in place to counter acts of terror—and they are much more likely to ...

Meanwhile ...
There is a strong belief that technology investment has ...

And ...
It is new products ...

... that the market needs,

but IP is a problem ...

... while technology management improves

TABLE OF CONTENTS

Executive summary ··· *1*

Section 1: Business
Outlook ··· *1*
QUESTION 2 – REGIONAL BUSINESS OUTLOOK ································· *1*
QUESTION 3 – GLOBAL DEVELOPMENTS IMPACTING BUSINESS ·················· *3*

Section 2: Human
Capital ·· *4*
QUESTION 4 – TECHNOLOGY MANAGEMENT RETENTION PROGRAMS ·············· *4*
QUESTION 5 – TECHNOLOGY MANAGEMENT SKILLS WITH HIGHEST IMPACT ·············· *5*

Section 3: Technology
Alignment ··· *6*
QUESTION 6 – COMPETITIVENESS OF TECHNOLOGY INVESTMENTS ··············· *6*

QUESTION 7 – ALIGNING BUSINESS AND TECHNOLOGY OBJECTIVES ························· 7

QUESTION 8 – ALIGNMENT OF TECHNOLOGY RESOURCES WITH BUSINESS
OBJECTIVES ··· 9

Section 4: Technology
Innovation ·· 10
QUESTION 9 – TECHNOLOGY INNOVATIONS WITH GREATEST BUSINESS
IMPACT ·· 10
QUESTIONS 10, 11 & 12 – PAST, CURRENT & FUTURE COMPETITIVENESS
OF TECHNOLOGY INNOVATION ·· 12
QUESTION 13 – FACTORS FOR SUCCESSFUL INNOVATION . ······························· 14

Section 5: Strategic Project and Process
Management ··· 16
QUESTION 14 – CONFIDENCE IN EVOLVING TECHNOLOGIES ···························· 16
QUESTION 15 – MOST CONFIDENT STATEMENTS ·· 17
QUESTION 16 – LEAST CONFIDENT STATEMENTS ·· 19
QUESTION 17 – EFFECTIVENESS OF OUTSOURCING PROGRAM ····················· 21
QUESTION 18 – CONTINGENCY PLANS FOR ACTS OF TERRORISM ················ 22
QUESTION 19 – OVERALL CONFIDENCE IN TECHNOLOGY MANAGEMENT ·········· 23

Appendix A: Pairs analysescharts ·· i

Appendix B: Profile of GTCI Senior ExecutivePanel ·· iii

Appendix C: GTCI questionnaire, Volume II, 2003 ··· iv

Appendix D: Report methodology & definition ofterms ··· vii

Executive summary

The GTCI Index

In the summary of our inaugural report based on the results of our first survey, administered in May 2003, we stated that confidence was the dominating theme of our findings. Five months on, in November 2003, we find that confidence has not diminished but rather increased even more. Based on a value of 100 for May 2003, our first estimate of the new overall Global Technology Confidence Index is:

The GTCI Index = XXX. X

This index is a mixture of confidence in the business outlook and confidence in various aspects of technology management.

Business Confidence Index

The business confidence measure was where the increase came from, both for the world as a whole and, more specifically, for the U. S. in particular.

GTCI : *Business confidence Index (world) = XXX. X*

GTCI : *Business confidence Index (U. S. A.) = XXX. X*

This striking increase in bullishness is explained in more detail in section 1 of this report.

Technology Confidence Index

Three quarters of the weighting of the overall index, however, is taken by three measures of technology confidence and here there has been no rise since last May, but rather a small fall from the incredibly high levels we found last time.

GTCI : *Technology confidence Index = XXX. X*

Further details on our findings for confidence in technology innovation, strategic project management and technology management are presented in the relevant sections of this report.

Business Outlook

We find great confidence that business will be. . .

(Continued). . .

Sample potential & opportunities report for Electrical Pty Ltd

This sample report is intended to give you an idea of the structure of the Potential and Opportunities report outlined in <u>Business Planning</u>.

Contents

1. Introduction

2. Business Breakdown by Customers

3. Market Breakdown by Competitors

4. Market Breakdown by Customers

5. Potential & Ability

6. Current Performance

7. Segment Surplus

8. Forecasts

9. Investment

10. SWOT Analysis

Appendix 1 – Data Tables

Appendix 2 – Instructions

1. Introduction

The information presented in this report is based on details provided as input for stage one of the BIZPEP Business Planning and Coaching Program. This information has been distilled(提取) and utilized in models to highlight(使显著,突出) business potential and opportunities. The document is designed to provide insight into the business and instigate(鼓动;发起;促成) actions to improve business performance. It forms the basis of Stage two, Decisions and Actions. Data tables not presented in the body of the report are included in Appendix 1. The methodology(方法学,方法论) is outlined in the input instructions. A reference copy is provided in Appendix 2. Green table cells represent data provided as input.

A combination of tables, charts and findings are given for each section. The SWOT Analysis acts as a summary of key points identified during input and processing. Consider the points given and their effect on your business. Use them to develop a vision of potential and opportunities. The next stage is to convert the vision to Decisions & Actions. To achieve this BIZPEP will provide a worksheet(工作表) to distill and define your actions. It will be processed using our Decision Assistant Model. This will indicate possible outcomes (helping you to make the best decision) and establish means to monitor performance.

Follow these guides to gain the most out of this report:
- Review the contents.
- Do not over analyze.
- Consider the points raised and their value to your business.
- Identify the points that add most value.
- Develop a vision for your business.
- Define the areas you wish to focus on.

To convert the vision to reality set a time to complete the Decision & Actions stage. This requires approximately one hour of your time and should be undertaken within one week of receiving your Potential & Opportunities report.

2. Business breakdown（细目分类）by customers

Business Breakdown by Customers

Customer Segment	Number of Customers in Segment	Auera go Number of Sales per Customer	Average Revenue per Sale	Revenue by Customer Segment	Unsecured Revenue
Real Estate Agents	3	120	100	36,000	7,000
Industrial R & M	5	75	400	150,000	0
Local Councils	1	25	1,500	37,500	35,000
General R & M	150	1	580	84,000	0
Installation	5	1	3,000	15,000	0
Total Business Revenue	164	6	352	322,500	42,000

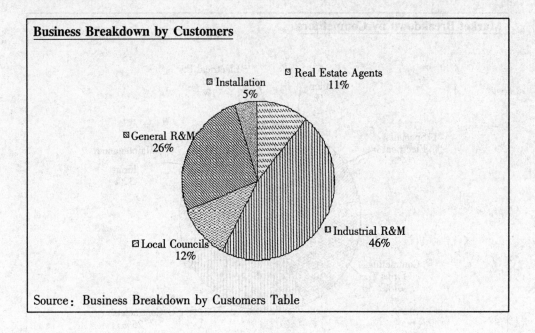

Source: Business Breakdown by Customers Table

Critical（评论的,批评的）findings:
- Customers are spread across four main segments（节,段）providing a broad base but this may contribute to resource conflict from different customers. Does the business know what it wants to be? What are its strengths and how do they support each customer base.
- Unsecured（不稳当的,未固定的）revenue（ $ 42,000 ）exists with current customers, why does this go to competitors?

3. Market breakdown by competitors

Market Breakdown by Competitors

Competitor Groups	Number of Competitors in Group	Average Revenue per Competitor	Revenue by Competitor Group
Maintenace Firms	9	1,000,000	9,000,000
Individual Contractors	70	100,000	7,000,000
Contracting Firms	20	300,000	6,000,000
Specialist Electrical	10	400,000	4,000,000
Other	20	100,000	2,000,000
Electrical Pty Ltd	1	322,500	322,500
Developed Market Size			28,322,500

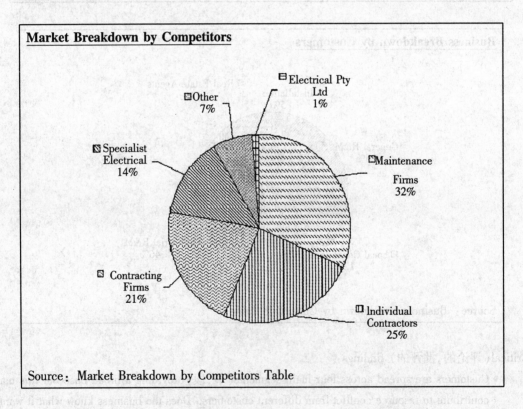

Market Breakdown by Competitors

Source: Market Breakdown by Competitors Table

Critical findings.

- Small market share (1%) presents opportunities to target competitors(订约人,承包人)core customers. This could provide substantial revenue increases with limited competitor impact or reaction.
- High number (70) of competitors in Individual Contractors segment. Successful differentia-tion(区别,差别；划分)would place the business above the crowd providing customers with

real choice.

- The high average revenue of Maintenance firms (1,000,000) may present a specialist opportunity by targeting a specific customer base. These competitors account for the largest portion of the market 32%. This also indicates an opportunity for development.

4. Market breakdown by customers

Market Breakdown by Customers

Customer Segment	Number of Customers in Segment	Auera go Number of Sales per Customer	Average Revenue per Sale	Revenue by Customer Segment	Business Share of Customer Segment
Real Estate Agents	85	120	100	1,022,500	3.5%
Industrial R & M	367	75	400	11,000,000	1.4%
Local Councils	8	25	1,500	300,000	12.5%
General R&M	5,357	1	560	3,000,000	2.8%
Installation OK	4,333	5 0	59.5	28,322,500	1.1%
Undeveloped Market Data & Control Systems	100	1	150,000	15,000,000	

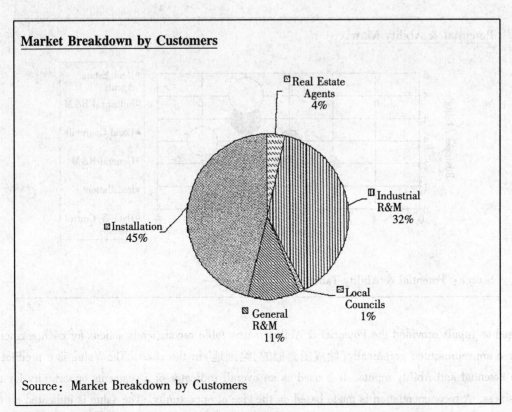

Market Breakdown by Customers

Real Estate Agents 4%

Industrial R&M 32%

Local Councils 1%

General R&M 11%

Installation 45%

Source: Market Breakdown by Customers

Critical findings:

- Revenue opportunity in excess of $ 1,000,000 exists in all segments except Local Councils.
- The highest market share (12.5%) is held in the segment offering the least growth opportunity, Local Councils.
- Two segments, Industrial R & M and Installation, offer revenue opportunities in excess of $ 10,000,000.

5. Potential & Ability

Potential & Ability Matrix

Customer Segment	Segment Potential	Business Ability	Value	Action
Real Estate Agents	4	4	16	Review
Industrial R&M	4	5	20	Develop
Local Councils	3	3	9	Review
General R&M	2	2	4	Divest
Installation	3	2	6	Divest
Data & Control Systems	5	3	15	Review

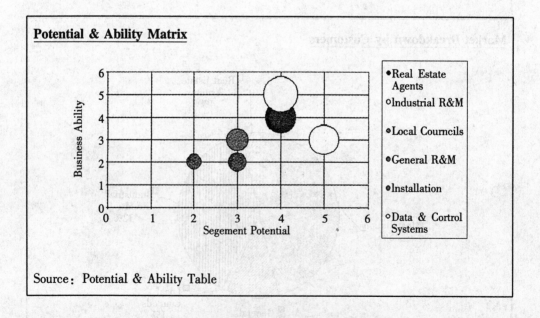

Source: Potential & Ability Table

Based on inputs provided the Potential & Ability matrix table recommends actions for each segment. These are represented graphically(绘成图画似的，绘画地) in the chart. The Value is a product of the Potential and Ability inputs. It is used as an overall indicator of a segments opportunity for the business. A recommendation is made based on the size of opportunity. The value is indicated on the chart by the size of the bubble(气泡;泡).

Critical Findings：
- Industrial maintenance provides the best Value and consideration should be given to developing this segment.
- Three segments Real Estates, Data & Control Systems and Local Councils are rated as review.
- Effort directed in other segments should be minimized.

6. Current performance

Breakeven Point Business Surplus

Breakeven Point	Yearly	Monthly	Weekly
Revenue	190,696	15,891	3,667
Number of Sales	541.0	45.1	10.4

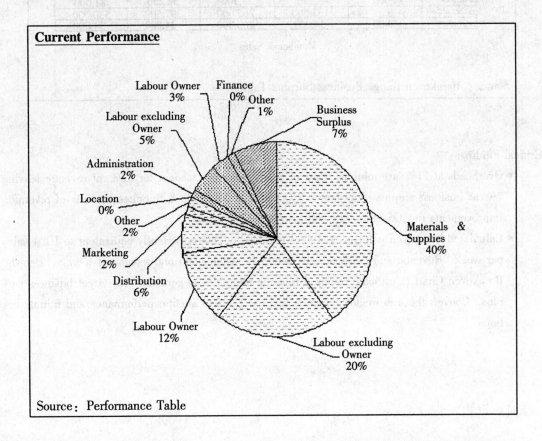

Current Performance

Labour Owner 3%
Finance 0%
Other 1%
Labour excluding Owner 5%
Administration 2%
Location 0%
Other 2%
Marketing 2%
Distribution 6%
Labour Owner 12%
Business Surplus 7%
Materials & Supplies 40%
Labour excluding Owner 20%

Source：Performance Table

Using the performance(成绩,业绩) data provided, a Breakeven(无亏损) Point has been determined. This represents the number of sales and revenue required for the business to generate(产生,

发生)a surplus (profit). This is provided as yearly, monthly and weekly values in the Breakeven Point Business Surplus table. The Breakeven Business Surplus plots(图) Overheads(上面的,位于上部的) Cost of Sales and Business Surplus over a range of sales quantities.

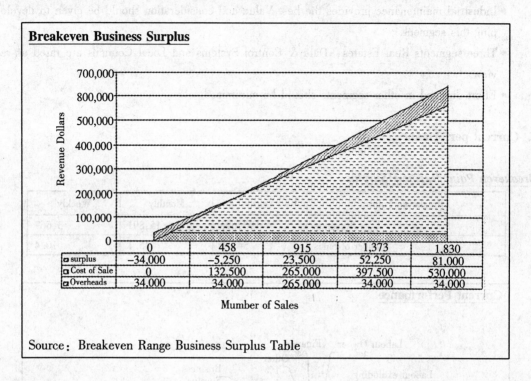

Breakeven Business Surplus

	0	458	915	1,373	1,830
surplus	−34,000	−5,250	23,500	52,250	81,000
Cost of Sale	0	132,500	265,000	397,500	530,000
Overheads	34,000	34,000	265,000	34,000	34,000

Mumber of Sales

Source: Breakeven Range Business Surplus Table

Critical Findings:

- Overheads at 11% are minimal, Cost of Sales expenses account for 82% of revenue leaving 7% as business surplus. The largest COS item is Materials & Supplies, at 40% of revenue. Improvements in COS efficiency will provide high returns.

- Calculated breakeven point is $ 3,667 per week. This is currently equivalent to 10.4 sales per week. Revenue and Sales targets should be established and monitored weekly. Use the Breakeven Chart to estimate required revenue and sales to generate your target business surplus. Convert these to weekly numbers and use them to monitor performance and initiate actions.

7. Segment surplus

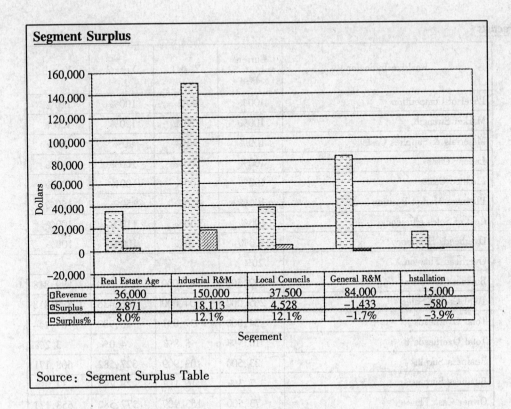

Segment Surplus

	Real Estate Age	hdustrial R&M	Local Councils	General R&M	hstallation
Revenue	36,000	150,000	37.500	84,000	15,000
Surplus	2,871	18,113	4,528	−1,433	−580
Surplus%	8.0%	12.1%	12.1%	−1.7%	−3.9%

Segement

Source: Segment Surplus Table

To assess the "profitability" of customer segments the level of segment surplus has been estimated. This is based on the revenue generated for each segment and an allocation of service costs based on the level of resources utilized.

Critical Findings:

- A negative surplus (loss) is indicated in the General R & M (− $ 1 ,433) and Installation (装设)(− $ 580) segments. These are diluting(冲淡,变弱)business performance. Effort should be redirected into segments that provide improved return on resources.

- All other segments provide comparable and acceptable surplus for effort. The best returns are secured in the Industrial R & M and Local Council segments.

- Industrial R & M contributes 77% of the current business surplus.

8. Forecasts

Forecasts

Realtive Indicator	Current Year	Year 1	Year 2	Year 3
Level of Competition	100%	90%	100%	110%
Market Strength	100%	120%	120%	120%
Materials & Supplies Costs	100%	90%	90%	90%
Labour Costs	100%	100%	100%	100%
Finance Costs	100%	100%	100%	100%
Business Market Position	100%	150%	150%	150%
Cost of Sales efficiency	100%	100%	110%	100%
Overheads Efficiency	100%	110%	100%	100%
Overhead Flow-on	20%			
Business Revenue	322,500	645,000	1,161,000	1,899,818
Total Cost of Sales	265,000	504,000	786,436	1,899,818
Total Overheads	34,000	37,091	46,982	61,144
Total Overheads%	10.5%	5.8%	4.0%	3.2%
Business Surplus	23,500	103,909	327,582	608,171
Business Surplus%	7.3%	16.1%	28.2%	32.0%
Owner Cash Flow	73,500	153,909	377,582	658,171
Owner Cash Flow%	22.8%	23.9%	32.5%	34.6%

Forecasts adjust the current performance data based on the relative indicators provided. To improve business performance, actions must be undertaken which impact on its costs, market position and, efficiencies. For the forecast to be realistic, the impact of these actions must be equivalent to the relative indicators used. The level of competition relative to market strength will tend to level out unless a business is able to establish a unique position from the customer perspective.

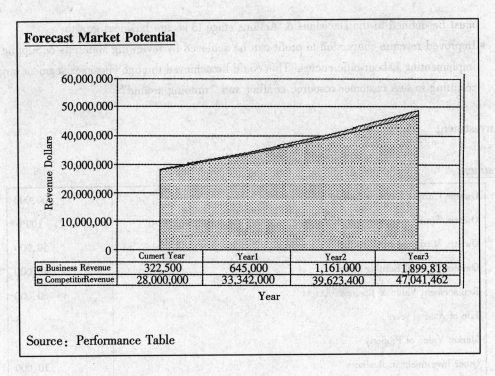

Forecast Market Potential

	Cumert Year	Year1	Year2	Year3
☑ Business Revenue	322,500	645,000	1,161,000	1,899,818
☐ CompetitorRevenue	28,000,000	33,342,000	39,623,400	47,041,462

Year

Source: Performance Table

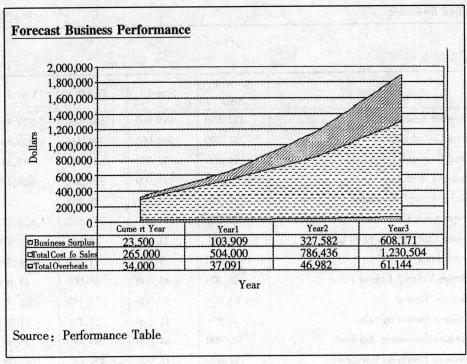

Forecast Business Performance

	Cume rt Year	Year1	Year2	Year3
☑ Business Surplus	23,500	103,909	327,582	608,171
☐ Total Cost fo Sales	265,000	504,000	786,436	1,230,504
☐ Total Overheads	34,000	37,091	46,982	61,144

Year

Source: Performance Table

Critical Findings:
- Solid growth in revenue and profit is achievable with limited impact on competitors.
- To secure increased revenue, real revenue generating actions must be undertaken. These

must be defined in the Decisions & Actions stage to secure business growth.
- Improved revenue conversion to profit can be achieved by reviewing Materials & Supplies and implementing Labour efficiencies. This could be achieved through customer segment targeting resulting in less customer resource conflict and "running around".

9. Investment

Investment

Owners Current Business Labour Earnings	500,000
Owners Time Commitment to Business	100%
Owners Maximum Business Labour Earnings	50,000
Owners External Earning Power	45,000
Replacement Value of Business Assets	60,000
Life of Assets(years)	8
Market Value of Property	0
Other Investment in Business	10,000
Total Investment	70,000

Return

	Current Year	Year 1	Year 2	Year 3
Business Revenue	322,500	645,000	1,161,000	1,899,818
Total Cost of Sales	265,000	504,000	786,436	1,230,504
Total Overheads	34,000	37,091	46,982	61,144
Business Surplus	23,500	103,909	327,582	608,171
Business Surplus on Sales	7.3%	16.1%	28.2%	32.0%
Owner Cash Flow	73,500	153,909	377,582	658,171
Owner Cash Flow on Sales LESS	22.8%	23.9%	32.5%	34.6%
Depreciation	7,500	9,000	11,400	14,836
Owners External Earning Power	45,000	45,000	45,000	45,000
Business Return	21.000	99.909	321.182	598.334
Business Return on Sales	6.5%	15.5%	27.7%	31.5%
Business Investment Adjusted	70,000	84,000	97,440	109,841
Business Return on Investment	30.0%	118.9%	329.6%	544.7%

Critical Findings:
- The business currently generates a low Business Return on Sales 6.5%. This could be substantially improved.

· 314 ·

- Business Return on Investment is strong due to the low investment level. Low investment requirements result in lower barriers to entry for competitors. In these instances the business must differentiate itself or compete on cost with a large number of competitors.

Forecast Rate of Return

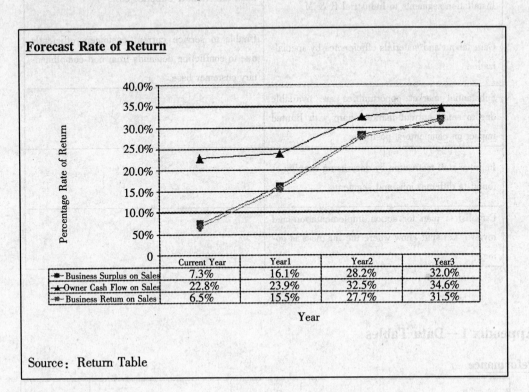

	Current Year	Year1	Year2	Year3
Business Surplus on Sales	7.3%	16.1%	28.2%	32.0%
Owner Cash Flow on Sales	22.8%	23.9%	32.5%	34.6%
Business Return on Sales	6.5%	15.5%	27.7%	31.5%

Year

Source: Return Table

10. SWOT analysis

Strengths	Weaknesses
Personality and character of owner.	Limited management expertise of owner.
Industry knowledge of owner, particularly Industrial R & M.	Skills of staff.
Strong industrial base with 100% of current customer business secured.	Maintaining quality staff.
Low investment requirements.	General R&M and Installation segments are not providing a surplus, recommend disposal.
?	Resources are spread across four main segments, two are generating losses.
Opportunities	**Threats**
Data & Control Cabling.	Resources stretched.
Targeted development of Industrial R & M segment. Become experts, which will provide customer and staff benefits.	Large number of competitors with limited differentiation.

Strengths	Weaknesses
Redirect resources used in General R & M and Installation segments to Industrial R & M.	High Materials & Supplies cost.
Gain labour and materials efficiencies by specialization.	Unable to service current customers efficiently due to conflicting demands from non-complimentary customer base.
Substantial market opportunities are available due to small current market share with limited impact on competitors' positions.	
Improve staff motivation by decreasing running around to different jobs and segments.	
Establish a plan for action implementation and review. Let staff know where the business is going.	

Appendix 1—Data Tables

Peformance

	Current Year	Year 1	Year 2	Year 3
Developed Market Size	28,322,500	33,987,000	40,784,400	48,941,280
Competition Revenue	28,000,000	33,342,000	39,623,400	37,041,462
Business Revenue	322,500	645,000	1,161,000	1,899,818
% of Developed Market	1.1%	1.9%	2.8%	3.9%
Expenses				
Cost of Sales				
Materials & Supplies	130,000	234,000	344,618	507,529
% Revenue	40.3%	36.3%	29.7%	26.7%
Labour excluding owner	65,000	170,909	307,455	530,298
% Revenue	20.2%	26.5%	26.5%	27.9%
Labour Owner	40,000	39,091	36,182	32,017
% Revenue	12.4%	6.1%	3.1%	1.7%
Distribution	20,000	40,000	65,455	107,107

		Current Year	Year 1	Year 2	Year 3
	% Revenue	6. 2%	6. 2%	5. 6%	5. 6%
	Marketing	5,000	10,000	16,364	26,777
	% Revenue	1. 6%	1. 6%	1. 4%	1. 4%
	Other	5. 000	10. 000	16. 364	26. 777
	% Revenue	1. 6%	1. 6%	1. 4%	1. 4%
	Total Cost of Sales	265,000	504,000	768,436	1,230,504
	Total Cost of Sales%	82. 2%	78. 1%	67. 7%	64. 8%
	Gross Profit	57,500	141,000	374,564	669,314
	Gross Profit%	17. 8%	21. 9%	32. 3%	35. 2%
Overheads					
	Location	0	0	0	0
	% Revenue	0. 0%	0. 0%	0. 0%	0. 0%
	Administration	5,000	5,455	6,909	8,992
	% Revenue	1. 6%	0. 8%	0. 6%	0. 6%
	Labour excluding Owner	15,000	16,364	20,727	26,975
	% Revenue	4. 7%	2. 5%	1. 8%	1. 4%
	Labour Owner	10,000	10,909	13,818	17,983
	% Revenue	3. 1%	1. 7%	1. 2%	0. 9%
	Finance	0	0	0	0
	% Revenue	0. 0%	0. 0%	0. 0%	0. 0%
	Other	4,000	4,364	5,527	7,193
	% Revenue	1. 2%	0. 7%	0. 5%	0. 4%
	Total Overheads	34,000	37,091	46,982	61,144
	Total Overheads%	10. 5%	5. 8%	4. 0%	3. 2%
Total Expenses		299,000	541,091	833,418	1,291,648
Business Surplus		23,500	103,909	327,582	608,171
	Business Surplus%	7. 3%	16. 1%	28. 2%	32. 0%
Owner Cash Flow		73,500	153,909	377,582	658,171
	Owner cash flow%	22. 8%	23. 9%	32. 6%	34. 6%

Segment Surplus

By Customer Breakdown? Yes	Real Estate Agents	Industrial R&M	Local Councils	General R&M	Installation	Total
Revenue	36,000	150,000	37,500	84,000	15,000	322,5
	11%	47%	12%	26%	5%	OK
Volume of Sales	360	375	25	150	5	9
	39%	41%	3%	16%	1%	OK
By Revenue(R)or Sales(S)?						
Revenue						
Cost of sales						
Materials & Supplies	100%	100%	100%	100%	120%	108%
Effort	11%	44%	11%	27%	5%	98%
Expense	14, 016	58, 401	14, 600	35, 975	7, 008	130, 00
% of Segment Revenue	30%	32%	32%	35%	35%	OK
Distribution	120%	50%	50%	120%	100%	88%
Effort	15%	26%	7%	36%	5%	89%
Expense	3, 418	5, 935	1, 484	7, 976	1, 187	20, 00
% of Segment Revenue	9%	4%	4%	9%	8%	OK
Marketing	110%	100%	100%	110%	100%	104
Effort	12%	45%	11%	28%	4%	100
Expense	592	2, 242	561	1, 381	224	5, 0
% of Segment Revenue	2%	1%	1%	2%	1%	OK
Other	100%	100%	100%	100%	100%	100%
Effort	11%	47%	12%	26%	5%	100%
Expense	558	2, 326	581	1, 302	233	5, 0
% of Segment Revenue	2%	2%	2%	2%	2%	OK
Overheads						
Total Overheads	100%	100%	100%	100%	100%	100%
Effort	11%	45%	11%	28%	5%	99%
Expense	3, 682	15, 343	3, 836	9, 451	1, 688	34, 00
% of Segment Revenue	10%	10%	10%	11%	11%	OK
Surplus	2, 871	18, 113	4, 528	-1, 433	-580	23, 5
Surplus%	8. 0%	12. 1%	12. 1%	-1. 7%	-3. 9%	OK

Break even Range Business Surplus

Average Revenue per Sale	352					
Current Number of Sales	915					
Number of Sales		0	458	915	1, 373	.
Revenue		0	161, 250	322, 500	483, 750	645, 0
Cost of Sales	82. 2%	0	132, 500	265, 000	397, 500	530, 0
Overheads	34, 000	34, 000	34, 000	34, 000	34, 000	34, 000
Surplus		-34, 000	-5, 250	23, 500	52, 250	81, 000
Surplus%		N/A	-3. 3%	7. 3%	10. 8%	12, 8

Appendix 2—Instructions

INPUT SHEETS
BIZPEP BUSINESS PERFORMANCE ENHANCEMENT
PROGRAM (BPEP)
(Stage 1) POTENTIAL & OPPORTUNITES

Confidentiality	It is acknowledged that all information utilised in program implementation is confidential and is not to be disclosed to any external party. This includes the business details and systems utilised by BIZPEP, its distributors and clients. It is also acknowledged that no guarantees of future performance are given or implied by BIZPEP or its representatives. BIZPEP provide tools to support business. The specific suitability of these tools must be independently assessed. BIZPEP acknowledge acceptance of these terms upon issue of this agreement. If you do not accept these terms dose this program immediately, delete all copies held by you and notify non-acceptance to morcom@ powerup. com. au. By proceeding acceptance acknowledged.

Outline	The BIZPEP Business Performance Enhancement Program (BPEP) consists of three stages. Each stage is designed to be economical, efficient and effective. Stage 1, Potential & Opportunities, uses models to provide business insight. The models are derived from your input data covering business performance and drivers. The input should be based on your subjective views. These are translated into quantifiable values for model operation. There is no need to provide "perfect" answers. Use your industry knowledge to make informed estimates. The goal is to provide a streamline tool which indicates possible outcomes. A recent business tax return will assist in determining values for the Performance section. Approximately one hour will be required for completion. The results provide a basis for BPEP Stage 2, Decisions & Actions. Save a backup of this file before you commence, just in case.
Inputs	All input for processing is on the Data and SWOT sheets. Sheets are accessed by clicking the appropriate tab. Green Cell s require input. In these text or values are recorded. If all available positions are not required simply delete any text or values associated with them. Blue cells indicate calculated values which may be replaced with input values. If you input values in blue cells the formulas will be overwritten. If you need to reinstate them copy and paste the blue cells from the Protected Blue Cells table located to the right of the Market Breakdown by Customers table. Orange cells indicate calculated values which should be checked to verify your inputs are reasonable. If the Orange cell values are unrealistic you must adjust the related input. Instructions for each section are included. To view the instructions and input at the same time open a new window with the data sheet and arrange as horizontal. Increase your screen size with view full screen. You may also print these instructions.
Processing	Processing details are provided at the end of the instructions. A Process Code will be allocated upon receipt.
Contact Details	Should you have any questions email us: morcom @ powerup . com . au or phone (07) 5445 5325 from within Australia or for international calls (617) 5445 5325 during business hours Australian Eastern Standard Time.
SECTION 1	Details
Business Name	Input your business name.
Form completed by	Input the name of person completing the sheet.
Date	Input the date of form completion.

SECTION 2	**Business Breakdown by Customers** This section review your current customer base. Use previous performance to estimate the current annual revenues generated by each customer segment.
Customer Segment	Input up to five descriptive names for segments of your customer base or the names of individual customers. Segments may be defined based on customer location, type, age, buying habits, number or value of sales, interests, or any attribute you choose. Delete default data as required. The descriptions used here are also applied to the Market Breakdown by Customer and must cover all developed (currently buying from you or your competitors) customer segments in your market. This encompasses all customers who are currently serviced by you, or could be serviced by you but are currently serviced by your competitors.
Number of Customers in Segment	Input the number of customers by segment for your business.
Average Number of Sales per Customer	Input the average number of sales per annum for each customer by segment for your business.
Average Revenue per Sale	Input the average revenue per sale by segment for your business.
Revenue by Customer Segment	Calculated as Number of Customers x Number of Sales per Customer x Average Revenue per Sale.
Unsecured Revenue	Input the annual value of unsecured revenue from your customers by segment for your business. If you secure all your customers business this value is 0. If they spend 50% with you and 50% with your competitors this value will equal your Revenue by Customer Segment. Consider only your customers and revenue for services you could provide.
Total Business Revenue	Check that the calculated Total Business Revenue equals the annual revenue of the business. If not adjust the related input data.
SECTION 3	**Market Breakdown by Competitors** This section reviews the competitors in your market. The developed market for your business consists of your current and potential customers. Potential customers and the unsecured component of your current customers are serviced by your competitors. The input data should encompass all your competitors.

Competitor Groups	Input up to 5 descriptive names for groups of competitors or the names of individual competitors. The fifth group is best used for those competitors who do not fit into a defined group i. e. "Other". However it can be given a defined group description if desired.
Number of Competitors in Group	Input the number o f competitors in the group or 1 for an individual competitor.
Average Revenue per Competitor	Input the average annual revenue of competitors in the group or the annual revenue of the individual competitor.
Revenue by Competitor Group	Calculated as Number of Competitors x Average Revenue per Competitor.
Developed Market Size	Check that the calculated Developed Market Size is realistic. If not adjust the related input data.
SECTION 4	**Market Breakdown by Customers** This section reviews the customers in your market. The program calculates possible values (blue cells) by assuming that the number of customers, revenue per sale and proportional revenue per segment for the market are the same as for your business. If this assumption is correct, no inputs are required in this section. To adjust the blue cells input your values. The values input must result in the Developed Market Size by Customers equalling the Developed Market Size by Competitors (section 3). If you input values in blue cells the formulas will be over written. If you need to reinstate them copy and paste the blue cell s from the Protected Blue cells table located to the right of the Market Breakdown by Customers table.
Customer Segment	Customer segments are as defined in the Business Breakdown by Customer.
Number of Customers in Segment	Calculated as Revenue by Customer Segment / Average Revenue per Sale / Average Number of Sales per Customer.
Average Number of Sales per Customer	Input the average number of sales per annum for each customer by segment for your market if the calculated values are not correct. Calculated as Average Number of Sales per Customer from Business Breakdown by Customers (section 2).

Average Revenue per Sale	Input the average revenue per sale by segment for your market if the calculated values are not correct. Calculated as Average Revenue per Sale from Business Breakdown by Customer (section 2).
Revenue by Customer Segment	Input the annual revenue of each customer segment for your market if the calculated values are not correct. Calculated as Developed Mark Size from Market Breakdown by competitors (section 3) Revenue by Customer Segment from Business Breakdown by Customer (section 2) / Total Business Revenue from Business Breakdown by Customer (section 2). This calculation allocates market revenue to customer segments in the same proportion as business revenue was allocated to customer segments.
Developed Market Size	Check that Developed Market Size by Customers equals the Developed Market Size by Competitors. If it does OK appears and the adjust customer segments by value is 0. If not adjust the related input data (blue cells). The amount of adjustment required in the Revenue by Customer Segment is shown as the adjust customer segments by value.
Business Share of Customer Segment	Check that the business share of each segment is realistic. It must be 0% to 100%. If not adjust the related input data (blue cells).
Undeveloped Market	Input a descriptive name for any customer segment in the market which is currently not serviced by you or your competitors. It could be a new product or service. If there is no undeveloped market no values should be entered.
SECTION 5	**Potential & Ability Matrix** This section establishes the relationship between customer segment potential and the ability of your business to service them. A rating is applied to each segment for these attributes. This rating is a number from 1 to 5. One indicates low potential or ability, three is neutral and live indicates high potential or ability.
Customer Segment	Customer segments are as defined in the Business Breakdown by Customer and the Undeveloped Market segment in the Market Breakdown by Customer.
Segment Potential	Input a number (1 to 5) to indicate the Segment Potential. Consider size, growth, profitability, customer satisfaction, competition levels, and risk. One indicates low potential, three is neutral and five indicates high potential.

Business Ability	Input a number (1 to 5) to indicate your Businesses Ability to service and develop the segment. Consider your expertise, market share, distribution, marketing, and resources. One indicates low ability, three is neutral and five indicates high ability.
SECTION 6	Performance This section reviews the current performance of your business for a full year period. This is designed to assess the level of expenses which vary with your sales (Costs of Sales) and those that dont (Overheads). It also allocates a realistic labour cost for the owners effort. The focus is on cash flow excluding asset purchases, depreciation and taxation. Broad expense categories are provided. Values can be based on the previous years tax return adjusted for current trading. Inputs do not have to be perfect but should reasonably reflect your business operation.
Cost of Sales	Cost of Sales (COS) vary with the volume of product or service you provide. Only include these costs in this section and allocate them into one of the six categories.
Materials & Supplies	Input the annual COS expense for materials and supplies directly related to producing your product or providing your service.
Labour excluding Owner	Input the annual COS expense for labour (excluding the owner) directly related to producing your product or providing your service. Labour expenses should include associated on-costs such as superannuation and benefits.
Labour Owner	Input the annual value of labour provided by the owner which is directly related to producing your product or providing your service. This COS expense should reflect the effective labour effort and can be estimated as the cost of an employee who could replace the owner. Labour expenses should include associated on-costs such as superannuation and benefits.
Distribution	Input the annual COS expense for distribution of your product or service. This may include freight costs, packaging, vehicle running costs and any associated labour expense that has not already been accounted for.
Marketing	Input the annual COS expense for marketing. Include advertising, promotional publications, sponsorships, client functions, and any marketing or sales labour expense that has not already been accounted for. Marketing is not essentially a COS expense, however it is assumed that marketing does influence the level of sales and a relationship exists between the level of marketing and the level of sales. It is on this basis that it forms a component of COS.
Other	Input any annual COS expenses not already accounted for.

Overheads	Overheads (OH) are expenses which remain constant (up to a point) while the volume of sales vary. Only include these costs in this section and allocate them into one of the six categories.
Location	Input the annual O/H location expense. Include rent, power and light, maintenance, building insurance, security, and cleaning. If you own the property do not include purchase or finance costs.
Administration	Input the annual O/H administration expense. Include office phone, equipment costs, and stationary.
Labour excluding Owner	Input the annual O/H labour expense (excluding owner). This should include any labour expense not already accounted for in COS. Labour expenses should include associated on-costs such as superannuation and benefits.
Labour Owner	Input the annual value of O/H labour provided by the owner. This should include the value of any labour which has not already been accounted for in COS. This O/H expense should reflect the effective labour effort and can be estimated as the cost of an employee who could replace the owner. Labour expenses should include associated on-costs such as superannuation and benefits.
Finance	Input the annual O/H finance cost. Include only the interest component of loan repayments. Principle components reflect assets.
Other	Input any annual O/H expenses not already accounted for.
Owner Cash Flow	Check that the Owner Cash Flow appears realistic. If not adjust the related input data. The Owner Cash Flow should reject cash available to the owner for a full years trading excluding cash applied to assets. Cash applied to assets covers property & equipment purchases and capital reinvestment in the business. It also includes the principle component of any loan for these purposes. If the owner provides no labour for the business Owner Cash flow and Business Surplus will be equal. Business Surplus reflects surplus available to the business for a full years trading before cash applied to assets and alter paying the owners labour.

SECTION 7	**Segment Surplus by Revenue** This section reviews Customer Segment Surplus. This divides the Business Surplus between segments to indicate segment profitability. Each expense provides a resource. This resource is used to secure revenue from customer segments. The amount of resource required to secure a set amount of revenue varies by customer segment. Customer segments that consume more of a resource should contribute more to the expense that provided the resource. Expense allocations are determined using relative indicators. The "average" expense is indicated by 100%. This is the level of expense incurred by the business across all customer segments to secure a set amount of revenue. If a segment uses 10% more of the expense than "average" to secure a set amount of revenue its relative indicator is 110%. If 10% less its relative indicator is 90%. If it uses none of the expense its relative indicator is 0%. Simply provide a relative indicator for each expense by customer segment.
Cost of Sales	Cost of Sales expenses are treated individually.
Materials & Supplies	Input the percentage relative indicator to reflect the amount of expense utilised to secure a set amount of revenue in the customer segment.
Labour including Owner	Input the percentage relative indicator to reflect the amount of expense utilised to secure a set amount of revenue in the customer segment.
Distribution	Input the percentage relative indicator to reflect the amount of expense utilised to secure a set amount of revenue in the customer segment.
Marketing	Input the percentage relative indicator to reflect the amount of expense utilised to secure a set amount of revenue in the customer segment.
Other	Input the percentage relative indicator to reflect the amount of expense utilised to secure a set amount of revenue in the customer segment.
Overheads	Overhead expenses are treated together.
Overheads	Input the percentage relative indicator to reflect the amount of expense utilised to secure a set amount of revenue in the customer segment.
SECTION 8	**Forecast** This section considers factors which will influence future business performance. A relative indicator is used to reflect unit changes in these factors. The current year relative indicator for each factor is defined as 100%. Relative indicators for the next three years are applied to reflect likely changes in the unit cost or strength of the factor. Each indicator is relative to the prior year. A 10% increase from the previous year is reflected by a relative indicator of 110%. A 10% decrease from the previous year is reflected by a relative indicator of 90%. Relative indicators for costs reflect changes in the base unit of the expense such as labour costs per hour or material costs per unit.

Level of Competition	Input the percentage relative indicator to reflect the level of change from the previous year. Consider the number of competitors, competitor strategies, potential new entrants. This indicator has an inverse relationship to forecast Business Revenue. All things being equal as the level of competition increases Business Revenue decreases.
Market Strength	Input the percentage relative indicator to reflect the level of change from the previous year. Consider market growth, technology & regulatory impacts and customer needs. This indicator has a direct relationship to forecast Business Revenue. All things being equal as market strength increases Business Revenue increases.
Materials & Supplies Costs	Input the percentage relative indicator to reflect the level of change from the previous year. Consider the potential changes in supplier pricing, sources of supply, your bargaining power, demand for materials, and possible alternative materials. This indicator has a direct relationship to forecast Materials & Supplies expenses. All things being equal as the unit cost of materials and supplies increases this COS expense increases.
Labour Costs	Input the percentage relative indicator to reflect the level of change from the previous year. Consider market forces and availability of skilled staff. This indicator has a direct relationship to forecast COS Labour excluding Owner, and Labour Owner expenses. All things being equal as the unit labour costs increase these COS expenses increase.
Finance Costs	Input the percentage relative indicator to reflect the level of change from the previous year. This is percentage change not actual values. For a current interest rate of 6% a relative indicator of 110% in Year 1 equates to 6.6%, a relative indicator of 110% in Year 2 takes this to 7.26%. This indicator has a direct relationship to forecast Finance expenses. All things being equal as interest rates increase this COS expense increases.
Business Market Position	Input the percentage relative indicator to reflect the level of change from the previous year. Consider your position in the market, and the impact of your current actions. If things will remain much the same input 100% indicating no change over the previous year. Actions contributing to the business position will be substantiated in the Decision and Actions stage.
Cost of Sales Efficiency	Input the percentage relative indicator to reflect the level of change from the previous year. This should reflect changes in the relationship between your COS and revenue. If COS efficiency will improve by 10% over the previous year input 110%. Consider changes in processes, distribution or the materials used. This indicator has an inverse relationship to forecast COS Materials & Supplies, Labour excluding Owner, Labour Owner, Distribution, Marketing and Other expenses. All things being equal as cost of sales efficiency increases less materials, labour, distribution and marketing resources are required resulting in a decrease in these expenses. Actions contributing to the Cost of Sales Efficiency will be substantiated in the Decision and Actions stage.

Overheads Efficiency	Input the percentage relative indicator to reflect the level of change from the previous year. Consider changes in administration processes and O/H labour requirements. This indicator has an inverse relationship to forecast O/H Administration, Labour excluding Owner, Labour Owner, and Other expenses. It does not apply to Location and Finance expenses. Actions contributing to the Overhead Efficiency will be substantiated in the Decision and Actions stage.
Overhead Flow-on	Input the percentage Overhead Flow-on. This indicates the estimated level of overhead adjustments to support revenue variations. Overheads are generally considered a constant expense, however large sustained revenue variations place pressure on overheads and usually result in an increased overhead expense. This may include larger floor area, more administration costs, or higher financing. The Overhead Flow-on percentage is the amount of increase in Overhead expense for a 100% increase in revenue. An overhead flow on of 20% reflects a 20% increase in Overhead expense for every 100% increase in revenue. This indicator has a direct relationship to all forecast Overhead expenses. All things being equal as the Overhead Flow-on increases the Overhead expense relative the revenue will increase.
SECTION 9	Investment This section reviews the value of the business to the owner. Consideration is given to the owners earning power outside the business, physical assets of the business, and financial investment incurred. This section utilises the Performance and Forecast inputs to determine values.
Owners Time Commitment to Business	Input the percentage of work time the owner commits to the business. This is used to determine the owners return for effort and indicates the avail able amount of owner resource. Available resource will be applied to any forecast labour increase in O/H then COS where the owner currently contributes.
Owners Earning Power Outside Business	Input the annual income the owner could earn if employed outside the business. Include superannuation and any benefits. This will be used in determining the owners return from the business.
Replacement Value of Business Assets	Input the replacement value of physical business as sets. Exclude property. Consider vehicles, plant and equipment. This forms a component of the total business investment.
Life of Assets (years)	Input the average life of the assets. The Replacement Value of Business Assets will be divided by the Life of Assets to provide an indication of annual asset depreciation expense. This will be used in determining the owners return from the business.

Market Value of Property	Input the estimated market value of property owned by the business. Property values are considered stable over the forecast period and no depreciation is allowed for. This forms a component of the total business investment.
Other Investment in Business	Input the value of any other investment made in the business. Consider operating capital and goodwill paid. This forms a component of the total business investment.
SECTION 10	SWOT Analysis This section is an initial analysis of your businesses Strengths, Weaknesses, Opportunities and Threats. List points for each section, one point per line.
Strengths	Input business strengths, these tend to be internal. Consider expertise, location, reputation, quality of product, service levels, price, guarantees, product range, image, processes used, responsiveness, amount of rework, business structure, business systems, technology etc. what makes customers use you instead of your competition?
Weaknesses	Input business weaknesses, these tend to be internal. Consider expertise, location, reputation, quality of product, service levels, price, guarantees, product range, image, processes used, responsiveness, amount of rework, business structure, business systems, technology etc. What makes customers use your competitors instead of you?
Opportunities	Input business opportunities, these tend to be external. Consider market changes, unmet customer needs, new products or services, technology, competitor activities, processes improvements. Build on your strengths to maximise your opportunities.
Threats	Input business threats, these tend to be external. Consider market changes, unmet customer needs, new products or services, technology, competitor activities, processes improvements. Turn your weaknesses into strengths to minimise your threats.

USEFUL WORDS & EXPRESSIONS

Chief Accountant	总会计师
Chief Architect	总建筑师
Chief Designer	总设计师
Chief Editor; Editor-in-Chief	总编辑
Chief Engineer; Engineer-in-Chief	总工程师

Chief of General Affairs	总务主任
Chief of the General Staff	总参谋长
Commander-in-Chief	总司令
General Accountant	总会计师
General Agent	总代理商
General Consul	总领事
General Designer	总设计师
General Dispatch Officer	总调度员
General Manager	总经理
General Secretary; Secretary-General	总书记；总干事
General Store Supervisor	总务管理员
Auditor-General	总稽查
Consul-General	总领事
Director-General	总干事
Chairman; President	总裁
Controller	总监；总管
Dean of General Affairs	总务长
Governor	总督
Head Clerk	总管
Business Office	营业部
Personnel Department	人事部
Human Resources Department	人力资源部
General Affairs Department	总务部
General Accounting Department	财务部
Sales Department	销售部
Sales Promotion Department	促销部
International Department	国际部
Export Department	出口部
Import Department	进口部

Public Relations Department	公共关系
Advertising Department	广告部
Planning Department	企划部
Product Development Department	产品开发部
Research and Development Department(R&D)	研发部
Secretarial Pool	秘书室
Head Office (Headquarters)	总公司
Branch Office	分公司
Board of Directors	董事会
Director	董事
CEO	首席执行官(总裁)
CFO	财务总监
Regional Office	区域性公司
Local Office	地区公司
Affiliate	附属(子)公司
Branch Office	分公司
Sub-office	支公司
Subsidiaries	下属公司
Liaison Office	联络处
Rep. Office (Representative Office)	代表(办事)处
Chief Representative	首席代表
Group Company	集团公司
Conglomerate	集团公司(企业集团)

EXERCISES

I. Imagine that you need to write a report. How would you collect the data necessary to it?

II. Using your imagination to supply the needed information, write an introductory paragraph for a section of a long, formal report.

III. Construct a complete, concise title for a bar chart that shows annual attendance at home football games at your school from 2000 to the present.

IV. As the office manager of a large company, you are requested to write a short report to the Managing Director, asking for his approval of changing the out-dated office filing system.

V. You and your colleagues at work have complained to the management that, as the number of staff in your office has trebled over the past five years, the staff canteen gets uncomfortably overcrowded during the lunch break between 12 noon and 1 pm. Several suggestions for overcoming the problem have been put forward by members of staff, such as enlarging the canteen issuing of luncheon vouchers so that fewer people use the canteen and staggering the break instead of everybody having lunch at the same time. Write a report on the situations and its possible solutions, stating the one you favor, and why, to the Managing Director.

References

1. A. Ashley,*Handbook of Commercial Correspondence* Oxford University Press,1986.
2. Richard D. *Business Communication – Theory and Application*（6th Edition）, Raymond V. Lesikar and John D. Pettit, Jr. Irwin, Inc. , 1989.
3. Pamela S. Rooney and Robert Supnick, *Business and Professional Writing—a problem-solving approach*, Prentic-Hall, Inc. , 1985.
4. Jane W. Gibson & Richard M. Hodgetts, *Business Communication* Harper & Row, Publishers, Inc. , 1990.
5. Walter Wells, *Communications in Business – Fourth Edition*, Kent Publishing Company, 1985.
6. F. Stanford Wayne and David P. Dauwalder, *Communicating in Business – An Action-Oriented Approach*, Richard D. Irwin, Inc. , 1994.
7. James Payne, *Applications and Communication—For Personal and Professional Contexts*, Clark Publishing, Inc. , 2001.
8. Jacqueline Trace, *Style and Strategy of Business Letter*, Prentic-Hall, Inc. , 1985.
9. Robert F. Wilson and Erik H. Rambusch, *Conquer Resume Objections*John Wiley & Sons, Inc. ,1994.
10. R. G. Mellor & V. G. Davison, *How To Pass English for Business*, Logophon Lehrmittel Verlag GmbH, 1994.
11. 陆墨珠编著,《国际商务函电》,对外经济贸易大学出版社,1994.
12. 付美榕编著,《现代商务英语写作》,北京理工大学出版社,2000.
13. 李平等编著,《国际商务英语应用文》,中国国际广播出版社,1997.
14. 徐以敬主编,《国际商务函电》,山西经济出版社,1994.
15. 甘鸿编著,《外经贸英语函电》,上海科学技术文献出版社,1996.
16. http: //resume. moster. com/articles/recommendation/
17. http: //www. guazell. com/Businessletter
18. http: //www. rmc. ca/acade
19. http: //www. dynotech. com/reports/attitude. htm

图书在版编目（CIP）数据

商务沟通：理论与技巧＝Business Communications：Theory and Technique/曹荣光，胡宏斌编著．—昆明：云南大学出版社，2006（2013 重印）
ISBN 978－7－81112－082－0

Ⅰ．商…　Ⅱ．①曹…②胡…　Ⅲ．商务－英语－写作　Ⅳ．H315

中国版本图书馆 CIP 数据核字（2006）第 003361 号

Business Communications—Theory and Technique
商务沟通——理论与技巧

编　　著：曹荣光　胡宏斌
策划编辑：熊晓霞
责任编辑：叶枫红
封面设计：刘　雨
出版发行：云南大学出版社
开　　本：787mm×1092mm　1/16
印　　张：21.5
字　　数：533 千
印　　装：昆明市五华区教育委员会印刷厂
版　　次：2006 年 2 月第 1 版
印　　次：2013 年 2 月第 2 次印刷
书　　号：ISBN 978－7－81112－082－0
定　　价：39.00 元

地址：云南省昆明市翠湖北路 2 号云南大学英华园内
电话：0871－5033244
邮编：650091